ONE BREATH

FREEDIVING,
DEATH,
AND THE
QUEST TO
SHATTER
HUMAN LIMITS

ONE BREATH

ADAM SKOLNICK

CORSAIR

First published in the United States of America in 2016 by Crown Archetype,
a division of Penguin Random House LLC
First published in Great Britain in 2016 by Corsair

1 3 5 7 9 10 8 6 4 2

A CIP catalogue record for this book
is available from the British Library.

ISBN: 978-1-4721-5202-2 (hardback)
ISBN: 978-1-4721-5203-9 (eBook)

Printed and bound by CPI Group (UK) Ltd, Croydon, CR0 4YY

Papers used by Corsair are from well-managed forests
and other responsible sources.

MIX
Paper from
responsible sources
FSC® C104740

Corsair
An imprint of
Little, Brown Book Group
Carmelite House
50 Victoria Embankment
London EC4Y 0DZ

An Hachette UK Company
www.hachette.co.uk

www.littlebrown.co.uk

For his family,

and his many tribes

Contents

1

DEAN'S BLUE HOLE
LONG ISLAND, BAHAMAS
NOVEMBER 17, 2013

The warm Atlantic sloshed in Nicholas Mevoli's ears as he floated into the competition zone at Dean's Blue Hole. He looked calm, but appearances can be deceiving. When Vertical Blue kicked off he had ambitions for a bronze medal and two more American records. Yet after a year of intense preparation and winning an overall gold in another competition only weeks earlier, plus silver at the world championship a month before that, he'd proceeded to flub every single dive that week. This was the Wimbledon of freediving. Aside from worlds, it was the only competition that mattered to him, and most others in the sport, and Nick was out of juice. Every muscle in his body hurt. Even his lungs hurt, but he wasn't about to give up. It was game day, and he was preparing to descend to 72 meters, or 240 feet, and back on a single breath.

"Six minutes!" announced Sam Trubridge, a theater director from Auckland, New Zealand, and the older brother of William Trubridge, the greatest freediver of them all. Standing on the platform, Sam loomed over Nick, who lay on his back, clipped to the competition line. His eyes stayed mostly closed, but when he opened them they flashed with focus and determination.

The competition zone was delineated by a set of white PVC pipes that formed a 6-meter square within the dark blue of the hole. Inside were a photographer, a videographer, and three judges, including lead judge Grant Graves, one of the longest-tenured professionals in the sport. Also within the zone were five safety divers clad in long bi-fins, led by Nick's friend, Ren Chapman, a former college baseball star from Wilmington, North Carolina. It was the safety divers' job to meet the athletes once they reached a depth of 30 meters while ascending from their dive. That's where pressure underwater shifts, and where lactic acid buildup and hypoxia (lack of oxygen) can begin to cause problems.

Clinging to the floating boundaries were a handful of fans and several of Nick's rivals. Folks like Mike Board, forty-four, the UK record holder and a former Royal Marine. Half-Chinese, half-English, six feet tall and all muscle, Mike patrolled the infamous Baghdad Airport Road as a private military contractor during the Iraq War, and earned good money dodging suicide attacks and ferrying high-dollar clients to the safety of the Green Zone. Afterward, he used his earnings to build a flourishing freedive center in Indonesia's Gili Islands, which enabled him to train year round. In terms of global standing within the sport, Mike and Nick were among the elite national record holders, and both hoped to be contending for world records soon. Also in the water was Junko Kitahama, another national record holder from Japan. She watched him carefully. Their conversation on the beach had thrown her and she was worried.

"Five minutes!"

So were his friends and family. They were aware that Nick was hurting, and they also knew that when others took breaks, he doubled down on training. While many kept a less ambitious competition schedule, Nick Mevoli took every opportunity to dive. That's what made him the best American freediver in less than two years of competition. But mulling past victories wasn't going to help him now. Frustrated, he clenched his eyes tight to silence his brainspeak, to switch off and calm down. He took a cleansing breath and leaned back, submerging his face, stimulating the nerves around his eyes, and sparking the mammalian dive reflex, a physiological response that, if developed, helped an average man become Aquaman, capable of freediving to unheard of depths for minutes at a time, without feeling any anxiety or the slightest urge to breathe.

"Four minutes!"

He inhaled long and slow and exhaled twice as slow, twice as calm. Each time purging his system of negativity and carbon dioxide, the buildup of which spurs that urge to breathe and can turn a relaxed, peaceful adventure into excruciating toil. If a stray bolt of fear bloomed in his mind, he'd slow his breath down even more. That was the only way to lower his heart rate, and keep his demons at bay.

"Three minutes!"

He knew them well, his demons. They'd trailed him his entire life. They fueled him. His broken home, his feelings of inadequacy, his frustration with a society attuned to greed and waste, were what drove him into the water in the first place. They also blessed him with uncommon generosity. On land, Nick wasn't the fierce competitor he was on the line, and beneath all of that anxiety, pain and loss, brainchatter and seawater sloshing in his ears, he knew something else, too: he had one more dive left in him, and he was going to tear that Velcro tag from the bottom plate, come up clean, and claim his record.

"Two minutes!"

He visualized the dive. Something his friend, William Trubridge, a fifteen-time world record holder and owner of Vertical Blue, taught him when they'd roomed together during the Caribbean Cup in Honduras the previous May, where Nick made the dive of his life and became the first American to swim to 100 meters on a single breath. He used a monofin that day. On Sunday, November 17, he would dive without fins, which ratcheted up the difficulty several degrees. Will stood on the beach, barefoot as usual, watching Nick breathe up. Typically he stayed away from the hole when he wasn't diving, but he didn't miss Nick's dives. Nobody in the history of the sport had gotten to 100 meters so fast, and Will knew he was witnessing someone special, someone capable of breaking world records one day and going deeper than any human had before.

"One minute!"

As the clock ticked below thirty seconds, Nick's breathing pattern changed and he began sipping the air, attempting to fill his lungs to the limit—from the depth of his diaphragm to those little-used air pockets between and behind the shoulder blades—and in so doing, pack as much oxygen into his system as possible. He would need it. If all went according to plan, he wouldn't breathe again for nearly three minutes.

DEAN'S BLUE HOLE bloomed onto the freediving scene in 2005 when Will began living and training there. At the time he was not yet a champion, but an aspirant frustrated by the lack of accessibility to deep water and good conditions on a consistent basis. He found both on Long Island, Bahamas, and within a few short years, he became one of the best, if not the best freediver on earth. Freedivers soon flocked to train alongside him, and those that were instructors brought students. That's how Nick found it in 2012, when he was about to come out of nowhere to break his first American record.

Eighty-one miles long but less than four miles across at its widest point, Long Island is splayed like a twisted egg noodle between the frothing blue Atlantic Ocean and the placid, turquoise Caribbean Sea. Etched from limestone by wind, surf, and rain, its stubby hills and plains are blanketed in thick, tropical scrub rustling with wild boar and feral cats, stitched with mangroves, and blessed with a series of exquisite, virgin beaches.

On his maiden voyage in 1492, Christopher Columbus navigated the northern tip of Long Island (he named it Fernandina), anchoring on the Caribbean side of what became known as Cape Santa Maria. A single strip of asphalt leads from there toward the southern terminus, and after about an hour's drive, in the town of Dean's, a gravel and dirt road branches east over low-lying hills and around a bend to Will's beloved blue hole, where the wind is almost always muffled and the current ever gentle, even in stormy weather.

That's because it's sheltered by a concave semicircle of thick limestone bluffs that rise over fifty feet high. Its insides, grooved with giant primordial brush strokes, are drilled with shallow caves and punctuated by phallic stalactites that dangle over a sea so dark blue it has no business being just three steps from a silky white sand beach. Where Will stood, watching, as the clock wound down on Nicholas Mevoli. Sam ticked off the seconds: "10, 9, 8 . . ." When he got to zero, Nick submerged, face first with his arms extended. He looked like a human arrow shooting into the darkness.

Dean's Blue Hole is an underwater cavern flipped vertically, shaped like a carafe. As Nick swam, he passed a rugged reef, which sprouted from sloping white sand that led to a ring of sheer limestone 10 meters below the surface. He'd reached the rim of the hole where sand spilled over the edge in a series of mesmerizing sandfalls that look exactly like a photo negative of a waterfall. Within five powerful breaststrokes those cliff walls receded beneath a sloped ceiling where small schools of giant tarpon or silver barracuda often hunkered in the shadows. After another few strokes and another 10-meter drop there was a second set of cliffs, and the walls receded again. Soon the hole was darker than midnight, and about twice as wide as the entire cove appears from the surface. The rim of the hole has a 35-meter diameter. Below

20 meters, the diameter is estimated at more than 150 meters. Nick had stopped swimming by then. His arms at his side, his chin tucked, he became as streamlined as possible. It was time to freefall. The part of a dive that feels like floating through outer space. He closed his eyes and surrendered to the soft, slow sink into dreamtime.

AT 202 METERS, Dean's Blue Hole is the deepest of its kind in the world. Only one diver, Jim King, has ever been to the bottom and made it back alive. King pulled it off in 1994 by breathing a safe mixture of gases from his open-circuit scuba system. He found a pyramid of sand, built up from the sandfalls, and a tidal current suggesting that through one of the limestone caves was a passage to the Atlantic, which helped explain why the hole wasn't completely filled with that sand that never stops falling. Of those inclined to wear tanks, only an experienced tech diver willing to breath helium can make it back from such depths, because beyond 60 meters, air is lethal. But tech divers aren't the only ones who can trump recreational scuba divers. Experienced freedivers like Nick reach depths most scuba divers will never know, and they do it on one breath.

Despite its surreal beauty, many locals don't go near Dean's Blue Hole, and if they do, they certainly don't swim to the center. The island's original inhabitants, the Lucayan people, told a myth of the Lusca, a Loch Ness–type creature that lives below, and will rise up and take down anyone who dares tempt him. Today, locals often swear that unpredictable whirlpool currents arise like vertical riptides and can take a diver down without warning.

The fearful point to lives lost as proof. Three tourists from Nassau died there in 2009. That tragedy unfolded when one of them lost her footing. She'd been strolling the shallows and didn't realize how close the shore was to the lip of the hole. She couldn't swim, so her daughter dove in to rescue her, and soon both were panicked and dragging each other down. Instead of running or calling for help, the third woman dove in, too. All three died that day.

Then in 2012, Theron Mailles, a nineteen-year-old local and gifted lobster diver, lost his life on Bahamian Mother's Day, while his whole family was at the beach celebrating. The prevailing belief is that he was strapped with too much weight, blacked out at or near the surface after repeated dives, and nobody saw him slip below. By the time they realized he was gone, he was already spiraling to the bottom. His bones lie there still.

When Nicholas Mevoli arrived on the beach on the morning of November 17, he slipped into his wetsuit not far from a plaque bearing the names of the three women lost in 2009, and he wasn't in great spirits. He'd been on the island since October, living in a rented house, and training with New Zealand's Jonathan Sunnex, aka Johnny Deep. When they arrived, Johnny and Nick were equals. Johnny was also an up-and-comer and an elite diver, yet while he and Mike Board had progressed steadily, Nick had not.

Just two days before, his attempt to reach 95 meters in a different freedive discipline called Free Immersion had gone awry when he had to be assisted to the surface, blood dripping from his mouth. Furious, he screamed and cursed, certain he had blown his left eardrum, an injury similar to one that ended his competition after just one dive the year before. As he sulked on the beach afterward, he understood where he went wrong.

"I wasn't relaxed on the way down and I lost air," he said, "and kept going instead of turning around. I just wanted to get there. Fucking stupidity."

Though Nick was still green enough to be prone to such rookie mistakes, he was accomplished. He'd won medals and had his one American record, but his preseason goal had been to break all the American depth records, and he hadn't achieved it yet. Vertical Blue was the final competition of the year—his last chance—and disqualification would be a gut punch. Lucrative sponsorships in freediving are rare, and Nick, like most divers, was self-funded. A prop man in New York film and television production, he'd spent $34,000, his life's savings, traveling and competing in 2013 alone. Right or wrong, if he didn't manage at least one other record at Vertical Blue before diving back into months of wage labor, he would consider his entire year a failure.

He was certain the competition doctor, Barbara Jeschke of Germany, would disqualify him when she examined him later that day, but she told him that his ear was sound, and he never complained about his lungs. If she had placed her stethoscope on his back and listened to him breathe, she might have heard the rattling of edema, thanks to yet another lung squeeze—what happens when capillaries hemorrhage blood and plasma into the alveoli (the lung's air sacs), often causing damage to the tissue. Nick had several lung squeezes over the previous two years, and like most freedivers he treated them like a nuisance that hindered training. Few took them seriously and nobody considered them fatal. After all, the alveoli aren't one big sac, but resemble a bunch of grapes, each berry capable of oxygenating blood through its own membrane. The prevailing thought was that even if a few berries were bruised, the rest should function just fine. Which is probably why Nick never told her he'd been spitting blood all afternoon.

She cleared him.

The following evening he attended a potluck dinner at Greenwich Lodge, a fly-fishing compound twenty minutes from Dean's Blue Hole near Deadman's Cay, where Ren and his safety team stayed. Such meals are a staple of the sport's competitions and several of the athletes spanning sixteen countries were there, frying fish they'd speared themselves, making rice and salad, playing guitar, and chilling out in a spacious lobby lounge that spilled onto a wrap-around deck overlooking the mangroves and the Caribbean Sea beyond. Nick sipped a cold Kalik—a Bahamian lager—with dinner, and his light brown eyes sparkled with calm and good humor. He looked confident, ready, content. His eyes were lying.

Nick and Johnny shared a rental car as well as a house on Long Island, and as they loaded their gear on the morning of November 17, Johnny offered a piece of advice. "If the dive doesn't feel right at any point," he said, "stop the dive." There is only so much one can hide from a roommate, and the fact that Nick was hurting was not lost on Johnny, who doubled as a sought-after instructor. In a sport with a slim margin for error, Nick's was nonexistent. When Nick saw Junko on the beach at the check-in station moments later, he gave her a long, warm hug and said something that would stick with her.

"I hope I see you again," he said, unsure.

"What are you talking about?" she asked, startled.

"I thought . . . um . . . aren't you leaving today?" he stammered.

"Yes, but I dive right after you. I'll see you on the beach later." Distracted, he turned and strolled toward the sea.

"**THIRTY METERS,** thirty-five meters, forty meters." Sam's voice rang out as a swirling wind whipped the sixteen national flags strung above the hole. Spectators stood on the beach or clung to the floating boundaries as they listened, rooted, and hoped. Junko was on the platform behind Sam, literally on deck, tracking her friend's progress.

Cheers of "Come on, Nick," and "Let's go, Nick," rang out as Sam squinted at his sonar feed and announced each new depth with authority.

"Fifty-five meters, sixty meters!" All was progressing smoothly until Nick hesitated at 68 meters. "Looks like he's turning around," Sam announced as the audience groaned. Several seconds passed, an eternity in freediving, as Sam waited for Nick to ascend. He didn't budge, and when he did start moving, he wasn't heading for the surface. "Wait, he's still . . . yes he's descending again."

Mike Board squirmed with discomfort, recognizing Nick's decision was a dangerous one. Instead of heading to the surface at the first sign of trouble, he was making the same mistake he'd made just two days before. Only this time he'd made a second questionable choice. According to footage of the dive, obtained by a GoPro camera mounted on the bottom plate adjusted to the diver's goal depth, it appeared that Nick was having a hard time equalizing, so he reversed his body position, turned upright, and stayed at 68 meters for nearly thirty seconds. Anybody who has ever scuba dived, or simply kicked and dived down to a reef, knows the feeling of their head being squeezed in the vice grip of barometric pressure.

Scuba divers equalize by pinching and then blowing through their nose. Freedivers, especially those attempting record depths, can't equalize that way. Instead, as their lungs shrink due to increased pressure, they move air from their lungs into their mouth. During freefall, their job is to close off their throat and keep their cheeks inflated with that air, like a chipmunk with a mouthful of acorns, so they can funnel it into the sinuses through the soft palate to equalize along the way. It's a delicate technique that can be hard to master and especially difficult to execute under the glaring lights of international competition, when divers often attempt depths they've never achieved before. It's harder still if a diver is already injured.

Yet with the clock ticking, in the midst of a record attempt, Nick managed to do it and began descending again, this time falling feet first. Within seconds, he was at the bottom plate, searching for the tag that would prove he made depth. Because of his reversed position and the pitch darkness of the hole, it took time to locate the plate, and he made subtle yet visible arm motions to tread water until he finally found it. In a flash, he ripped away one of the tags, secured it in his wetsuit, and rocketed toward the surface, swimming hard, and once again looking very much in control.

That footage was not available in real time, so nobody on the surface knew what he was going through. Still, the vibe was uncomfortable if not eerie. "Diving to that depth with no fins, that's a hard, physical dive," said Mike. "I was thinking, 'okay, he's going to have a hard time getting up.' "

Sam announced the time and depth as Nick rose, and was worried enough to address the safety team directly, something he had never done before. "You better be ready for this one," he said.

Defying the odds, Nick shot to the surface, under his own power, after a dive of three minutes and thirty-eight seconds, nearly a minute longer than planned. He flashed the okay sign and attempted to complete the surface protocol that would make his attempt official by saying the words, "I am okay." Unfortunately, his words were garbled, and he never removed his nose clip. He'd fumbled the protocol so his dive was nullified, but he didn't black out, at least not right away. For nearly a minute he clung to the line with both hands, still conscious, laboring to breathe, before falling back into Ren's arms. Ren held him and called his name, hoping to keep him alert and connected to this world.

Ren and Nick had trained together and even sailed together to Jamaica and Cuba on Ren's boat, *Nila Girl*. Ren's safety team, all of whom were certified in life-support techniques, closed in around him. They included an Australian paramedic, Joe Knight. Ren and Joe hefted Nick onto the nearby platform, where he faded into unconsciousness. Dr. Jeschke moved in to try and revive him. That's when the scene turned nightmarish. "There's a problem with his lung," shouted Marco Consentino, one of the safety divers. The team turned Nick onto his side and blood seeped from his mouth, pooling on the platform before dissipating into the sea. Will jumped into the water and swam over to join the effort. Their attempts to revive their friend included three shots of adrenaline, but nothing worked.

After about twenty minutes, Ren and the others transported Nick by bodyboard from the platform to the beach, and lifted him into a Honda station wagon, the event's de facto ambulance. It was a ten-minute ride to the Vid Simms Memorial Health Centre, a rugged and remote 2,000-square-foot clinic founded by American missionaries and set on a promontory.

With water-stained ceiling tiles and rusted air-conditioning vents, Long Island's clinic is equipped to handle general illnesses and trauma common to the island's 3,000 residents. It's not the emergency room you'd hope for in a matter of life and death. By the time Nick arrived there, he had no vital signs, but his friends kept fighting for his life. Ren, Joe, Will, and Dr. Jeschke took turns continuing CPR, in the Honda and in the clinic, where they were joined by a local physician, Yvette Carter, who declared him dead at 1:44 p.m. According to AIDA (International Association for the Development of Apnea), the governing body of the sport, that's when Nicholas Mevoli became the first athlete to die in an international freediving competition.

Within minutes of his arrival at the clinic, athletes and their families began converging on the hilltop. A tight-knit group in the best of times, most sat on a patch of grass under a young jacaranda tree, the boiling sea visible in the distance. Some joined hands in prayer. Others embraced. A light rain fell. A rainbow bloomed.

Ren emerged from the clinic, shirtless, his wetsuit dangling from his waist, and addressed the gathering. "We wish Nick luck in his new world," he said, his voice cracking with emotion. "He died doing what he loved to do, I know that."

"It's an extreme sport," Mike said, still mulling Nick's crucial decision at 68 meters. "We all make split-second decisions, and sometimes we pay the consequences. But his will to get the job done and win is what made him such a great freediver."

It wasn't just his competitive fire that was recalled in the aftermath. Others mentioned how the year before Nick eschewed a hotel or rental house to sleep in the rectory of a local Catholic church. He helped repair the roof of the church's hurricane-damaged bazaar grounds, and ferried some of the island's poor, elderly residents to the bank to cash their pension checks and then on to the store to buy groceries in the church pickup.

"He was universally loved," Grant Graves said.

That point was underlined at around 3:30 p.m., when, after most of the competitors had filtered back toward their respective rental homes, Junko led a Japanese contingent to the clinic's doorstep, flowers in hand. They asked to see Nick and pay their respects one last time. Ten people visited his remains, wrapped tightly in a pristine white sheet, his hands rested in prayer. One by one his fellow divers took turns whispering in his ear, sprinkling white blossoms on his heart, and softly sobbing into one another's arms.

In the days after his death, Nick Mevoli's story went viral, and a niche sport's tragedy became front-page news all over the world, sparking a public debate. Readers wondered why freedivers bother to do it at all. What could possibly be the draw to a sport where athletes plummet to the very edge and risk so much to achieve records in relative obscurity? What Nick's critics couldn't grasp is that it isn't external glory these divers are after. The dive itself is the glory.

"I really enjoy going on this journey where other people can't go," Mike said. "The feeling of being deep underwater, somewhere you're not meant to be, and feeling this sort of mastery over your body and your mind and it being so peaceful. It's a real achievement."

The way Mike and the others describe it, freediving is both an athletic quest to push the limits of the body and mind, and a spiritual experience. When they overcome their fears and surrender to the sea down deep, they become a speck of pure consciousness in a vast dark abyss. Time slows down, and the deeper they fall, the tighter the sea seems to squeeze, until they feel a merge, a total loss of I.

Skeptics might consider such feelings to be rooted in a string of chemical reactions, where pressure exerted on the human body can compress organs and lead not only to nosebleeds, bloody tracheas, and hemorrhaged capillaries, but also to nitrogen narcosis, until the diver feels a throbbing euphoria that's as close to an acid trip as it is enlightenment. But to freedivers that's beside the point. They still need their fix, which is why Nick spent his life savings roaming the globe, from competition to competition, to dive ever deeper, to disappear into the darkness so he could see the light. But if all he and these other great athletes care about is the dive, if the results don't matter as much as the feeling, why compete at all? And why didn't Nick simply come up when he hesitated at 68 meters?

Nick Mevoli's death put an end to Vertical Blue 2013, and the next day a memorial was held. A crowd of eighty mourners, including all the competitors and several local residents who knew and loved him, gathered on the crescent white-sand beach on the edge of Dean's Blue Hole. Some wore their Sunday finest. Others dressed in beach gear. Three women linked arms beneath a parasol. A Bahamian couple arrived and passed out wildflowers. One woman rested her bouquet against the heel of the craggy limestone cliff. The Shins crooned from the Vertical Blue PA system, but all other traces of the competition had been removed. The platform where Nick had been treated the day before was anchored down the beach, in postcard-perfect turquoise shallows that extended for half a mile. In contrast to those shallows all around, Dean's Blue Hole looked a deep purple, ripe for a farewell dive.

Reverend Carl Johnson, a pastor at nearby Millerton Seventh-Day Adventist Church, launched the ceremony with the story of Lazarus. "Life gives you these experiences that you think you're ready for, but you're not," he said. Though he was referring to the emotional complexity of grief, he may as well have been referencing the death of Nicholas Mevoli and the sport of competitive freediving.

In the wake of tragedy there remained a mystery. How did Nick die? This tight community of misfits, daredevils, yogis, and renegades had been rehashing the episode in small groups for twenty-four hours. Over a year later, their discussion would still be simmering.

"It was an event we haven't seen in freediving before," Will Trubridge said after the memorial, "and until we know exactly what happened, there is no way of knowing if it's some sort of freak occurrence or something that happened on the dive."

Most agreed that it was his decision at depth that was Nick's undoing, yet some were beginning to come to grips with a haunting realization. Up until November 17, 2013, the freediving community would dismiss loss of consciousness, nosebleeds, and even lung squeezes as inconveniences. AIDA pointed to its spotless safety record in competition to prove the point. Nick's was the first fatality in more than 35,000 competitive dives. Afterward, they were forced to admit that nobody could say for sure how repeated dives to superhuman depths impacted the body, especially the lungs. This wasn't a matter of conflicting science; research was almost nonexistent. Once Nick died, the prevalence of lung squeezes became competitive freediving's dirty open secret, and their root cause is linked to something all divers do, whether they admit it or not.

Competitive freedivers dive for numbers. Top athletes often say that fixating on a number pulls their focus away from the feeling of the dive, and that the only way to dive deeper is to forget about the number they're aiming for and stay with the feeling. Yet, there is no escaping the fact that when an athlete dives along a line, getting deeper is the intrinsic goal. Which is why at its core, freediving can be a mindfuck, a Zen koan, a shape-shifting riddle impossible to solve.

Each time an athlete hits a new depth, he feels a new charge, a new pride. When he goes to bed that night, he revels in accomplishment, and when he wakes the next morning, he sets a new goal, a new depth—a new number. One he has a hard time letting go of until it's in his rearview. That's true for beginners, for competitors gunning for records, and it was especially true for Nick Mevoli. "We all know how he was," Ren said. "He wanted it so bad that he hurt himself."

There is no doubt that Nick wanted numbers, but he didn't use them to inflate his ego. He wasn't the type to peacock and preen. He gave away the trophies and medals he'd won, not interested in them at all. His mother, uncle, and older sister, his closest loved ones, never even knew that he was the best American freediver of them all. So what was it that he wanted so badly? Who was Nicholas Mevoli, and what would happen to the sport he loved? Would top athletes begin to temper their ambitions, or would his death simply raise the stakes for those conditioned to push past their fears, right up to the edge of their mortality?

At the memorial, Sam Trubridge read a poem sent by Nick's mother, Belinda Rudzik. It was "A Song of Living" by American poet Amelia Josephine Burr.

I have longed for death in the darkness and risen alive out of hell.
Because I have loved life, I shall have no sorrow to die.

With that, everyone swam together to the edge of Dean's Blue Hole and formed a circle. They tossed their flowers into the center, took a collective breath, and dove down to the underwater cliff's edge. The divers, balletic and graceful as ever, swam through wild ginger blossoms and bougainvillea, past the sandfalls into deep darkness. When they surfaced, Grant huddled the group close.

"When we have a new national or world record, the tradition is to splash the hell out of the diver. Let's celebrate Nick's life, like we celebrated his record in Honduras. Let's splash it out for him."

Together the divers, consumed with sadness and anxiety, knowing their sport would never be the same, began beating and kicking the water in fury, in celebration, with release. There was laughter. There were tears. The hole foamed and frothed.

2

WATER CHILD

It was another sunny Gulf Coast morning when Josephine Owsianik led her eighteen-month-old grandson, Nick, through the kitchen door and onto the pool deck, carrying an armful of laundry. It was one of those mornings that make anyone grateful to be alive, and to be alive in Florida. Josie was doubly blessed. Not only had she fled her frigid New Jersey neighborhood for a few weeks, she was with her toddling grandson, the light of her life.

A long-legged New Jersey beauty in her day, Josie adored these quiet mornings with Nick when her daughter and son-in-law were at work and his older sister was at school. It was just the two of them. Unless she counted Smokey, the black-and-white cocker spaniel mix, who shadowed Nick everywhere, and Lion Bear, his other best friend. Wherever the boy went, that stuffed bear went too. Still new, it was already patched together, thanks to his habit of dragging it along the ground. It had a music box embedded in its fluff, so when he dropped it, she'd hear a lullaby. Words were just starting to come when Lion

Bear first arrived around Christmas, and he promptly named his new friend, refusing to believe it wasn't both lion and bear.

The year 1983 was still fresh when Josie watched Nick toddle and drag Lion Bear by the hand in the backyard of one of St. Petersburg's newest homes. Although it had a pool, the house was a modest single-story 1,200-square-foot cinder block construct, sided with stucco, wood, and stone. Nick's folks bought it for $50 down, when there were just three houses on a block shaded by Chinese flame trees. These were heady times in one of America's fastest-growing states. Weather was sweet, property was cheap (this house went for $21,500), and all seemed possible. Neighborhoods would sprout from barren ground, almost overnight.

Josie looked up at blue sky, closed her eyes, and felt the sun on her face, then began hanging laundry on the lines. A few seconds later, Smokey charged through the back door and bumped Nick, who toppled and slipped soundlessly into the pool. The dog barked furiously. Lion Bear sang his lullaby, and Josie turned to see Smokey peering into the pool and glancing back at her, guilty as charged.

Panicked, she rushed toward the edge and kicked off her shoes, but before she jumped in she looked down. There was Nick, his pudgy cheeks puffed out, his two big brown eyes shining like flying saucers, happy and calm as he could be. When he was older she'd tell him, "I knew right then, you were gonna be a fish."

Nicholas Lawrence Mevoli III was born at the stroke of midnight on August 22, 1981. His father, born Nicholas Jr. but known as Larry Mevoli, met Nick's mother at Tusculum College in Greeneville, Tennessee. One of Larry's fraternity brothers set him up with Belinda and they went to a dance. They knew nothing about one another, except that they were both from large, ethnic Jersey families, which was no small thing at a tiny, rural Tennessee college in 1970. He was Italian. She was Polish, which felt to her like common ground. Also, Larry had some moves. He spun Belinda around that dance floor to doo-wop and early rock and roll, and for a moment the two streetwise kids from working-class East Coast neighborhoods felt like they were back home.

They fell in love and Belinda became pregnant later that year. Larry, who had enrolled in college to avoid the draft, had to leave school to make ends meet, and worked two jobs. He punched the clock in the school cafeteria's kitchen for $1.25 an hour by day and bused tables at a Greeneville dive bar for $1.75 an hour by night. They moved into a trailer on Belinda's professor's property, and got married on the steps of a New Jersey city hall. By the time Jennifer, or Jen, was born, Larry was a line cook and bartender at that same Greeneville dive, but they weren't long for the Tennessee hills.

Jen was born in 1972, Belinda graduated in 1973, and almost immediately, they packed and drove to West Florida where Larry's parents, Nick and Dolly, had recently moved. Belinda was seduced by her new hometown. A series of interlocking islands and bridges, with wide white-sand beaches on the green Gulf of Mexico and placid marinas on Tampa Bay, St. Petersburg was a place of stucco and sunshine, East Coast attitude and tropical rain, cheap gas and imported food. It meant easy living with wide, smooth roads and no traffic. A good Catholic girl, Belinda harbored some guilt about the nature of her marriage, so there was something about the distance from her own family and the newness of St. Petersburg that appealed to her. To Belinda, St. Petersburg was a blank slate. It had no memory.

It wasn't even well populated yet. The snowbirds hadn't yet flocked. And when they did, not all the retirees enjoyed retirement. Larry's father certainly did not. Nick the First was a butcher who owned a successful neighborhood grocery, called Nick's, in Oaklyn, New Jersey, for thirty years. He sold it to move to the sunshine and try to do nothing, and soon found that doing nothing was boring as hell. He was not a golfer, or much of a fisherman. The man had no hobbies, so while

Larry was working the mainframe computer in the billing department at Florida Power, his dad got back into the meat business, opening George's Market in 1974.

Larry, who cut meat in the original store growing up, took a job at the new branch, with the understanding that when his father finally retired for real, the market—which would soon gross over $500,000 a year—would belong to him. Around that same time it was becoming apparent to Belinda that she and Larry weren't well matched. Larry was a social animal, with slicked-back hair and a thousand stories—real and exaggerated—on the tip of his tongue. Belinda, who was a teacher at a private Catholic school, was an introvert, an observer, drawn to quiet corners where she could hide in plain sight. Larry liked the flash and pop. His wife blended into the wallpaper, and as the years went on, it would be difficult to find two people with less in common.

There were good times. Larry had charm, and Belinda wanted to love him. One afternoon they took a long drive around St. Petersburg to the nearby hamlet of Seminole, a suburb in waiting. They bought a plot of land and Larry promised his wife that one day he'd build her their dream home. A couple of nights later, on a sweltering summer evening, they enjoyed a midnight skinny dip while eight-year-old Jennifer slept. They made love and conceived a water child.

The pregnancy was a surprise to both, but they embraced it. The store was a smash hit and Larry began devoting nearly all his waking hours to the family business. Belinda would often come to George's in the afternoon for groceries, and she happened to be there when her water broke. Perhaps it was a sign of the times, when American culture was different and less was expected of husbands, or maybe it was a personality flaw that Larry would never shake, or could be he just screwed up when he gave Belinda some plastic bags to sit on in the car and walked her to the door. It was the afternoon rush, he said.

He was needed at the store. Belinda drove herself home, and it wasn't until after the store was closed a few hours later that Larry showed up and drove her to the hospital, so she could give birth to Nick.

Such slights, large and small, exacerbated the distance between them. With two children there was twice as much work to do, and Larry was devoted to the store first. Belinda felt abandoned and betrayed. She was expected to do all the parenting and the housework, while working full time. Jen pitched in where she could. She would change diapers, make lunches, read to her baby brother, and lie with him while he faded off to sleep at night, but capable though she was, she was still in elementary school.

Through it all, Nick was a happy kid, at least at first. After Smokey pushed him in the pool, he couldn't get enough of the water. For his second birthday he got toy dive gear. There was a set of tanks and a mask and he'd often strap them on and jump into the pool, staying down as long as he could. The fights didn't start until Nick was four years old. Whenever his parents argued, Jen and Nick escaped. She would wander the backyard or stroll the street out front, while he would hide in the pool, hanging onto the lowest rung of the ladder. He'd surface just long enough to hear if it was all over. If the shouting continued, he'd inhale and go back down.

One evening, Belinda handed Larry divorce papers. She'd served him dinner, and this was dessert, foisted on him without warning. She'd even packed his clothes. Larry was baffled when Belinda cleared his plate, handed him his bags, and showed her husband the door for the last time, but he didn't fight her. He blew off the hearing but accepted terms. He got the car, George's market, and the lot for their dream home. Belinda kept the house and won her freedom. Nick was five years old.

Jen and Nick's parents both remarried in 1988. Fred Rudzik, a music teacher at Belinda's school, moved in with Belinda and the kids. Meanwhile, Larry was an apparition. He'd commit to picking Nick up at school or at the house and show up hours late, leaving his son to wait on the curb, alone. Sometimes he didn't show at all. When Jen and Nick did hang with Larry, it was never just the three of them. Larry's three stepchildren were always there.

Larry did get his dream house: a 10,000-square-foot McMansion he built for his new wife, Mary. One afternoon, he took all his children to the construction site. The store was his by then and he was doing $1.5 million in business annually. Larry pointed out where Jen's and Nick's rooms would be. He promised them that when the house was finished, things would be different. They could stay with him and have their own rooms, their own space. But when the house was finally complete there were no rooms for Jen and Nick, and when they'd visit, usually on holidays, they felt out of place while Larry was consumed with the needs of children they didn't know and a wife who was too overwhelmed to pay them any mind. Kids would scream, dogs would bark, Larry's steady stream of guests would mingle day and night, and Jen and Nick would sit on the couch, lean into one another, and watch their father's odd, dysfunctional universe spin.

They were two happy accidents, a blend of introvert and extrovert, loud and soft, prone to deep thinking, sensitivity, and adventure. They walked the same twisted road, and though it would make them sad sometimes, it also made them, and their bond, resilient and strong.

Jen was sixteen by the time her parents remarried. She was gorgeous—olive skinned and big eyed, and embraced her type A impulse, filling her schedule to the brim, leaving no time to think, which was exactly what she needed. She spent most of her time involved with her church group, playing on the school volleyball team, and studying with her boyfriend, driven to make the national honor society. Nick was still a young boy, and he rarely complained; in fact, he rarely spoke at all. He was a brooder who internalized his pain. He still loved the water, but his talent might have remained untapped, if not for his Uncle Paul.

Paul Mevoli, Larry's brother, wasn't even thirty when his mother called him one summer day in 1989. Just out of dental school and starting his practice, Paul still lived like a college kid. Beach chairs were his living room furniture, and take-out dinners in front of the ballgame would do just fine. For Paul, house was not yet home, but shelter between adventures. He raced cars, and once a year he'd rent a house with his best buddies down on Marathon Key and go lobster diving and spearfishing. He was young, handsome, and making money, and life was good. But the news on the other end of the phone did not sit well. Larry had been skipping out on visiting Nick and Jen, and the day before had kept Nick waiting for five hours before taking him to the mall with his stepkids. Nick's grandmother was worried about how quiet he had become and thought he was in desperate need of guy time. Nine years younger than Larry, Paul wasn't too concerned about Jen, who was getting ready for college, but he worried about Nick, and it didn't take him long to figure out what to do.

A few days later, Nick was at the Daytona International Speedway, during one of Paul's weekend races in the Sports Club Car Racing Series. Between heats Paul zoomed his GT into the garage area where he and Nick rotated and changed the tires, worked on the engine and refueled the vehicle together. Paul called Nick his one-man grease monkey pit crew and with his nephew's help, he took the checkered flag in the final heat.

As much as Nick loved the racetrack, he enjoyed their trips to Marathon Key even more. After she heard about his little adventure to Daytona, it took some lobbying to get Belinda's blessing to join the lobster hunt with Paul's *Bonzo* crew. There was Craig, the handsome executive; Tim Scott, the happy-go-lucky wiseass with the preacher's soul; and David Schilt, aka Sailor Boy, a six-foot-four Irish American New Yorker turned Florida detective. Every year for the past decade the four friends had gone to Marathon for lobster season. On Nick's first trip he was just nine years old.

Though Key West, at the southern terminus of Highway 1, and Key Largo, farther north, get all the press, Marathon is the most beautiful of the famed Florida Keys. There are no big hotels, and no chic or trashy restaurants and bars either. Marathon is about the water. A flat, wide island fringed with mangroves and marinas, with the green Gulf on one side and the blue Atlantic on the other, it's a place of second homes and hard-core commercial fishermen who make their living selling grouper and lobster. But before commercial lobster season opens, there is a mini-season for recreational fishermen like the *Bonzo* crew who scout holes for days to prepare for those forty-eight hours in late July when it's legal to score lobster.

On opening day, the Gulf is always filled with hundreds of gleaming fishing boats, thanks to the droves that descend from across the state and beyond. Back in 1992, Paul and his buddies owned the worst boat of them all, a 1973 Pro Line with a duct-taped engine cover, patched-up hull, and flaking fiberglass deck. The thing looked like it had been pulled straight from a dumpsite, and Nick fell in love with it from the very first time he boarded "*Bonzo*." Even as a kid, Nick enjoyed fixer-uppers.

"Why do you call it *Bonzo*?" Nick asked when he was hosing down the deck after a long day of scouting.

"You never heard of Bonzo the Wildman?" Paul asked, sipping a beer. Nick shook his head. "He used to be part of a traveling carnival. You would have loved him. Tell him about Bonzo, Sailor Boy." With that, Sailor Boy gathered up his best vaudevillian mojo.

"Come one, come all! Come see Bonzo the Wildman! He has no asshole!"

"But, but, but mister, how does he take a shit?" Paul asked in childlike wonder.

"He don't, sonny, that's what makes him so wild!"

Nick cackled along with his uncle and Paul's friends, who couldn't get enough of Sailor Boy's antics. The first night the *Bonzo* crew hung out together in Key West, Sailor Boy launched into his Wildman shtick in every bar they found. Not everybody understood it or found it funny, but the *Bonzo* crew didn't mind. Inside humor was as much a part of their bond as lobstering, and Nick picked up both with ease.

Throughout their week in Marathon, Nick had been the gofer. He'd gathered the gear, opened the beers, put together the weight belts, counted lobster nets, and helped scout holes. His Uncle Paul (aka Captain Bastard) did most of the pointing and shouting. But Sailor Boy, Craig (aka Salty Seaman), and Tim (aka Scotty) filed their share of requests, too. Nick worked all day tirelessly, and whenever he got the opportunity he dove underwater. All of it was new, all of it exciting, and none of it compared to the exhilaration he felt on opening day of his first lobster season.

It began with a 4 a.m. wake-up call. Captain Bastard shook him awake from his bedroll on the living room floor. "Rise and shine, buddy," he said. "Time to get us some lobsters." They walked outside to a sky full of stars. A light, hot breeze filtered through the mangroves, which sheltered their neighborhood marina, and it was still dark when Paul piloted *Bonzo* from the backwaters out onto the Gulf of Mexico. As the sun rose, the sky and water seemed to merge. Dawn colors clung to the atmosphere, the clouds streaked pink, orange, and gold. The Gulf looked endless to Nick, but it was one giant bay: shallow, warm, green, and crawling with lobsters, which hid in her cracks and holes cratered in a seafloor caked in mud.

Paul kept his nose in the *Bonzo* nerve center, a dog-eared binder of GPS coordinates—fishing holes they'd been tipped off to or discovered on their own, and kept guarded from their rivals, who occasionally buzzed past in state-of-the-art fishing boats. "Looks like the damn Spanish Armada," Paul said to Nick, who glared toward another of the shiny new vessels that came too close, hoping to piggyback a lobster hole. Paul played possum and pretended to be lost, adrift.

"Did you send out that SOS? We can tow you to shore after we get our fill," joked the other captain. His crew pointed and laughed at the decrepit *Bonzo*. Outnumbered, the *Bonzo* boys kept their mouths shut. Nick was especially ticked.

"It don't matter what the boat looks like, Nick," Paul told him when their rivals sped away. "What matters is who's in the boat. Now drop one of those markers, right over there." Paul flashed his Q-Beam on a dark spot in the green and Nick dropped a glow stick into a foam buoy and tossed it into the drink, illuminating the hole. Craig and Scotty strapped on their weight belts and scuba tanks and dropped in to grab their first bugs of the season. Nick dove in after them, with just fins and goggles, to hand them nets and ferry their catch to the boat.

When Scotty and Craig had enough, Paul did some freediving with Nick, taught him to equalize and how to use a metal tickler, to chase lobsters out from their craggy hiding places, and into his net. At first they got away, but Nick was determined and stayed with it as Paul rose for another breath. When he went back down, Nick was still on the bottom, with a lobster in his net, another in his left hand, and a big bright smile on his face. The kid was a natural.

Of all their secret spots to catch lobster, Paul's favorite was Grouper Gorge, a narrow depression fringed by a few boulders in the channel on the west end of Marathon, where the Gulf of Mexico meets the Atlantic Ocean and unpredictable currents thrash the pilings of Seven Mile Bridge. But as challenging as the currents were to navigate, the rewards were even greater; because of the flow of nutrients, life bloomed in the gorge like nowhere else.

The sun rose higher as they approached Seven Mile Bridge. Nick tossed the marker, and Sailor Boy took the wheel as Scotty, Craig, Paul, and Nick dove in. The current was hammering, and Craig and Scotty had to hold on to the reef to gather lobster while Nick swam and spun with ease. He dove down to twelve feet, and effortlessly kicked his fins to stay in place. He wore weights, which helped, and in minutes he had three lobsters. Ten minutes later he'd caught thirteen. The team found a bounty in that hole and kept pulling up fat bugs. Paul sent Nick back to the deck to fetch his speargun, and Nick dove down with it. With the holes clear of lobster they checked for grouper, a flaky whitefish and a staple for seafood lovers in the Florida Keys. It was clear that Nick already had the longest breath hold, and Paul would soon learn that he had an eye for grouper, too. When Paul missed one behind the rocks, Nick never did, and when Paul surfaced for air, Nick stayed down, hunting shadows. During one such respite, Sailor Boy stared at Paul with wonder.

"Where the hell is Nick?"

"What do you mean? He's down there."

"He's been *down there* for a minute and a half."

"With that current, I don't know, Paul," said Scotty.

"You guys are making me nervous now," Paul said, adjusting his mask. "I'll go get him."

Paul went back down and couldn't find Nick. Ten long seconds passed, and Paul started to panic when he caught a glimpse of his nephew worming between two rocks pointing exactly where he wanted Paul to shoot. Paul handed him the gun. When they finally surfaced with their third ten-pound grouper of the day, Nick had been underwater for nearly three minutes. "Sailor Boy was worried about you, Nick," Paul said.

"How the hell does he do that?" Scotty asked. Paul chuckled. "I'm serious. What's with this kid?"

"I don't know, Scotty. Apparently he was born for this shit." The *Bonzo* crew laughed with relief, as Nick smirked and tossed his grouper at Sailor Boy's feet.

They'd found dozens of lobsters in the gorge, which put them above their legal limit. Paul instructed Nick to measure them and throw back the smallest ones, several of which he had collected in the exuberance of his first hunt, and were still alive. "It's fun to catch them," Paul said, "but we're good stewards of the environment out here. We can't screw this place up, and we don't take more than our share. Remember that." Nick nodded, and with Paul's guidance, winnowed the catch down to thirty prime lobsters. They'd hit their maximum after less than two hours at sea. Tradition called for beers, so the kid passed out a round of Bud Light, and grabbed a Coke for himself. They thrust their cans together, and Paul led a cheer.

"Gooooooo, *Bonzo*!"

The guys joked, drank, and enjoyed the sun and sea, still anchored in the channel just above Grouper Gorge when the boat they'd seen two hours earlier motored toward them. "Geez, how many lobsters did you guys find down there?" the captain asked, envious.

"How many have you found out there?" Paul asked, cracking another beer.

"We haven't had much luck, to be honest."

"Yeah, that's too bad," said Scotty, as he opened up two coolers filled with lobster and grouper. The *Bonzo* crew glanced at their catch, then each other, then back at their rivals and exploded in laughter one more time.

3

WHAT IS FREEDIVING?

"The most broad definition would be having fun underwater," said Will Trubridge, when asked to define his sport. "It could be spearfishing or it could be going for depth, distance, and time. Anything that would involve testing your limits underwater would qualify, but you don't have to test your limits. Just as you could climb a mountain to look at the view, you can do the same thing in freediving."

"It is a lifestyle," said former world champ, Carlos Coste. "It's a philosophy of life around the sea. It's exploring your limits, your abilities, and improving yourself all the time."

"To me," said Mike Board, "it's a sport that combines a physical challenge with a mental challenge. I get to overcome another barrier or break through another perceived limit."

"It's total freedom," said Yaron Hoory, an Israeli record holder. "You're floating. You merge with the water. You're at one with the elements. It's this meditative state I don't get in any other situation, a switching-off kind of thing. It's therapy. It's therapy for many people. Once they discover it, it becomes addictive. We alter our lives for it."

Ask a hundred freedivers the same question, and you will get that many unique answers, but one thing is certain. Freediving is universal. Anybody who has ever kicked and dived down to the bottom of a pool or to a reef has done it, and for millennia, all over the world, it's proven to be more lifestyle than competitive sport.

In ancient Greece there were sponge divers—and there still are in modern Greece, and in Greek American towns like Tarpon Springs, Florida. In the fourth century, Roman freedivers were used like early Navy SEAL teams to erect and destroy underwater barricades during an invasion. The Ama, a culture of Japanese and Korean women, have been freediving for oysters and pearls for over two thousand years, and lobstermen and spearfishermen have been hunting this way in the waters of Europe, Africa, Polynesia, and Southeast Asia for centuries.

Spearfishing remains the most popular form of freediving. It's also the bridge that links aboriginal hunter-gatherers to modern competitive freedivers, many of whom are expert ocean hunters, too. Like hunters on land, spearfishermen wear camouflage (in this case, "camo" wetsuits) and stalk prey with passion, but they are also part of the food chain. Their catch can lure bull, tiger, and oceanic whitetip sharks, even great whites, all hoping to scavenge. The wise fishermen toss them some free lunch. The unlucky don't just lose fish. Whether they are competing or hunting, however, the techniques are the same. Both groups have learned to master their own physiology, push past discomfort and fear, kick down to blue water, and hold their breath for minutes at a time.

Freediving didn't become a competitive sport until 1949, when Italian Air Force captain Raimondo Bucher dove to 30 meters in a lake on the island of Capri to win a fifty-thousand-lira bet. He rode weights to get down, dropped them at the bottom where he handed a scuba diver a package to prove he made depth, and finned to the surface. Part stunt, part athletic feat, it took tremendous courage because doctors at the time believed it impossible to survive a freedive to such depths.

Those doctors pointed to a seventeenth-century law of physics discovered by Robert Boyle, known today as Boyle's law. It states that pressure and volume are inversely proportional. As atmospheric pressure goes up, the volume of a gas will decrease at the same rate. Consider a balloon. At the surface it can inflate to its normal size and the volume of gas inside remains constant. Under pressure, however, that balloon will shrink, and as a result, there will be less room for air inside. As far as freedivers are concerned the balloon is their lungs, and the gas is the air they inhaled on their last breath.

Like the balloon, on the surface the amount of pressure exerted on the human body is neutral, and is measured as 1 ATM (atmosphere, a unit of pressure), but as a diver descends, the pressure begins to increase because water is much more dense than air. At 10 meters, the diver is at 2 ATM, at 20 meters he is at 3 ATM, and scientists know that as the pressure cranks up, the lungs will continue to compress. At 2 ATM the lungs shrink to half their normal size, and at 3 ATM, they are one-third. At 30 meters, where Bucher touched down, his lungs were one-fourth of their normal volume, and scientists were certain there would be nothing to stop his rib cage from collapsing, which would cause fatal internal bleeding. Bucher proved them wrong, launching a never-ending race to become the deepest man in the world, and even more important, expanded the limits of human understanding. Over the years, early freedivers continued to push the known limits of physiology, while doctors continued to wag their fingers in warning.

In 1966 (seventeen years after the Bucher bet), the great Italian freediver Enzo Maiorca extended the record to 62 meters, only to be eclipsed by a US Navy submarine sailor and pioneering technical diver, Bob Croft, when he dove to 64 meters in Ft. Lauderdale. Both men rode weights down and climbed back to the surface along a line. Croft broke his own record twice more, nearly going bankrupt to cover the cost. He and Maiorca never bothered to deeply relax before their dives. Croft was known to smoke cigars and drink whiskey until 1 a.m. the night before a record attempt. What they had was an enormous lung capacity, which meant they had more oxygen for their muscles to use. Back then lung capacity was what separated underwater studs like Maiorca and Croft from mere mortals.

Their feats dazzled because with each dive they were risking their lives. Nobody knew where that unknown human limit was. If the thorax didn't collapse at 7 ATM, would it collapse at 8 ATM? Who would be the sacrificial daredevil to find out? On the day of his dive to 64 meters, Croft's commanding officer, a master scuba diver, took him aside and said, "You know you're gonna die, right?"

Almost every scientist who was paying attention agreed. Even the navy's dive manual—Croft's bible—said that if anybody went below 120 feet (about 35 meters), he would die from a thoracic squeeze. Croft was nervous, his stomach twisted in knots. "If you're doing something that could possibly kill you and you don't have at least a small amount of apprehension," he said, "you're either a liar or a fool."

It made sense that scientists would be concerned, because they knew that pressure at depth squeezes with incredible force. At 70 meters, the vice grip of pressure is nearly 17,000 pounds per square foot. How could the human body withstand that? What would be revealed to researchers was that Maiorca's and Croft's bodies were undergoing physiological changes in response to that pressure. While their lungs compressed, it was as if an alarm sounded in their brains. To avoid the skeleton from collapsing in on itself, something had to be done. Cue: the physiological hack.

The vessels in their arms and legs involuntarily constricted, pushing that blood to the core to fill the vacuum with fluid, which is incompressible. Think about a plastic water bottle on an airplane. If it remains full from runway to runway, the bottle's shape remains intact, but if you drink some, leaving space inside, that bottle gets crunched. This shunting of blood was a lifesaver, and few knew it was happening.

One Swedish scientist working in the states, Per Scholander, was the first to discover it in 1962 when, after observing blood shift in Weddell seals, he put a group of humans through a range of underwater calisthenics and found a similar response. Two other scientists had an inkling. Robert Allison, like Scholander, had measured blood shift in sea lions during deep dives and hypothesized that the same phenomenon would take place in humans. He called Karl Schaefer looking for a daredevil. A former U-boat officer who immigrated to the States from Germany after the war, Schaefer led the test diving program at the submarine base in Groton, Connecticut, where Bob Croft happened to work. Allison and Schaefer teamed up to measure blood shift in Croft, who went through a series of experimental dives in a wet hyperbaric chamber. The so-called wet pot simulated the effects of depth and pressure, though Croft's head was just a few inches underwater. He hit over 70 meters in that chamber, and afterward, Schaefer's confidence and Croft's intuition told him that he'd survive a similar dive in open water, which is why he went for Maiorca's record.

Allison and Schaefer, who had monitored Croft's heart, lungs, and brain, as well as his blood shift, also noticed a sharp drop in his heart rate at depth, which jived with the sea lions Allison observed. We're talking about a pulse in the twenties and thirties. Until then, heart rates that low had only been observed in Tibetan monks deep in meditation. The average Joe's rate is over seventy. Additional physiological changes in freedivers wouldn't be discovered for decades. For instance, instead of constricting, the blood vessels in their hearts and brains dilate, flooding them with oxygen molecules, and their spleens contract, sending a fresh supply of red blood cells into the circulatory system. Blood is made of plasma, which is the fluid, and blood cells. Oxygen travels from the lungs to the muscles and organs by hitching a ride through that river of plasma on red blood cells. When Maiorca and Croft held their breath, they had cut off their regular oxygen supply, which the brain needed to remain alert and function. But when their spleen contracted, and the blood vessels in their brain and heart strategically dilated, it allowed oxygen to get where it was most needed, more efficiently. This phenomenon—the blood shift, bradycardia (that extreme lowering of the pulse), and all the rest—is now known as the mammalian dive reflex. Maiorca and Croft weren't enlightened monks and they weren't daredevils either. They were becoming dolphins and seals.

As the sport matured, athletes would come to learn how to maximize the mammalian dive reflex thanks to Frenchman Jacques Mayol, an early rival of Maiorca and Croft who first integrated yoga practice and philosophy into freediving. As he stretched and meditated before a dive, his competitors laughed at him. They relied on their massive lungs and their fearlessness. They knew they were tempting fate and had trained their minds to blast past their fears and dive farther than anybody else. Mayol believed there was another level to mind over matter. His theory was that if he relaxed, emotionally, psychologically, and physically before the dive, he'd become even more oxygen efficient and perform better because his heart rate would be lower than normal before he ever went down.

Proving his theory, Mayol would be the first to eclipse 100 meters when he touched 101 meters in 1975, and extended his record to 105 meters in 1983. Maiorca had his share of victories in between, beating Mayol for world titles here and there, but he wouldn't eclipse triple digits until 1988, when he hit 101 meters. Their gripping friendship and rivalry inspired Luc Besson's seminal freediving film *The Big Blue,* which in turn inspired a generation of freedivers, Nick Mevoli included, but it was Mayol's concepts that would push the sport deeper.

Among the most important was the yoga pose Uddiyana Bandha, or upward abdominal lock, which serious competitive freedivers practice nearly every day. Although the diaphragm is a muscle everybody uses to breathe, in most people it's an independent contractor. It gets the job done, but very few know how to manage it. However, those who become proficient in Uddiyana Bandha, like Will Trubridge and other elite freedivers, have complete control of their diaphragm. They can pancake it against their spine or suck it up beneath their ribs until it disappears. They can even ripple it in waves like a contortionist. Mayol also pioneered stretches for the intercostal muscles, which increased his rib cage flexibility. Combining the two allows modern-day freedivers to pack their lungs in excess of 20 percent over their normal lung capacity, and helps their bodies withstand the effect of increased barometric pressure.

Records for self-propulsive freediving were recorded for the first time in the 1980s, when weighted freediving was still king and had been tagged with the name No Limits. In No Limits, competitors would ride weighted sleds to depth and inflate a balloon to rise back to the surface. When Pipin Ferreras took a sled down to 112 meters in his native Cuba in 1989, he became the deepest man in the world. For the next decade, Ferreras would battle Jacques Mayol's protégé, Italian Umberto Pelizzari, for that title.

Pelizzari broke the 150-meter barrier in No Limits in October 1999. Ferreras never eclipsed it, but in a feat that shocked the world, American Tanya Streeter did when she dove to 160 meters in the Turks and Caicos Islands in August 2002, breaking the world record for both men and women.

That set the stage for one of the sport's biggest tragedies. Ferreras's wife, Audrey Mestre of France, attempted to break Streeter's record less than two months later with a dive in the Dominican Republic to 171 meters. Mestre touched down, but when she turned the knob on the air tank that was to inflate the balloon that would bring her to the surface, nothing happened. A safety tech diver came to her aid and brought her up partway but couldn't immediately swim to the surface or he would die. Ferreras finally swam down with a scuba tank, risking decompression sickness to bring her back.

Mestre was underwater for 8:38 and never revived. Her death was the subject of two books and an ESPN documentary entitled *No Limits*, which revealed that her air tank was empty and that Ferreras, who trained and pushed Mestre to make the attempt, was in charge of filling it that morning. Rumor also seeped out that Mestre was preparing to leave Ferreras, and many of her friends suspected foul play. Their accusations were tempered by his daring rescue attempt, and no charges were filed.

Mourned by her competitors, Mestre's death didn't stop them from continuing to push limits. Austrian Herbert Nitsch was the first to surpass 200 meters, as the No Limits world record inched closer to certain suicide. Venezuelan world champion Carlos Coste suffered a major stroke caused by an air embolism (when an air bubble blocks a blood vessel) while training for a No Limits world record attempt in Egypt in 2006. Nitsch had a similar accident during an attempt to break his own No Limits record in 2012 with a dive to 248 meters. Although he's made vast improvements, his speech is still slurred, and his left side remains partially paralyzed. With each passing year, a full recovery becomes less and less likely.

That run of injuries convinced AIDA officials to end sanctioned No Limits attempts. Their decision was a de facto admission that humans may have met their physiological limit in that discipline when Herbert Nitsch hit 214 meters in 2007. Where the human limit lies in the six disciplines that make up competitive freediving, the sport practiced by Nick, Will, and the rest, remains a mystery.

The oldest competitive freediving organization was founded in Monaco in 1959 as the Confédération Mondiale des Activités Subaquatiques (CMAS), which translates as the World Underwater Federation. They officiated the battles between Mayol, Croft, and Maiorca, and held popular pool competitions as well, but in the early 1990s they stopped running depth competitions to focus on pool events exclusively. In the void, a new organization was formed in Nice called the Association Internationale pour le Développement de l'Apnée (AIDA; International Association for the Development of Apnea).

Although corporate sponsorships are few, and events are often run on a shoestring budget and are managed by the athletes themselves, there are a whopping 140-plus annual competitions on the AIDA calendar. Depth competitions include three main disciplines. In Constant Weight, divers dolphin kick to depth wearing a monofin, which looks like a dolphin's tail. The weight refers to any weight they carry around their waist or neck, but unlike in No Limits, if they use weight to descend—and almost all do—they must swim it back up. In Free Immersion, athletes pull themselves along the competition line to depth, then back to the surface without wearing fins, and the same weight rule applies. The most difficult event is Constant No Fins, where competitors dive using a modified breaststroke, wearing no fins at all, and adhere to the same weight rule.

It's this type of self-propulsive freediving that has exploded in popularity in recent years because it's so pure. There are no bulky sleds or tanks and no air-lifting balloons. There is only the diver, who relies on the bare minimum of equipment, a trusted routine, the laws of physics, and his or her own innate physiological response to pressure, to go deep and come up clean without assistance. More than the No Limits dive pioneers of the past, it's today's competitive freedivers who are coming as close as anyone has before to bridging the evolutionary gap between humans and marine mammals, one elegant dive at a time.

Of course, every athlete knows that in order to be a star in the open water, it helps to train and compete in the pool. Pool events include Dynamic and Dynamic No Fins. In Dynamic, a diver attempts to swim as many laps as possible on a single breath with a monofin. Dynamic No Fins is also a distance event, in which divers use the breaststroke.

Static Apnea is the simplest and perhaps the most challenging discipline. All competitors do is place their face in the water and hold their breath as long as possible. But without the motion and flow of water to distract their swirling minds, the athletes have only the long strand of time and the violent intensity of an endless breath hold to keep them company, while CO2 builds up and their thorax shudders and contracts. Translation: it hurts. AIDA judge Grant Graves describes it this way: "Imagine placing your testicles in a drawer and slamming it shut over and over again." With a time of 11:54 seconds, Serbia's Branko Petrovic is the Static king. The women's record is 9:02, held by Russian Natalia Molchanova.

Pool training is important for deep divers because they know that to dive to 100 meters, they must be able to hold their breath for close to six minutes on the surface. And by training in the Dynamic disciplines, athletes like Will Trubridge and Mike Board build up lactic acid and CO2 tolerance, which helps on deep dives, when they must fight through both, as well as negative buoyancy, to get back home.

Negative buoyancy is underwater gravity. When an athlete duck dives, he must kick hard to get to neutral buoyancy at 10 meters. It takes about half the power to kick from 10 to 20 meters, and when negative buoyancy takes over at 20 meters, the diver sinks like a stone. On the way up, the athlete has to kick against that negative buoyancy, as if swimming against a stiff current, to reach 10 meters, when positive buoyancy floats him to the surface. The point is, on deep dives the hardest work begins when the athlete has already been underwater for a long time.

No matter the discipline, upon surfacing, divers must face the judges, clear their face of all equipment (mask, goggles, and/or nose clip), make the universal "okay" sign, and say the words, "I am okay," in that order. If they do it within fifteen seconds after surfacing, their surface protocol is clean. They earn a white card and score points. If they don't, they get a red card and no points. Penalties may also be assessed for cutting a dive short and turning early, putting their face in the water before letting go of the line, or breaching the surface of the pool with their fin or body on Dynamic dives. In such cases, divers earn yellow cards. They're docked points and their dive won't count as a world or national record.

One would think, considering humans have been freediving for millennia, that someone would have already hit the physiological limit in all six disciplines by now. But that's not true. Today's competitive freedivers are swimming deeper and longer, and holding their breath for a greater amount of time than anybody ever has in human history. In that way, competitive freedivers aren't just watermen, they're Aquamen.

Most serious freedivers play a variety of roles in their sport. They might compete in an event, judge the next, and act as a safety diver in the one after that. Several top athletes are coaches and almost all are teachers. Two early schools jump-started freediving education worldwide: Umberto Pelizzari's Apnea Academy and Kirk Krack's Performance Freediving International (PFI), which he founded with former world record holder Martin Stepanek.

Winnipeg born, Kirk Krack was a tech diving instructor and owner of a scuba shop in the Cayman Islands when he discovered freediving. Soon after, Pipin Ferreras and Audrey Mestre approached him to organize a world record attempt—though not the fateful one. Kirk was one of the first to bring high-octane performance philosophy to the sport when he designed apnea exercises and breath hold sequences, as well as pool and depth workouts for Brett LeMaster, an American from New Mexico who broke the Constant Weight record in 1999. At that time Pelizzari and Ferreras were at the top of the sport, and nobody had ever heard of LeMaster. Kirk helped him hit 81 meters and shock the freediving world, and would go on to train his wife, Mandy, Mestre's contemporary, to seven world records.

Kirk, who these days trains Red Bull athletes, US Navy SEALs, and movie stars like Tom Cruise, who he trained to a 6:30 breath hold for an underwater stunt in the 2015 film *Mission: Impossible—Rogue Nation,* launched PFI in part to stem the epidemic of spearfishing deaths. It's estimated that at least a hundred people die from spearfishing accidents each year. Almost all of them die from surface or shallow-water blackouts, a natural physiological response to hypoxia that competitive freedivers often experience as well.

Oxygen is the brain's fuel, and on a deep freedive, the overall amount of oxygen in the system burns as the diver kicks and free-falls. However, at depth the brain is duped into thinking that there is plenty of oxygen available because when the lungs compress thanks to increased barometric pressure (remember that balloon example), the remaining oxygen molecules take up a greater percentage of the available lung space. The illusion is over as the diver ascends, the pressure reverses, the lungs expand to their normal capacity, and the true percentage of available oxygen registers in the brain. That reversal is at its most intense during the last 10 meters of an ascent when barometric pressure is cut in half. As the now buoyant diver accelerates toward the surface, there is no hiding that the tank is empty, and if oxygen levels are too low, the brain will shut down to prevent damage. That's why a diver blacks out.

"Ninety percent of all blackouts happen at the surface," Kirk said, "9 percent happen within that first 10 meters, and .9 percent happen below 10 meters." Freedivers call that the "rule of nines." But blackouts aren't what kill spearfishermen. Competitive freedivers black out just as often if not more so, and Nick was their first death in over 35,000 dives. Spearfishermen die when they black out alone. With no safety divers or dive buddies to bring them around, they sink and drown. Safety protocols are integral to PFI courses and those given at newer schools like Mike Board's Freedive Gili and Ted Harty's Immersion

Freediving, where Nick studied. But with a profusion of new schools come even more students, and some arrive on a quest to get as deep as possible, as quickly as they can.

A fundamental sea change in the sport began with the publication of an equalization document from Eric Fattah, a former world record holder considered by Will Trubridge to be one of competitive freediving's top innovators. He was the first to attempt a depth record with a monofin and he invented fluid goggles, swim goggles adapted to withstand pressure at depth. But his most significant and controversial impact on the sport came in 2001, shortly before he set his world record, when he published a document online entitled "Frenzel-Fattah Equalizing Workshop." It spelled out the deep equalization technique, known as "three-stage mouthfill," in an easy and user-friendly way.

"Everybody laughed because they didn't know who I was," he said, "and I'm not entirely certain it was a good decision [to publish it]. It's become the bible of equalization, I've never made a penny on it, and instructors aren't even teaching it properly."

Before Eric Fattah, athletes were already funneling air from their lungs into their mouth using what's known as a grouper call, storing it there for the rest of the dive, and using it to equalize their sinuses through the soft palate. But they weren't grouper calling until at least 50 meters because they were worried that if they brought their air up too soon, they'd swallow it before they reached their goal depth. Eric knew that there was a lot more air in his lungs at 20 meters than there would be at 50 meters, and hypothesized that if he grouper called at 20 meters, he could store more air for equalization. The trick would be keeping that air in his mouth without swallowing it, so he added exercises, which enabled him to close off his throat effectively and maintain his 20-meter mouthfill all the way down.

It was as if he'd cracked a code. Until then the only thing that stopped divers with long breath holds from going deep was equalization. For years, athletes experimented in the dark, attempting new techniques on their own, slowly adapting to pressure and inching their way down. Eric's document threatened to change everything, which is why he included an important disclaimer:

> *If your diving depth is currently limited by equalizing, the techniques explained in this document, if properly learned, may dramatically increase your depth potential in a short time. Please take care in your progression to new depths as all the risks normally associated with freediving deeper without proper preparation will still apply!*

At first, Eric's document largely benefited only elite athletes because experienced teachers knew not to share the Frenzel-Fattah technique with new students until they were better adapted to pressure. Even Will Trubridge and his main rival, world record holder Alexey Molchanov of Russia, progressed deliberately. It took Alexey two years to get to 80 meters and another three years to get to 100. Will dove to 40 meters in 2004 and to 89 meters in 2008. But soon something would go terribly wrong.

Marco Consentino, the Vertical Blue safety diver and longtime Apnea Academy instructor, can pinpoint the year the freediving community lost perspective. "There is a kind of line from what was [competitive] freediving in 2011, and what [competitive] freediving became after that point," he said. "Until then people who were competing had adapted to the depths. They were people with a lot of experience, with hours of depth behind their shoulders. So everything was much more under control. Since then I've seen lots of newcomers doing incredible depths without any knowledge about their physiology and how it adapts."

The trouble was that freediving schools had opened everywhere. Anywhere there was deep water—Hawaii, Egypt, Indonesia, Greece, Russia, Slovenia, Tenerife, California, Florida, Israel, and, of course, the Bahamas—there were newly minted freediving instructors spreading the gospel that it didn't require years of training to go deep. Humans were born to do it, they'd say, which is why the mammalian dive reflex is a hardwired genetic response. All someone needed was a decent breath hold, proper instruction, and Eric Fattah's technique, and they too could go from everyman to Aquaman.

Like Marco, Will Trubridge sees a direct link between the wide dissemination of Eric's technique and the proliferation of lung squeezes in competitive freediving: "The [three-stage] mouthfill has enabled divers who don't have a great deal of flexibility in the diaphragm to equalize to 70, 80, 90, 100 meters, and because they don't have the flexibility, their system becomes brittle and any small tweak will cause damage to that brittle structure. For example, maybe you are a little too panicky on the bottom and pull a little too hard on the rope in Free Immersion or you have a contraction that's a little too strong. Anything that deviates from that perfect beautiful fall down to depth, slow turn, and cruise back up will start to incede on those structures."

"I love the sport and I love to go deeper and deeper, but meter by meter, year by year," Marco said. "You need time, you need experience, and you need hours of training. Newer generations want it all and they want it now. Something has to change. I've seen too many guys spitting blood. I've seen too many guys going down without proper preparation. You cannot just go for more depth because you want. The sea is listening to you, and if you are doing things without proper preparation he will not forgive you."

For decades the limiting factor separating the deepest freedivers from the rest was almost always equalization, which took patience and dedication to master. After 2011, there was a new limiting factor in the sport: the lung squeeze.

Nick Mevoli took his first formal freediving course in 2011.

4

PUNK-ASS VEGANS

On his first day at Lincoln High School, Nick Mevoli wore what would become his uniform: a secondhand flannel shirt, jeans, and a studded black belt crowned with a fat vintage Americana belt buckle. He rode to school on his BMX and coasted to the front gate across the brick plaza in front of the auditorium, where students gathered in groups beneath the sycamore trees.

Set in Florida's western panhandle, Tallahassee shared more traits with the Deep South than it did with South Florida. There were sprawling oak-shaded streets, rolling green hills, antebellum homes with wide front porches, and like most small Southern towns, a legacy of segregation. The black kids and white kids mostly kept their distance.

Justin Pogge noticed Nick ride up, standing in the saddle, weaving between students. Justin was skinny, with a bookish, pale complexion, bright blue eyes, and a mop of dark brown hair. Compared to him and all his friends, this new kid looked like a grown man. He was tall and strong, with massive sideburns, olive skin, and a thick brown mane. Maybe he was an escaped felon posing as a student, or worse. A narc. Justin enjoyed conjuring possible past lives for Nick as he locked up his bike and disappeared into the low-lying complex of brick buildings that made up campus.

When Belinda and Fred told him they were moving, Nick bucked and kicked. He didn't like the idea of leaving his friends and girlfriend, and switching high schools midstream, but the decision had been made. They had two daughters of their own at that point, and Fred had left teaching and become an attorney. When his meth-head client stole his car, they decided to ditch the Tampa area and its rising tide of crime. Fred landed at the Florida Department of Revenue in Tallahassee and his family landed in a cramped two-bedroom apartment where Nick shared a small room with his two baby sisters.

Later that day Justin found himself sitting next to Nick in his English class. Justin grew up outside of town in an intentional community called the Miccosukee Land Cooperative. It was a commune of sorts, founded in the back-to-the-land, free-love daze of the early 1970s. This one had a private property twist that enabled its sustainability. Families owned their individual plots, but there was a mix of shared property too. Most of it designated as open space. Roads were unpaved and named for Beatles songs. There were organic gardens and ancient oak trees, and trails winding through ninety glorious acres of woods and wetlands. There were also lots of parties. It was the kind of place where new people constantly blew through.

Perhaps that's why Justin was a "connector," attracted to anyone and anything new. He offered to show Nick around town after school. Justin seemed harmless enough, so he agreed. After the bell rang, they swerved streets shaded by mossy oaks, cut corners through mini-mall parking lots and gas stations, hopped curbs and ran red lights. They talked about music. Nick had started to enjoy straight edge punk bands like Minor Threat, which was precisely what Justin was into. Minor Threat's song "Out of Step" summarized the straight edge scene:

I don't drink
I don't smoke
I don't fuck

For kids like Justin and Nick, that song felt like an anthem of rebellion against the excess and indulgence of modern life. Unlike almost all rock, pop, and hip-hop acts since the dawn of the music industry, straight edge bands were antihedonistic and yet engaged in the world. Their most fervent devotees got the letter *X* inked on the back of their hands, inspired by the *X* stamped on the hands of underage kids at shows. It was supposed to mean they couldn't drink, but straight edge kids adopted the mark because they had no intention of drinking. Justin had the *X* tattoo, the first iteration of what would be a mosaic of ink on his left side traveling from his hand to his collar. Nick noticed. The new friends discussed straight edge philosophy and their favorite bands as they lapped the state capitol and made their way to the Civic Center, an arena complex where Florida State's basketball team plays their home games.

Still a block away, Nick spotted a house on a small rise above the sidewalk with a fifteen-foot slope running toward the street. He rode up the driveway without warning and bunny hopped off the slope, sticking the landing and coasting into the Civic Center parking lot with ease. Justin was stunned, but Nick was just warming up.

Nick had been riding and competing on a BMX bike since middle school. Back in St. Pete, he'd won races and moved up the Florida rankings, but didn't care much for the spoils. The day after winning a race, he'd ride over to the post office and ship the shiny trophy to his Grandma Josie in New Jersey. He had no use for it and figured it would make her happy. To him it was about the win itself and the thrill of the ride.

These were the so-called dark days of BMX. X Games were rising, and even the best track riders were abandoning the race circuit to freestyle in the streets. They rode rails, jumped stairs, and worked on tricks on half-pipes and jumps they built themselves. Nick and his pal, Ryan Cullen, took after them. Although riders are pulling 540s these days, back then a 360 was the Holy Grail, and only the great Todd Lyons was doing midair back flips. Nick wanted to accomplish both.

He and Ryan scouted a grassy embankment off a freeway extension near Ryan's house where the slope was steep and abutted a deep channel linked to a bayou. This was Florida, after all, where swampland was the new suburbia. Nick brought his dive gear to the channel—he had it all by then, weights, tanks, mask, and fins—and cleared it of rusted shopping carts and stolen bicycles. He made sure nothing dangerous cluttered the drop zone, and only then did they build their jump.

"He was so creative and always pushing himself to the limit, with whatever he was into," said Ryan. "I remember he had to build the biggest, craziest jump. It wasn't necessarily built correctly, but he made it work."

Their plywood ramp was six feet high, eight feet long, and about four feet wide. They called it Lake Jump, and when it was finally ready, Nick took the first run. He duct-taped two-liter water bottles to his handlebars and frame to make the bike float, and hiked to the top of the embankment. At the apex he could feel the draft of hundreds of cars whipping down the interstate in a blur and see the channel meet the bayou in the distance. When he came charging downhill, his buddies cheered. He flew twenty feet in the air, higher than any of them had ever been before, and came splashing down in the murky channel, unscathed.

Before long he was pulling the tricks of his dreams. He mastered the Superman, where he'd grab the seat and the bars and kick his legs straight back in a flying position; landed a "no-footed can can," with both of his legs kicked out over the top tube, like a Rockette; and one day, he even pulled a 360. Soon it became easy for him to do it over the water, but he never could land it on solid ground. Whenever he launched at a skate park he would hit the back wheel first and flip over the front of the handlebars. Afterward he'd be livid, scream and curse, and brood about it for hours.

His best trick came when he rode over to Lake Jump on his mom's bubble-gum-pink beach cruiser. He pushed that heavy mess to the top of the embankment and flew downhill, pulling a back flip over the water. Ryan and Nick laughed their asses off, then hosed it down, so he could ride it home before Belinda knew a thing.

There were injuries. One evening when Jen was home from college, Nick snuck in the back door with a wad of bloody napkins over his left eye and found her in the bathroom applying makeup, getting ready to go out.

"Oh my God! What happened to you?!" Jen shrieked.

"Shhh! Mom'll freak out."

"Fine, let me see it," she said. Nick peeled the napkins away, revealing a three-inch gash centimeters from his eyeball. The white of his eye was clouded with blood.

"Is it bad?" he asked. Jen nodded. She could barely speak it looked so terrible. It also looked painful, but Nick didn't seem to be in pain. She'd picked up on Nick's tremendous pain tolerance when he was a small child, and as he'd grown, his tolerance for pain and discomfort had grown as well—traits that would eventually help him achieve greatness underwater, but might also become his Achilles' heel.

"We're going to the hospital," she said sternly. That evening, Jen, in heels and big hair, dressed to the nines; Nick, in his bloodied, muddy bike gear; and Belinda, in sweats and flip-flops, spent six hours in the ER. His next hospital visit came when he was sixteen, after breaking his wrist at the BMX track. His mother forbade him from riding until the cast came off. Nick waited four days before sawing out the wedge between his thumb and first finger, so he could duct-tape that hand to his handlebars and practice his tricks with a broken wrist. He had X Games ambitions, after all, and couldn't miss any training time. A few weeks later, when he felt even stronger, he sawed the remainder of the cast into two pieces, rode with both arms free, then expertly duct-taped it back together before heading home.

JUSTIN WATCHED IN awe as Nick built up speed and glided across the Civic Center's concrete apron toward two long flights of steel-tipped stairs, lined by black iron railings. Nick hopped onto the railings to grind both sets in a single shot. It was immaculate, and the best trick Justin had ever seen in person. Nobody rode like that in Tally. Not until Nick showed up.

Justin ushered Nick into his straight edge crew. Among them was Clayton Rychlik, a gifted musician who would go on to play drums for Of Montreal. Clayton also lived at Miccosukee and went to school with Nick and Justin. Lincoln was an open campus and the boys would spend their lunch hours gobbling vegan food at New Leaf Co-op, sitting among Tally's hippie, stoner set. Nick's new friends were all vegan, but they weren't hippies.

After school the guys usually gathered at Railroad Square, where Justin had rented an old railroad warehouse and was in the process of converting it into an all-ages punk rock venue, dubbed Mega Rock Arena, with his pal Soliman Lawrence. Nick rode over one day and bunny hopped onto the loading dock. That was the first time Soliman had ever seen the new straight edge kid who was a monster on a bike.

"You're a unique sort of creature," Soliman said with a side glance. Nick looked like an athlete, and athletes bored him. Nick took stock of Soliman, as well. He was short, his hair was close cropped, and his wire-framed glasses made him look tense and earnest, like a big-brained intellectual who acted more sure of himself than he was. "I'm Soliman. Most people call me Soli."

"Soli, huh?" Nick said. "What if I call you Sol [soul]?"

"Sol. I guess that's okay."

"You don't go to Lincoln, do you, Sol?"

"No, I go to the high school for dropouts, hippies, and weirdos. It's a class size thing. My parents are cuckoo for small class sizes. Supposedly we learn more 'optimally' in more 'personalized' environments. Studies have shown. But, you know, whatever."

"Right, studies have shown."

"I think unschooling is the wave of the future, though. Have you read much about unschooling? It's the most radical invention ever to hit education, because it's not really education at all, except it totally is. The premise is that education itself is the problem with society. Not the solution." Sol went on to explain the virtues of letting young kids explore the world in feral delirium, learning from their Tom Sawyer-esque adventures. Nick could tell Sol liked to talk about ideas, and he enjoyed listening. They clicked immediately.

"The point of staying sober and lucid is to see things as they really are, so we can engage with the world," Sol said, as they painted the Mega Rock Arena's stage. "Change shit. That's what Mega Rock Arena is all about. If we think Tally is boring and fucking lame and all about sports and sorority girls and fucking football, and it is, then let's do something about it. If we don't like that all the good shows around here are twenty-one and over, or eighteen and over, then let's throw our own damn punk shows, you know?"

Nick did know. He'd always seen the world as imperfect, because his world certainly was, and he set about altering it in the ways he saw fit. Whether that was modifying his $1,000 bike, building his own jumps, removing his own cast, or even asking for and receiving dive weights when he was nine so he could stay down deeper and longer. The world was his canvas, and it would stay that way.

Nick's Tally crew didn't hide their disdain for consumer culture and industrial food. To them, mainstream American life was dysfunctional, the American Dream a hoax. Happiness wasn't bundled in thirty-year mortgages or well-paid careers or a thick steak. Not if everything they bought with their hard-earned cash was disposable and animals were tortured for their sustenance. But while most dealt with teenage ennui by numbing the truth and marinating their minds with herb and booze, Nick and his friends wanted to stay angry. Their melancholy would be a force of good, though it didn't always feel that way at home.

During his first week in Tallahassee, Nick came home late for dinner while Belinda was putting a platter of sliced tenderloin on the table. He glimpsed it on his way to the kitchen and said, "I don't eat that stuff anymore."

"You don't eat steak?" she asked.

"Meat. I don't eat meat. And that butter stuff. You gotta stop putting that in the vegetables. I don't eat that either."

"Okay," she said. Nick's sisters, six-year-old Kristine and four-year-old Katie, took it all in. "Would you like to tell us why?" He came back into the dining nook, wearing the most disgruntled expression he could muster.

"Do you guys have any idea how they make butter and beef? What the cows are eating? How they're killed? It's disgusting. It's an industry of murder and you're participating. Not me. Not anymore." Sol and Justin had downloaded the basics to Nick, who retreated to the kitchen and opened a pack of tofu. Fred and Belinda watched as he rattled pans, found cooking oil, and began slicing bland globs of tofu into cubes.

"You won't eat steak, but you'll eat that?" Fred asked. Belinda glared at him.

"Don't worry, from now on I'll make my own meals."

It wasn't cool to be happy in Tallahassee in 1998, at least not among Nick's crew, but from a distance, Nick certainly looked that way. He got a job busing tables at a farm-to-table restaurant called Kool Beanz, which eats better than the name suggests, and began riding with one of the chefs at Tom Brown Park, where he helped build a proper BMX track.

The park was large and leafy with pines, poplars, and southern live oaks, but when Nick first saw the BMX track, he found the terrain modest and cramped, with just two manmade hills that lacked the pitch or depth Nick needed. X Games tryouts were in a few months and he needed a proper course, so he shaped it himself, one shovelful of earth at a time. Clayton and Justin used to see him cruise into school in the morning in his beat-down Chrysler ragtop, his clothes caked in mud from digging and molding the dirt track since dawn. His hard work paid off. Soon Nick was pulling 360s and even getting close to landing his backflip. But with a few weeks to go before tryouts, he put his seat post into his leg, inches from his femoral artery. It was a bad enough gash to knock him off his bike for a month and dust his X Games dream. Jen happened to be in Tally that weekend and, once again, she and Belinda took Nick to the ER.

"You almost lost an eye, now you almost punctured your artery," Jen said. Nick sat between them, his leg elevated, as they awaited a prescription for pain meds he wouldn't swallow. "When is this gonna stop?" Nick didn't say a word.

"Don't. Just. No more. I can't take it," said Belinda. The three of them stared into the distance for a few minutes until Belinda saw tears streaming down Nick's cheeks. She rested her head on her son's shoulder as he wept and mourned his dashed X Games dream.

That night he watched his favorite movie for the twentieth time: *The Big Blue*. Later, when his family was asleep, he locked himself in the bathroom and filled the tub with warm water. He slung his wounded thigh over the edge of the shallow tub, checked the time on an old wristwatch he'd balanced on the ledge, and dipped his head beneath the surface. The pain started to build in the third minute. His body shuddered with contractions, the urge to breathe manifesting in physical demands he would stave off. Each time his muscles contracted and his rib cage rattled, his smile got wider.

The Mega Rock Arena lasted less than a year, but it had its moment and it helped cement Railroad Square as Tally's coolest corner of town. In a few months they'd turned a defunct 500-square-foot space into a thriving punk palace. They booked name bands, like Converge and Dillinger Escape Plan, on the come up, and their shows were a dissonant thrashing of metal and angst, hope and release.

After it fizzled, Justin, Clayton, and Sol frequently road-tripped around Florida to see their favorite straight edge bands live. They'd usually hit festivals that Nick seldom received clearance from Belinda to attend. Like Jen before him, now he was the babysitter, but after Nick had spent all his free time for months helping Fred build their beautiful new home by hand, she greenlit his weekend pass to the Gainesville Fest, North Florida's hottest music festival.

Giddy, the boys piled into Justin's van on a perfect blue-sky Friday afternoon. An hour outside of Gainesville they stopped for gas at the kitschiest truck stop they could find, and Nick noticed a cattle truck parked between two semis, the driver nowhere in sight. He peered through the wooden slats, and caught a pair of sad cow eyes. She stuck her nose between the planks and Nick petted her snout. Next to her was a doe-eyed calf teetering on spindly legs. Was she days old? A week? Maybe two? He looked back into that mama cow's beautiful eyes, which seemed to be peering deep into Nick's novo vegan soul. What if they were bound for Larry's blade at George's Market? What if the calf was about to become veal? Would he do something to stop it? He checked the back gate. No lock. Delicious mayhem bloomed in his brain.

To Justin and Clayton it seemed to happen in slow motion. While another friend, Tim, flung open the back gate, Nick hopped into the trailer and guided the mama cow and her calf to the pavement. The rest piled out in a hurry. Cows wandered the parking lot. Some looked scared. Others amused. A few made a beeline to a patch of green grass near the air and water station and started to munch and empty their bladders. Cars stopped short. Patrons at gas tanks watched in wonder. The driver tore out of the diner and charged after Nick and Tim, who sprinted toward the van. Justin sped over with his side door slid open, the boys jumped in, and Justin peeled out, all of them in hysterics. The truck driver kept running after them. Justin picked up speed. By the time sirens rang out they were but a whisper.

On the day Nick graduated high school, he rented a house with Justin and three other friends and moved out on his own. Theirs was a perfectly lovely middle-class home, in a perfectly lovely middle-class neighborhood of midcentury brick houses, with American flags and basketball hoops, on a street lined with towering pine and oak trees. They called the place The J Spot. When Nick and Justin showed up with their boxes, their neighbors braced for the worst, and just as they feared, weirdos descended all day, every day. One of them had hitch-hiked into Tally from a small farming town a few hours south the year before.

When Aaron Suko arrived in their world, Justin was hosting a gathering storm of a party while Nick was in the midst of writing a letter to his new crush, Michelle, a twenty-one-year-old, pink-haired lead screamer of a band called Scrotum Grinder. He couldn't get into the mood in his room, so he moved his desk, floor lamp, desk chair, and sofa into the backyard to write alfresco. He typed feverishly, in a zone, his eyes aflame. Aaron was curious. "What are you doing?" he asked, sinking into the sofa.

"Writing the most important letter in my entire life," Nick said, still typing.

"Oh," Aaron said, getting up. "Sorry to intrude."

"You're not an intruder," Nick said. He finished his thought, leaned away from the desk, and motioned for Aaron to sit back down. "You're always welcome. We have a strict open door policy around here. I'm Nick, by the way."

Aaron was from Auburndale, Florida, the kind of God, mom, and football town where it ruins a childhood to be labeled a nerd, which is what happened to whip-smart, quiet kids with Coke-bottle glasses, especially if their mom was the school librarian and their dad a truck-driving Christian mystic. The night he graduated high school, Aaron hitchhiked to Tallahassee, where he enrolled in Florida State to study linguistics. He excelled in the classroom, but was still lost socially, because small talk and typical college parties weren't for him. Through word of mouth he landed at The J Spot.

"Aaron. Who's the letter to?"

"This girl."

"Of course."

"A woman, actually. She's amazing. The way she thinks. She's so creative and has this tenderness, but refuses to take any shit. She inspires me, and needs to know that, but we can't be together the way we want because she's in Tampa and I'm here."

Earlier, Aaron had been in the living room eavesdropping on Sol, who raved about the virtue of direct action and the importance of an upcoming protest in DC against the International Monetary Fund. And he'd met Justin and Clayton in the kitchen where Justin had gushed about plans for his own vegan café in Tallahassee, while Clayton strummed a stray guitar ever so beautifully. Now, here was Nick, who he'd soon learn had dropped out of community college and starred in a handful of FSU student films. It was a party full of oddballs, obsessed with interesting, even fleeting, passions. There was no small talk to suffer through, and for the first time, Aaron didn't feel like the weirdest dude around. He'd finally found somewhere he belonged.

"Fucking geography," Aaron said. Nick smirked. Aaron smiled back.

Y2K was fast approaching, and on New Year's Eve Nick's Tally crew stormed the commune to hear Clayton's dad's band, the Harvest Gypsies, play. It was a Miccosukee tradition, and Nick dressed for the occasion by wearing a Speedo, cowboy hat, and windbreaker and nothing else. The friends all danced around a bonfire, set off fireworks at midnight, then drove out to the beach to start a new century. Nick was still in his outfit, looking brash, beautiful, intense, and weird, and as dawn threatened to launch a new year, he relaxed into the sand to think. Aaron and Sol found him there and slumped down on either side of him. Nick threw his arms around their shoulders as a pink thread spread across the horizon.

"What's on your mind, freedom cowboy?" Sol asked.

"Death, I guess."

"Death? But the world didn't end, did it? Y2K was a hoax, right?" Aaron joked. "This isn't a dream. It can't be!"

"We're gonna make it, won't we Nick?" Sol took the baton, and kneeled at Nick's feet. He and Aaron were in full movie cliché mode. "Tell us, Nick. Tell us, we're gonna make it!"

"Damn right we are," Nick said, unable to resist. "You know why? Because we're Americans! And we'll get through this thing together!" As the sun rose, the friends were shredded with laughter and sleep deprivation, but soon Nick grew pensive again. "Death's the wrong word, I guess. I'm thinking about life."

"That is a different word," said Sol.

"As in the meaning of life?" Aaron asked.

"As in life insurance," Nick said. "That's what my dad got me for my eighteenth birthday this year. Life insurance."

"Wow. Who does that?" Aaron asked.

"Larry Mevoli apparently," Nick said. "$100,000. That's what I'm worth."

"If you're dead," Sol said with a smile.

"Probably depends how he dies," said Aaron. Nick couldn't help but laugh.

"You know what's really funny? The policy was supposed to be a gift to me, but he only bought it because his stepson is selling life insurance now. So really, it was a gift for him. You know, first sale to make him look good."

"That's fucked up," said Aaron. "I'm sorry, Nick."

"Consider it one more reason to get the fuck out," Sol said. Aaron looked confused.

"Sol's moving to Philly this year," Nick said. "He wants me to come. Gave me a sales pitch and everything. What did you say again?" Sol stood and cleared his throat.

"Life is urgent! Life is meaningless! Nothing matters! Travel! Seek! Live!"

Sol saluted and stood at attention. Nick tackled him. It was a clean takedown, and though he was outweighed and outmuscled, Sol was tenacious and would have fought back if only he could stop laughing. Aaron piled on top of Nick and soon they were all on their backs staring at a brightening sky, laughing until they couldn't breathe.

They laughed at the absurdity of life, at the crooked birth lottery, at their wide-open futures, their empty bank accounts, Nick's lucrative life insurance policy, and their refusal to give in to norms of any kind. They were part of a sacred generation torn between feeling everything way too much and not giving any sort of fuck at all. Fueled by the dueling influences of Jack Kerouac and *Jackass,* they stared into the sky, then out to the blue sea with a fresh new year—make that millennium—all laid out before them. Escape sounded damn fine. It was the only pure move to make.

"My whole life I've been in Florida," Nick said. "And there is a big world out there."

"Year 2000, man. Time to do the shit we've never done," Aaron said.

"Hell yes," said Sol, as golden light spread around them. "Let's do what we've never even imagined."

Later that spring, on one of Nick's last days as a Florida resident, he drove out to Wakulla Springs State Park, alone. Sixteen miles south of town, the springs gush 225 million gallons of sweet water each day and propel a river fourteen miles to the Gulf of Mexico. It's a pristine ecosystem of bullrush stands and five-hundred-year-old bald cypress trees, blue herons, gators, and manatees. There's a small swimming area just off a sandy beach, and about thirty feet below the surface is a network of limestone caves, where the springs bubble from the earth's crust.

That's where Nick liked to go. He'd never seen anybody down there, probably because nobody else had the balls. To Nick it was effortless. He'd wait for the ranger to turn his head, then swim through clear green water to the mouth of a cavern, and penetrate it a little at a time. Sometimes he'd jump off the fifteen-foot platform and dive with momentum. He was wise enough to know that without a light and a line, and no scuba tank, a diver could die in a cave. So he wouldn't go too far. He was happy enough to feel the serenity and silence underwater. There are only so many bath tub breath holds one man can enjoy before getting bored of being perpetually interrupted by his baby sisters banging on the door, with an urgent request to pee. At Wakulla he could take his time, dive deep. Explore. As much as he enjoyed his creative life—acting in student films, writing self-indulgent letters, and jamming on the drums and guitar with Clayton—underwater he could be an athlete again. Underwater he was free. Besides, lobster season was coming up, and he needed to get back in shape before joining the *Bonzo* crew for another mission.

On his final dive of the day, he saw three manatees drifting and twirling with sweet elegance. He swam with them for a minute. Maybe two. Long enough for the contractions to fade and his head to tingle as he kicked to the surface, where he slipped into a beautiful dream. He wasn't wearing weights, which probably saved his life, and woke up on his back, staring at the treetops with a ranger shouting and stomping toward him from the beach. "I've told you for the last time, no diving! You're done! Get the hell out of the water! Now!"

Disoriented, Nick swam to shore. He'd blacked out and wound up floating on his back. Years later he'd take a freediving class and learn how he'd succumbed to a surface blackout, and almost became a statistic. In the spring of 2000, Nick dodged a bullet, and he didn't even know it.

5

CARIBBEAN CUP 2014
ROATAN, HONDURAS

On May 27, 2014, about a dozen divers and spectators huddled on the bow of a fifty-foot catamaran overlooking the competition zone, a kilometer offshore from the island of Roatan. A handful of others gathered in the water, on the outside of the yellow ropes that delineated the zone, which was populated by the usual team of five safety divers and three judges. Ren Chapman was leading the safeties again, though he had an entirely new squad. The most senior judge was Kimmo Lahtinen of Finland, the president of AIDA. Over the next week, Kimmo, Ren, and their counterparts would paste their faces with sunblock and wrap every exposed morsel of flesh with cloth, looking like devout Bedouins facing a sandstorm, but it wouldn't matter much. Tropical sun always wins, especially when beating on the pale pigment of gringos surrounded by open sea for hours and days at a time.

But this was day one of the Caribbean Cup freediving competition, and the first man up was Walid Boudhiaf. The son of a Tunisian economics professor and a French doctor, he was born in Lyon and raised in Tunis. A gifted swimmer as a child, he spent hours in the sea and went spearfishing with friends whenever he could, but it wasn't until he moved to landlocked Bogota, Colombia, in 2005 that he discovered freediving. By 2007 he could hold his breath for over seven minutes in the pool and began taking long walkabouts on the Colombian island of San Andres, where he found a coach who took him offshore for depth training.

He'd made slow and steady progress since then, and as he floated into the zone with a goal of 102 meters in mind, he was confident. Not only had he won silver in Roatan in 2013, he'd hit 112 meters during training just days earlier. This was the first of what he hoped would be a succession of Free Immersion dives that would push him into the big numbers, closer to his personal limit and a potential world record. Nevertheless, 102 meters was still virgin territory. Walid had never before eclipsed 100 meters in a competitive environment.

The Caribbean Cup was most certainly that. In just its second year, it was one of the shining stars on the AIDA schedule. On hand were world record holders William Trubridge and Alexey Molchanov, as well as onetime world record holder and current American record holder Ashley Chapman, Ren's wife. Also here was former world champion Carlos Coste of Venezuela, the first man ever to swim past 100 meters.

The 100-meter plateau remains a standard on the men's side of the draw. To get there means having a strong breath hold, the ability to relax as barometric pressure cranks up, a tolerance for the throbbing swirl of nitrogen narcosis, and a strong handle on the Frenzel-Fattah mouthfill technique. Oh, and divers need to have the athletic ability to swim or pull back up against negative pressure, while their legs are on fire thanks to lactic acid buildup and their intercostal muscles contract, in a desperate impulse to breathe.

Pulling off such a feat in training is incredible, but to do it with the added stress of competition, when spectators and judges watch every move, is an even stiffer challenge. That's why any athlete who earns a white card for a clean dive of over 100 meters is finally taken seriously as an elite-level freediver. When Nick became the first American to hit 100 meters with a monofin the year before, his feat buzzed through the sport's forums, chat rooms, and Facebook pages. Deeper Blue is the largest of the freedive forums, with over 36,000 members all over the world, and over 200,000 unique visitors each month. His 100-meter dive lit up Deeper Blue. Though he'd been on the rise for a year, after that dive, freedivers from every corner of the globe considered Nick Mevoli a credible threat to break world records one day.

Walid was partial to Free Immersion, because given his strong upper body and reedy legs, it fit his physiology. Plus, the Free Immersion world record seemed the most attainable. Alexey couldn't be beat with a monofin, and Will's dominance in Constant No Fins was well known, but Walid's training dive to 112 meters gave him cause to dream that he might be able to get close to Will's Free Immersion record of 121 meters before the week was out. That dive had been super clean; he could equalize easily and didn't feel foggy at the surface. He knew he could do more, which is why he could hardly wait for the competition to begin.

Chiseled and lean, Walid was dressed in a low-buoyancy Orca wetsuit specifically designed for freedivers, with a lanyard jutting from the center of his chest attached to a carabiner. Lanyards are required safety equipment in all depth competitions, because they allow the athletes to clip onto a competition line that measures target depth, but is also attached to a weighted, counterballast system that if activated can pull divers back to the surface in seconds, even if they lose consciousness beyond the reach of the safety team. These days most prefer a Velcro quick-release lanyard, which they attach to their wrist or ankle like a surfboard leash. Walid's lanyard was old school. As he clipped in and the countdown began, he couldn't help but smile. Before him was a vast cerulean sea stretching to a long sweep of powdery white sand, shimmering in the sun.

On the southwest shore of the forty-mile-long island, West Bay Beach is a palm-freckled beauty, backed by voluptuous green hills swathed in scrubby jungle. Roatan, one of the famed Bay Islands of Honduras, attracts an offbeat mixture of package tourists from the States, high-class Hondurans from the capital, scuba divers from all over the world, and American retirees. Think bikinis, Speedos, and beer bellies; fanny packs, backpacks, and man purses; drunkards and explorers. They come to lounge on the sugar-white sand, drink piña coladas all day, and splash in the turquoise shallows. Some grab a mask and fins and kick out to a lovely reef that parallels the shore and slopes until it disappears into the Cayman Trench, a 12,000-foot-deep underwater canyon, the bottom of which nobody will ever see. It's Roatan's easy access to depth and consistent 30-meter visibility that made the Caribbean Cup such a choice addition to the freediving calendar.

When the countdown hit zero, Walid bent over backward with a reverse entry and began pulling down. "Walid Boudhiaf, Free Immersion, 102 meters!" shouted the announcer. "Dive time of three minutes and fifty seconds." Given the water's clarity, it took a while before Walid was swallowed up whole in blue.

It's a strange thing to wait at the surface for a deep diver, especially early in a competition in which all athletes get six dives to score once each in the three disciplines. In terms of the standings, early dives don't matter much. There's more tension later, when the athletes are in rhythm and pushing their limits, and each dive is critical to determining a champion. This, however, was the first dive in a major competition since Nick's death, and Walid's pace was troubling. He reached the bottom plate in less than two minutes, but his ascent was just faster than a sea snail's. "I have him at 90 meters," said the announcer. "Two minutes and twenty seconds!" It would take Walid another full minute before he'd reach 50 meters.

The safety team stirred in anticipation and Ren was the first to go down. Everyone else stared into endless blue, on edge, willing Walid to materialize. Could the sport suffer another injury or tragedy immediately after its first? Walid appeared from the shadows holding the answer. He moved in elegant rhythm. Right-hand pull, glide. Left-hand pull, glide. As he breached, he gripped the line hard and took three hook breaths, or sharp inhales, which he held for a second or two before exhaling. Depleted of oxygen, hook breaths helped Walid absorb it as quickly as possible. Of course, there is always a lag before that fresh rush of O2 reaches the brain, and with the first inhalation an athlete who has pushed their limits is in danger of becoming dizzy and losing motor control. If that happens and his mouth dips into the water, he earns a dreaded red card from the judges, and the dive is disqualified.

Walid never got dizzy. He barely looked out of breath. He was slow but strong, and the dive was as clean and relaxed as he'd hoped. Kimmo flashed a white card and the gallery erupted with celebration and relief. Walid had achieved a new national record for Tunisia, joined the 100-meter club, and gotten the 2014 season off to a splendid and safe start.

The night before the competition kicked off, the thirty-three divers who had signed up to compete in the Caribbean Cup gathered at the rustic San Simon Beach Club in West Bay. They were from Argentina and Chile, Colombia and Venezuela, Mexico and Honduras. Latino divers who usually have to travel to Europe to compete in world-class events were ecstatic to be diving in a Spanish-speaking country. Argentinean Esteban Darhanpe, who's lived on Roatan since 1999, founded the Caribbean Cup in 2013. He lost money the first year. He also lost his job running a dive center, and spent the rest of that summer installing floors in vacation homes, but he never considered folding the operation. "Year by year we get more competitors," he said, "and that's what I care about." He cares so much that he pays the freight for seven athletes. "I cover the champions, and the ones who are broke." This year, the broke included Venezuelan Iru Balic, the defending champ on the women's side. Though that was more the fault of her government than her bank balance.

As the cup was set to kick off, Venezuela's streets were roiled with civil disobedience and its economy was close to collapse. Shops had bare shelves and it was illegal and impossible for folks like Iru to take their money out of Venezuelan banks and use it overseas. In the past, the government had assisted Iru and Carlos Coste in their drive to compete on an international stage because their accomplishments were celebrated in the media back home. In May of 2014, those days looked to be over.

Kimmo opened the meeting by explaining the rules of play, as Iru sat with her friends from Colombia, a gardenia in her thick brown hair. However, he neglected to explain the scoring system before yielding the floor to Ren, who had something more important to discuss.

"There's something we've been talking about ever since the recent tragedy with our friend Nick," Ren said, "and that's squeezes." Six feet tall with a chiseled physique, blue eyes, ruddy cheeks, a wave of blond hair, and an easy North Carolina drawl, Ren, then forty, has a confidence, competitiveness, and charisma that draw you in without overpowering you. A natural athlete, he played baseball through college, then ran his own contracting business in Wilmington, North Carolina, until he quit to sail and teach freediving full time. "We're gonna be watching you, and if we see anything that looks out of the ordinary, you are gonna talk to Kerry and Steve." He gestured toward Dr. Kerry Hollowell, thirty-eight, and her boyfriend, Steve Benson, forty-six, a physician's assistant. The couple lived together, worked at the same hospital in Greenville, North Carolina, and also knew Nick well. "So take care of yourself and get rest, but if you start spitting up blood, just know that we have the ability to ground you."

"It's not grounding you," said Iru, "it's taking care of you." Iru was also close to Nick. The flower in her hair was a dedication to him, a nod to his habit of bringing her flowers each morning the year before, when she dominated the women's draw. The most accomplished Venezuelan woman ever in the sport, Iru was adorable, with big eyes and a sharp wit, and could effortlessly bring a room to life.

Standing beside Ren was his wife, Ashley, a tall, athletic all-American beauty, straight out of the Carolina countryside. Her long brown hair flowing over her shoulders, she cradled her nine-month-old baby in her arms. In 2012, she'd set a world record, and this would be her post-maternity comeback party. "I'm so stoked to be here and see all of you," she said, "but I'm not stoked to be here without Nick. We have to have each other's backs. We tried to have Nick's back, but we failed. We all failed, and I don't plan on losing any more of my friends." She paused to let her words sink in, and fight back tears. "Let's keep that in our minds in every competition we go to. He's the first death, and he was our friend."

The next morning, after Walid's nervy dive, Alexey Molchanov floated into the zone with his girlfriend and coach, Marina Kazakova, an athlete, actress, and model. Dressed in a hooded gold wetsuit, glittering in the sun, he remained upright and held the line with both hands, preparing to dive to 92 meters in his worst discipline, Constant No Fins. This would be a personal best and a national record, but to Alexey it was also a stepping-stone. For his entire career he'd put his energy into Constant Weight, which is why he owned the world record at 128 meters. In 2014 he would switch gears, hoping to close the 10-meter gap between his personal best and Will's Constant No Fins world record, and overtake his rival as the best all-around diver on earth.

Alexey's dive was devoid of drama. He announced a dive of 3:10, and he was on point the whole way. When he hit the surface, Marina kept her GoPro camera rolling and guided him through a clean surface protocol. "*Vichy,* Alex, *vichy,*" she said in their native tongue, beaming with pride. His sharp inhales anchored him back in this world as they awaited the judges' decision.

White card.

Soon it was Will's turn to slip into the drink. The first half of 2014 had been difficult. In January, he thought he'd landed a big-dollar deal with the National Geographic channel for a live televised world record attempt in Kona, but before he could sign on the dotted line, a tragedy on Mt. Everest killed sixteen Sherpas, shut down the climbing season, and killed a TV series the network had planned to air in 2014. When new network leadership arrived to pick up the pieces, they decided that a $3.5 million record attempt in a niche sport was too much of a risk. The deal was off. But it wasn't a missed opportunity that weighed heavily on Will's soul when he floated into the competition zone. It was his missing friend. He'd dedicated his first dive of the 2014 season to Nick Mevoli, announcing a depth of 72 meters in Constant No Fins.

It should have been easy for the world record holder, and his form looked solid on the way down, but his attention was divided, and narcosis crept in at the bottom plate. He took too much time finding the tag, and didn't ascend with purpose. When he breached, he looked disoriented. Luckily, Carla Hanson was there.

A Newport Beach native and onetime competitive freediver whom Will trained and certified at Dean's Blue Hole, Carla is an AIDA judge. In fact, she was one of the three judges at Vertical Blue when Nick passed, but when she's not working a competition, she moonlights as a valuable coach. As a former diver she knows exactly what her athletes need during breathe up, and her loud, high-pitched tone slices hypoxic haze during the critical seconds of a surface protocol. Will flew her in for just such a moment.

"Breathe!" she yelled. "Grab the line, William! Breathe!" He was only half-conscious, his peripheral vision obscured by the fluid goggles, but slowly all came into focus. "Goggles!" Carla screamed, and with some effort, Will pried the goggles off his eyes and moved them to his forehead. He blinked hard, twice. Then a third time as if waking from a stressful dream.

"I'm okay," he said, looking at the judges, making the sign and completing the protocol. When Kimmo flashed the white card, he smiled with relief. Yet even in tribute, it was not the sort of beginning to a competition that a contender hoped for. Alexey had looked smooth and strong. Will looked anything but.

As promised, Ren and Kerry had been watching. Ren signaled to Kerry, who called Will to the platform where she'd set up a clinic, stocked with emergency supplies. She would run a battery of tests on the deep divers, test their blood for oxygen saturation, ask them to cough to see if they would produce blood, and listen to them breathe through her stethoscope. Will checked out fine and was soon sitting on the platform, breathing oxygen to recover.

Such a thorough workup right after a dive was not typical protocol, and some athletes were annoyed to have to cough when they'd rather be breathing oxygen or grinding a protein bar, but 2014 wouldn't be a typical season. Like it or not, every event that year would operate beneath a shadow, and Kerry Hollowell was on a mission—to make sure what happened to Nick never happened again.

6

REVOLUTION

It was a winding river of discontent, a throbbing mass of civil disobedience. Protestors carried hand-scrawled placards reading: *Get Corporate Greed Out of Government, People Not Profits,* and *Raise the Minimum Wage.* There were peace activists who wanted the military budget slashed and dollars diverted to teacher salaries, and an LGBT contingent agitating for equal rights. Sol and Nick marched alongside them up Ben Franklin Parkway toward the Philadelphia Museum of Art—the same route Rocky Balboa made famous—when a call-and-response chant broke out. "This is what democracy looks like!" Someone called through a megaphone up ahead. Nick, Sol, and the rest of the activists roared their response.

"This is what democracy looks like!"

It went like that, back and forth, as they approached the museum, and when the chant died down, a feminist cheerleader squad took center stage. "My bush for president!" they yelled as they leapt into the air, their short skirts billowing upward, revealing hilarious merkins to the delight of the crowd. The lesson: there's no reason activism can't be fun.

For Sol and Nick it *was* fun. Philadelphia in July 2000 was part carnival, part revolution. They landed in the belly of a vital movement hungry for change. The two friends craved a world where profit and efficiency were tempered by justice and community, and so did the tens of thousands who had taken over Philadelphia. Most activists had a pet issue that motivated them, and each day had its own theme. One day the focus would be on wage disparity, the next would highlight environmental issues, and so on.

Black bloc activists known to throw bricks through the plate glass windows of McDonald's and Starbucks were there too, and as the convention approached, vandalism spiked. For city officials and local police, this was their worst nightmare. The Republican National Convention was slated to begin in two days, and the event's urgency muted law enforcement's distinction between nonviolent activists exercising their constitutional rights to protest (99 percent of the movement) and the anarchists. To the cops, it all became one problem to be solved.

This was a big moment for Philly. In the 1990s, Philadelphia had shrugged off its postindustrial, high-crime shroud to become a gleaming beacon of affordable housing and booming small business that promised the excitement of New York with less in-your-face hassle, and its weeklong turn on national television would make its comeback a national news story. Then activists started pouring in, and the mayor, governor, and business leaders had nightmare visions of Seattle the year before, when tens of thousands of activists marched, snarled traffic, barricaded themselves to buildings, scaled skyscrapers to unfurl banners, and for a short while even managed to shut down the World Trade Organization (WTO) meetings. The Battle of Seattle brought global economic issues into American living rooms, because their clashes with local law enforcement led the news for days. The way Nick and Sol saw it, the activists had exposed the WTO to be a network of developed nations, driven by big business, colluding to implement economic policies for the benefit of the few and at the expense of the many, in each and every country.

Sol's first foray into the movement (which after a period of dormancy would rise again as Occupy Wall Street in 2011) happened during a similar protest against the International Monetary Fund in Washington, DC, the previous April—the first major protest since Seattle. Afterward, he returned to Tally and told stories of activist girls who were brainy and sexy, tender and open-minded. He told Nick that Philadelphia would be the next target, and that anyone who showed up and was willing to march and squat in one of West Philly's beat-down old Victorians would be provided with a bed, a bike, and a date. That was the policy that convinced Nick.

As the convention loomed, the city urged, threatened, and begged protestors to utilize their "legal protest zone," a cordoned-off quadrant of sidewalk tucked away from the main entrance of the convention and most of the television cameras. Activists were in the mood for civil disobedience instead—the kind that if properly executed would shut the convention down.

The Friends Center on 15th Street and Cherry Avenue offered a welcome mat for the activists. A brick complex whose oldest buildings date to 1856, this was the city's main meeting house for people of the Quaker faith, one of the largest of its kind in the country, and a place where activists had gathered for more than a century. When it opened, it was where abolitionists met and organized. After the turn of the twentieth century it was the headquarters for the women's suffrage movement. It was also a shelter for antiwar protesters during Vietnam.

Nick met Sol and another activist, Jessica Mammarella, in the Friends Center lobby, which was packed with protesters. There were silver-streaked elder longhairs who'd been agitating since the sixties; painted, pierced punks of the new day; and church-rooted African American protesters young and old—some of whom had been fighting for equality and justice for decades. Jessica, born to a teenage mother and raised in the Philly suburbs, was in charge of logistics. It was her job to take that raw manpower and channel it. She led Sol and Nick from the Friends Center to the brand-new, state-of-the-art Convention Center with its multihued LED lights glowing on Broad Street, one block away.

"That's where W is to be crowned," she said.

"Gross," said Sol.

"We need the entire parade route sealed. Nobody gets nominated without a little chaos."

When they weren't on Ben Franklin Parkway or in the Friends Center, Nick and Sol were in West Philly at an old trolley turnaround. Jessica and her team rented the mammoth two-story brick warehouse in an impoverished neighborhood, across the street from the Mount Olive housing projects, for $500 from a man who owned a flooring company. This is where they'd build props and prepare for the signature moment of the Philadelphia protests: a puppet show.

A rather elaborate puppet show that would feature 141 twelve-foot-tall skeletons linked together with colorful chains. Built with the help of a famed political theater troupe out of Vermont called Bread & Puppet, they would be marched along a parade route carved through the city center by activists who would block traffic by locking themselves together with a contraption made from metal pipes. Day one of the Republican Convention was criminal justice day on the streets, and the skeletons symbolized the record 141 prisoners executed by Bush during his tenure as governor of Texas.

Sol led one of the lockdown teams. He recruited Nick to create a diversion with his bicycle and block traffic while he and the others could be locked in place, at which point Nick could ride away to safety. In the meantime, he became a gofer. Whenever Jessica needed something, she'd find Nick, whom she always called by his full name. As in, "Nick Mevoli, we need more plywood," or "Where's your bike, Nick

Mevoli, I need you to make a run to the dollar store." He would happily do her bidding, hit hardware stores and dumpster dive for supplies. Sometimes he would take care of his tasks alone, but he often asked Jen Kates to tag along.

Nick and Jen had noticed one another on his first day in the trolley house. She was twenty-one years old and pretty, with short dark hair she'd cut herself, fair skin, dark eyes, and a small mouth. Philly born, she'd only recently moved home from Asheville, North Carolina, to take part in the protests. Before Asheville she'd studied human rights law and Greek tragedy at Oxford; Nick wasn't anything like the intellectuals she was used to dating.

"He was beautiful, but with unusual features," she said, "and he was self-conscious. He didn't really know where he fit." Nick wouldn't engage in the political discussions. He'd do BMX tricks, and put Jen on his handlebars and ride her around a still-decrepit corner of her hometown with no fear. "He lived in an immersive way," she said. Whenever they went out for supplies he'd hit a coffee shop he liked, where old-timers played chess and the coffee was strong, or he'd have lunch at an Indian restaurant with a cheap vegetarian buffet. Nick told her every moment with her was an adventure to be savored. She would have kissed him, but he never tried. Didn't matter. Blurred lines only added to the urgency and romance of the task at hand.

On the morning of August 1, the day of the puppet show, Sol and his team staged their gear at the trolly house, while Nick slipped out and rode over to his favorite dive café for breakfast then coasted back in plenty of time to join the action. Or so he thought. As he made the final turn, he was stunned to find police cars everywhere. More than 150 cops had the trolley house surrounded, and his friends—Jessica, Sol, Jen, and seventy-two others—were being led off in zip-tie cuffs.

Days before the convention, four carpenters had showed up with union cards and were put to work. They were undercover state troopers. They joked with the activists as they helped build the puppets, while surreptitiously taking note of flooring chemicals and metal pipe in various sections of the warehouse. Didn't matter that the chemicals belonged to the landlord's flooring company, and the pipes were there to lock the activists together. What they reported was an explosives factory and a bomb plot, when all they did was shut down a puppet show.

The DA hammered the activists with an array of charges, and most were held until the convention was over. "It was a conspiracy to keep the city clean and conflict free during the convention," said Jessica, "and they succeeded because [the GOP convention] was a huge coming-out party for the city. And it was all Democrats doing it."

The city's infiltration into the activist community would eventually be proven illegal after it was revealed that the FBI and police tracked activist emails in the run up to the arrests, and to make matters more absurd, in the immediate aftermath, officials claimed the protesters were in league with communists. At a press conference weeks later, Stefan Presser, the legal director of the American Civil Liberties Union, said of the police report, "That document could have been written by Hoover's FBI." Still, it would take several months, and in some cases years, before all the charges would be dismissed.

Jessica was held for four days. Sol was released after posting a $250,000 bond twelve days after his arrest. Jen was locked up for two weeks. Nick stuck around for as long as he could, hoping to see her, but Paul and the *Bonzo* crew needed him in Marathon. It was lobster season, after all, and by the time she was released, Nick was already home in Tallahassee trying to figure out what to do next.

Within days, she called him from her grandparents' house in Boynton Beach, near West Palm, where she'd retreated to recover from her incarceration. "I'm taking you to the Keys," he said. "You have to see them."

"Yeah, that sounds like fun. When were you thinking?"

"I'll leave in fifteen minutes, and see you in, like, six and a half hours. Be ready."

"Nick, that's crazy. You can't drop everything because I randomly called you."

"Why not?"

"I don't know, because it doesn't make any sense. Nobody does that."

"Exactly!" he said. Her giggle was a yes.

Sol used to talk about how Clayton was good with girls because he could make them laugh. Justin would cuddle and watch movies all day, but Nick would take them on a magic carpet ride. True to form, he hung up the phone, packed a duffle, and checked the oil in the Chick Magnet, his 1976 Pontiac Grand Prix. His Uncle Paul named it when he drove it in high school, and gifted it to Nick when he turned seventeen. In minutes Nick was lead-footing it 427 miles to Boynton Beach.

He rang the bell just after dark and Jen found him on her grandparents' doorstep. Her grandfather was a World War II air force veteran, just like his, and Nick wanted to hear every story. They went through old pictures and talked for hours, and the next morning her grandmother packed them a lunch, sealed in waxed bags she'd salvaged from cereal boxes. Nick loved it. He did the exact same thing.

"You realize that you have the soul of a Jewish grandmother, don't you?" Jen asked on their drive into Little Havana for a cup of Cuban coffee before they hit Highway 1. He glanced over at her. "One that grew up during the Great Depression and refuses to throw anything away."

"Thank you," he said.

They zoomed the highway from Miami Beach and veered into the Everglades, stopping to scope gators and blue herons, watch snakes slither, and listen to the wind rustle the mangroves. They blitzed through Key Largo at sunset and landed at the foot of Seven Mile

Bridge as the half-moon rose high enough to illuminate the causeway, that minimalist marvel of engineering. The sky was clear and dark. They still hadn't kissed, but they undressed each other to their underwear before wading into the warm water on the Gulf side. He pointed toward Grouper Gorge.

"Let's go out there." Jen tensed up. "You'll be fine," he said, "I got you. Relax on your back." She trusted him and lay flat. He took her by the wrist and kicked farther out. As the current started to swirl he noticed phosphorescence rising from the surface with each stroke. He lifted his hand out of the water and droplets of blue-green light streamed down his wrist as he drizzled electricity on her neck, chest, and navel. They were surrounded by microscopic bioluminescent plankton, which turned the sea into an electric blue field of light—their magnificent biological ploy to distract predators.

"No way!" she said, watching liquid light pearl on her arms and cling to his eyelids. Nick duck dove and dolphin kicked in figure eights all around her. When he finally came up for air, she splashed him good, starting a delirious bioluminescent water fight, charging the night with a blue-green flash. The water rippled with an energy that connected them, the privileged Jewish intellectual from the Northeast and the dreamy son of a butcher from West Florida.

They spent that night curled up in the Chick Magnet and when the sun rose, took off again, blitzing up the west coast of Florida. They listened to Nick's mix tapes the whole way. There was a lot of Weakerthans and Pedro the Lion—all straight edge punk. They talked incessantly, stopped in a shitty motel when he got too tired to drive, and made love for the first time. They drove all the way to Tallahassee, where Jen hopped a flight back to South Florida. When she left they had no idea when they would see each other next.

Two months later Clayton and Nick made their way into 4040, an underground punk club in Philly that was on its last legs. The interior was dank and dark, the sound system wonderfully distorted, and the Weakerthans were about to take the stage. Nick was nervous with anticipation. He and Jen had barely spoken since their roadtrip, and tonight would be their reunion. The lights came down, the crowd cheered, and the two friends snaked through the compressed web of humanity toward the front of the stage where they found her.

"I know you," she said. He didn't say a word. He just stared into her eyes. She threw her arms around him, the band launched into "Confessions of a Futon Revolutionist," and he spun her around as the crowd hopped up and down, screamed and collided.

They stepped outside for a smoke break and watched each other silently as their breath fogged in the chill. Layered in a denim jacket and a hoody, Nick shivered, ill prepared for true winter. He had just moved out of his Tally digs—finally escaped Florida—only to land in a cold-water squat with no heat and no warm clothes. Jen decided there and then to take him home.

She brought him to her parent's colonial farmhouse outside the city, and the next day they started looking for a place to live. They never discussed boundaries. They never said I love you. Their lines remained blurred as they moved in together, renting a turn-of-the-century row house in a beleaguered, working-class section of South Philly. It was a dump. The foundation was cracked, and the splintering wood floors were sloped. Furniture, which they found on street corners and in alleys, would migrate, and there was no hot water, which was a big deal during a Philadelphia winter. As he heated bathwater for them on the stove, he held her close to warm up.

Jen got a job at a local bakery. Nick worked as a bike courier, the only one of his kind on a BMX. He liked everything about his job at Heaven Sent: the ancient dispatcher with her gravelly Philly brogue; the grimy wood-paneled office always percolating with Maxwell House; and the fact that he could learn the city on two wheels.

At home he created scavenger hunts for Jen, hiding letters and gifts around their hovel. One was a book of illustrations and poetry he'd created after their trip to the Keys. Another was a glass of seawater and shells sealed in wax. He even made a postindustrial dream catcher, crafted from an old glass lens, twisted wire, and feathers, all of which he found on the streets.

They'd take long bike rides, often to that Indian buffet in West Philly, which Jen didn't even like and was out of the way, but she'd always agree. It was completely unreasonable, but he was completely unreasonable, and she appreciated that about him. It was at the buffet when he confessed that he wanted to be an actor. "Nobody comes to Philly to be an actor," she said. "You have to go to New York." He shrugged, knowing it was true, and plopped a samosa on her plate.

On Saturday nights they'd get take-out pizza and eat while sitting on the brick paths of Rittenhouse Square, surrounded by sycamore trees dangling with white lanterns. On Fridays they'd join the midnight Critical Mass ride to the Pretzel Factory to pluck fresh, warm pretzels straight from the conveyer belt. But the trouble with undefined relationships is they don't often last. Jen stepped out on him and then moved out of the house completely. She expected him to hate her, and he was certainly hurt, but he told her he understood, that he wouldn't hold it against her, and he kept his promise.

Nick stuck around Philadelphia, working as a courier, and had just moved back into a West Philly squat when he heard about a Brooklyn film director who had come to town to shoot an independent movie about Philly's activists and squatters. There was an open casting coming up, and the director was hoping to hire real activists, which she called *actorvists*. Nick was intrigued.

The casting was held at a defunct video store near the University of Pennsylvania, and when Nick showed he was asked to fill out a form with his name and age, and write a short bio. He watched as a lineup of would be actorvists, some giggly and goofing off, others looking overwhelmed or on edge, took turns sitting in a plastic chair before the director, her assistant, and a camera operator.

The director had creamy white skin, red hair, brown eyes, and she spoke softly. When it was his turn, he handed her his reel of student films along with the questionnaire, and read his lines. She jotted down notes about his burning intensity and leading man's looks, but all she needed were side players. Glorified extras. She checked his age on the questionnaire. It said he was twenty-five years old.

Esther Bell was thirty when she and her assistant moved to Philadelphia to shoot her second feature film. She'd sold her first movie, *Godass,* about a gay father and his punk teenage daughter, to Showtime in 2000, and was approached to direct a fully financed independent feature based on the activists who had protested against the WTO in Seattle. She hated the script, but the opportunity to direct a film with a $300,000 budget was too good to pass up. She planned to rewrite it on the fly. The night after the auditions she lingered on Nick's audition tape late into the night and watched his reel. He was in.

Esther filmed cinéma vérité style, which meant the actors as well as the crew would become entrenched in the world they portrayed. Nick couldn't fathom his luck. He'd practically stumbled into his first professional acting gig, and he would do everything he could to help. He invited all fifteen members of the cast and crew to come live in his sprawling old Victorian that was once a mansion and was now a wreck. He also became the unofficial location scout, securing locations around the city, and a one-man craft services concession. After Philadelphia's wonderful Italian Market closed for the night, he'd root through the dumpsters of the delis and bakeries, olive oil purveyors and chocolatiers, sorting edibles from true waste. He had an above-the-rim policy. With Nick on the case and in the kitchen, the cast and crew ate like movie stars.

It was a twenty-one-day shoot and on one of her first nights in his squat, Nick and Esther found themselves alone in his room discussing the new pages she'd written. After running lines they locked eyes, exhausted and exhilarated. The room was a wreck. It smelled of piss and stale nicotine. His sheets were filthy. Cigarette butts were extinguished on windowsills. None of it bothered her. She was too turned on. He kissed her quickly. She was hesitant at first. She had a strict rule against on-set hookups, and here she was breaking it. Their kisses grew softer and deeper. She slipped off her top and turned out the light.

A few days later the financier pulled out. Esther had been self-funding the shoot, waiting for the promised $300,000 to land in her bank account. Now she was both screwed financially and heartbroken to have to break the news to her cast and crew. She confided in Nick.

Hers was the first in a night of revelations. She told him about her difficult teenage years in South Carolina, and he told her everything too, tagging life-altering events with dates that sounded out of place. "Nick, how old *are* you?" she asked, her head on his bare chest, his finger twirling her red curls. It was a muggy July night. Their skin was slick with perspiration. "Your audition sheet said twenty-five."

"Did it?"

"Oh my god," she said, sitting up. "You're a teenager, and I'm a cradle robber."

"Chill out. I'm twenty. It's perfectly legal."

"Barely." Esther was baffled. Nick was mature, thoughtful, capable, and hard working. He was a great cook—he had his own pots and pans, for god's sake—and he was wonderful in bed. How could he be so young? Then she looked around the room. It was filthy. The roof leaked. The walls had holes so big even plywood couldn't patch them. It was like something out of *Fight Club*, and unlike the rest of the cast and crew, he was living there before he got the gig. Only a kid could live that way without an end date. She lay back down and curled up close. "I just feel shitty about it is all."

The production folded, and Nick brought her to Union Station to catch her train back to New York. On the way, he told her that he and Aaron were headed to Cuba, flouting the US travel ban by routing through the Bahamas. Nick had never been abroad and was thrilled. Esther was excited for him, but a little sad too. He told her he loved her, and she wanted to believe him.

He handed her a letter and asked her to open it on the train. They kissed goodbye and he watched as she found a seat near the window, waving as the Amtrak rattled away. As Philadelphia receded and the train emerged into the countryside, she opened the envelope. Inside was a Polaroid he'd shot of a sunflower growing out of a garbage heap. She'd told him about being sexually abused and raped. She'd shared more with him than with anybody she'd ever known. "You've been through a lot of shit," he wrote, "but you are the flower that survived it." When she arrived at her Williamsburg apartment she climbed onto the roof, stared over the East River toward the Twin Towers and the beautiful Manhattan skyline, and read it once more. That's it, she thought, I'm in love. She had no idea when or if she'd see him again.

A little over a month later, Aaron and Nick were sitting in a patch of Cuban wetlands, on the edge of a limestone depression filled with clear freshwater. The scrub jungle that surrounded them seemed to sprout from a hollow crust, and beneath it was a network of caves that burrowed deep into the earth. Like on Mexico's Yucatan peninsula, the Cuban *cenotes* were prime snorkeling and scuba diving habitat, and a handful of tourists were in the water, splashing, scuba diving, and playing. One of them swam over.

He was a lifeguard from Havana, was upbeat and friendly, spoke raspy rapid-fire Spanish, and challenged the guys to see how deep they could dive. Aaron had never seen Nick dive deep, and though they'd been in Cuba for three weeks by then, the majority of their time had been spent in cities. They'd strolled Havana's magnificent *malecón* and spent vast tracts of time sitting in the shade, smoking cigars, people watching, and chatting with locals. They bought produce in local markets, prepared their own meals, hitch-hiked from town to town in open-bed sugarcane trucks then hopped a third-class train to Santiago, where they spent sweltering days strolling barrios and watching kids play stickball, and their nights in the palm-dappled plazas begging for a cool breeze. They drank coffee with *viejos,* flirted with beautiful *chicas,* and sipped Havana Club with local boys into the wee hours.

Thanks to Aaron's language skills the trip had been a free flow. Each new face offered a unique taste of what life felt like in the friendliest outlaw country in the world. They left each bar, park, and *casa particular* (Cuban B&B) with a recommendation for the next stop, and fueled up on cheap rum, drowning their straight edge past in 80 proof sugarcane spirit. When they found a beach, Nick enjoyed long swims but also made it a priority to try and teach Aaron how to equalize so they could explore the coral reefs offshore. No luck. Didn't matter, Nick was content to follow Aaron's trail, happy to be hanging with one of his best friends on the gritty road. Then came the challenge from a Havana lifeguard, and the promise of a bottomless limestone pit.

"How deep is it, do you think?" Nick asked the lifeguard.

"*Dios sabe. Mas que ciento metros, creo,*" he said. Nick nodded, and grabbed his mask. He had enough Spanish to know what 100 meters sounded like. "*Cuantos metros puede bucear.*"

"*Vamos a ver,*" Nick said, hopping in the water. He'd never actually measured how deep he could go, but he took stock of the guy and felt good about his chances. Lifeguard or no.

"Loser buys rum," said the lifeguard, flashing his English with a sly smile.

"*Bueno,*" said Nick.

Aaron counted down from ten, the competitors took their deepest breath, and then they were gone. Aaron peered over the limestone ledge, checked his watch and his wallet. They were traveling on a shoestring budget—$20 per day. Could Nick really beat a lifeguard on his home turf? In about thirty seconds he had his answer. The lifeguard was already shooting back to the surface.

"*Tu amigo donde está*?" he asked, breathless. Aaron shrugged. The lifeguard put his face back in the water, concerned. Nick had disappeared, he said. He just kept going farther and farther down until the lifeguard couldn't see him anymore. Aaron checked his watch. Nick had been underwater for a minute. In fact, he'd just passed a crew of scuba divers who'd materialized from a cavern and couldn't believe their eyes.

Just before the two-minute mark Nick materialized from the watery shadows, dolphin kicking through the blue. When he surfaced, Aaron offered a hand and pulled him up onto the limestone ledge. "All right," he said, only slightly breathless, "let's go drink some rum."

The lifeguard bought their bottle of blanco in the nearby village of Playa Guiones. They drank it out of small plastic cups on a powdery beach kissed by Bahia de Cochinos, aka the Bay of Pigs. Buzzed, Nick and the lifeguard took turns behind the wheel of his vintage Volvo, which thumped with distorted techno remixes of Nirvana, on the long drive back to Havana.

Rural Cuba unfurled as an analog dream. Horse carts pulled timber wagons. Fishing ports were crowded with colorful wooden canoes. They slalomed around jalopy trucks hauling sugarcane and tobacco, and putt-putting tractors on their way home from the fields. The lifeguard was passed out, sitting shotgun, when Nick and Aaron stopped on the side of the road to take a leak in the golden sun. "Dude, I knew you were good in the water, but I had no idea you were superhuman." Aaron said.

"I'm not," Nick said, "it's just kind of natural for me."

"That was not natural, man. *That* was amazing."

HER PHONE RANG a little after 9 a.m. on September 11, 2001. Esther's bohemian friends typically didn't wake until after ten and they rarely called before noon, so she assumed it was family and ignored it. It kept ringing. When she finally answered and got the news she placed the phone on the cradle without a word, stumbled to the stairs, and climbed to the roof of her building, barefoot. Still in her pajamas, she saw fire blaze near the top of Tower One and black smoke curl into the sky. It wasn't long before the second plane slammed into Tower Two, and within two hours both structures had folded in on themselves. She hadn't moved a muscle.

Aaron and Nick were supposed to fly home, via the Bahamas, the next day and when they reached the airport they still hadn't heard the news. By then US airspace was closed and a fellow passenger told them why as they boarded their flight. When they landed in Freeport, they learned that they'd be stranded on Grand Bahama Island in a mega casino resort for three days.

Esther didn't leave her apartment for nearly a week. To her and many New Yorkers, it felt like the world was falling apart, so she decided to hunker down and wait out the next big blow. She was sitting at her desk overlooking Berry Street on the afternoon of September 16 when she saw a U-Haul pull up to her building. She stepped to the windows to get a better view of whoever was about to emerge from the cab. Probably yet another hipster newcomer, she thought. Perhaps a Manhattan refugee shell-shocked from 9/11.

Nick hopped out of the truck instead. He squinted at a folded-over piece of notebook paper, hand-scrawled with Esther's address. In his other arm he cradled a sewing machine. He looked up and saw her staring down from her open window. "There you are!" he shouted, flashing his contagious smile.

"What's with the U-Haul?!"

"I'm moving, of course!"

"Moving where?!"

"Right up there!" he yelled. Her heart flip-flopped. Her lips curled toward the powder-blue Brooklyn sky. She wiped her left eye. A stray droplet trickled down her right cheek. He'd called her as soon as he got back on US soil, but never said he was coming to see her, much less move in. Wasn't that something people discussed?

"I love you," she whispered.

"What?!" he shouted.

"I said, I love you!"

7

CARIBBEAN CUP 2014
ROATAN, HONDURAS

West Bay's gifts were shining on day two of the Caribbean Cup while Ashley Chapman was in the competition zone. Onshore, the golden sun was high, the suntan brigade lay out in tiny bikinis on powder-white sand, and the piña coladas were flowing. Offshore, visibility was magnificent, and the blue world looked like heaven. Ashley hooked the line with her fingertips as she floated on her back, decked out in her silver hooded wetsuit, fluid goggles, a nose clip, and a monofin. As the spectators murmured, she visualized a fluid dolphin kick down to 20 meters, a streamlined freefall to the bottom plate at 75 meters, then a graceful yet powerful kick back toward the light.

Day one hadn't gone as planned for Ashley or for Christina Saenz de Santamaria, her chief rival, as both earned red cards. It's not uncommon for the best divers to start slow, but nobody wants to start a comp with two disqualifications. That would leave only four remaining dives to score three times. On day two, both needed to dive clean.

Christina wasn't the only athlete on Ashley's radar. Sophie Jacquin would be a handful as well. While Christina and Ashley were both tall and slender, with long arms and legs—all of which are ideal for freediving—Sophie was in the best shape of all. Born in France but based in Guadeloupe, a French Caribbean isle, she didn't have the height of her competitors but made up for it with lean yet strong arms, muscular legs, and a six-pack. On the first day of the competition, Sophie swam to 53 meters without fins. And just before Ashley got in the water, she rocked a 73-meter Free Immersion dive, pulling herself down to depth and back, setting a national record. When the white card was flashed, she screamed and pounded the surface in glee. Two dives, two white cards. Sophie was in charge.

Ashley didn't live in the tropics like Sophie or Christina, who lived on Ko Tao, Thailand, but she was born for the sport she loved. The average woman sports a 4.2-liter lung capacity. Ashley's is an incredible 9 liters. That's a larger lung volume than both Will Trubridge and Alexey Molchanov, who come in at 7 and 7.5 liters, respectively. Yet despite her athletic build, Ashley didn't play sports growing up and wasn't on the swim team. She was raised more beauty queen than killer athlete in the small town of Richlands, North Carolina. Less than a thousand people lived there and few of them imagined a life traveling the world or even aspired to college. Ashley wanted both. She studied environmental engineering near the beach at UNC-Wilmington, where she got into Ultimate Frisbee, a physically demanding game that is part rugby, part soccer, and has an extreme geek quotient. It says something about a person's quirk level when their first competitive sports experience involves a Frisbee. Ashley had always been quirky. She was also a badass, and it was her speed and athletic grace that caught Ren's eye on the Frisbee field.

Ren was a born competitor, and Ashley's skills were endearing to him. When she blew out her cleat in a big game, Ren bonded it with epoxy and duct tape. Ren was handy, sweet, fit, had a killer smile and two labradors, one chocolate and one black, that accompanied him everywhere. To work, to dinner, to Frisbee practice. She dug all three of them immediately. One afternoon after practice, she got in his F250 and told him she was a few weeks away from heading abroad with the Peace Corps. His heart flinched. He didn't. He told her about his job building playgrounds for schools and day care centers, and he invited her on a boat ride with him and his dogs.

They drove out to his house, a cute clapboard number on the Intracoastal Waterway, overlooking a spectacular estuary and less than two miles to the beach. Tied up to a boat ramp out front was a little runabout. The dogs bounded aboard. Ashley and Ren followed. They motored up the estuary, spotting herons and sea eagles, and watched the sunset ignite the western sky. She never did join the Peace Corps. She was too busy falling in love.

Ren's father had been a biologist, scuba instructor, and the head of water safety at UNC-Wilmington since the mid-1970s, and he had Ren scuba diving by the time he was six years old. Baseball and college life got between Ren and the ocean for a short while, but as soon as he graduated and started his business, he felt a deeper pull toward nature. He'd get his fix in the marsh, the nearby woods, and deep underwater. In 2007 he got into spearfishing and took a course with Performance Freediving International.

Ashley moved in with Ren, got into freediving too, and the couple soon dedicated themselves to their sport. They became instructors with PFI and began teaching courses from their sailboat, *Nila Girl*. They sailed the Caribbean and the Florida Keys, teaching, cruising, and training, and Ashley was a fixture on the competitive circuit. From 2010 to 2012 she competed around the globe, became captain of the US national team, earned five American records (two in the pool and all three depth records), and broke a world record. Ren was both her coach and a professional safety diver through it all. They even found time to get married.

When the countdown hit zero, Ashley sipped air until her lungs were fully inflated, and said a final prayer. Then she turned and disappeared. She breached the surface again in under 2:30, hooked the line, faced the judges, removed her nose clip and her goggles with ease, and flashed the okay sign, but she hadn't said those three magic words. Her lips were blue. She needed oxygen. She kept breathing as the seconds ticked away. "Say I'm okay!" Carla Hanson shrieked. "Say it!"

"I'm okay," Ashley said, revealing the tag, proving she'd made depth at 75 meters. When the white card came, she hugged Carla and rolled her eyes in relief.

Next it was Christina's turn. Her 78-meter dive the day before had been a bit too ambitious, so she downshifted to 76 meters. Not a big difference to mere mortals, but those who push their limits know that it becomes increasingly difficult to equalize with each meter, and if she could pull down to 76 meters and back up again, she would still be the deepest woman in the tournament thus far, one click deeper than Ashley.

Christina stayed vertical as she breathed up. Dressed in an all-black wetsuit, her husband and coach Eusebio Saenz de Santamaria was right next to her, whispering instruction and encouragement as she began sipping and then gulping air. Over the past ten years Christina had scored eight national records, including the Australian record of 85 meters in Constant Weight and 80 meters in Free Immersion. Like 100 meters for men, 80 meters is a serious number for women, and Christina is one of the deepest women in the world. Like Ashley and Sophie, she nailed her dive, and when the white card came, Eusebio grabbed her and kissed her on the mouth.

"I felt good today," she said as she toweled off on the catamaran, but insisted no matter who's in the field, the ultimate competition lies within. "In the end you are only competing against yourself."

Ashley saw it differently. "This is exactly what I needed," she said, nuzzling her baby, Ani, and nodding toward Christina from their patch of shade on the boat deck. "Points on the board."

"Ashley, you know all of our cell phones are infested with Ani's picture," Iru Balic said as she bent down to give mother and baby a hug. The freediving community is so well connected on Facebook, every Ani picture had become an online event. Ashley laughed and nodded, guilty as charged.

At five feet one, Iru, the defending champion, lacked size but made up for it in determination. Then just twenty-eight years old, she had overcome both family tragedy and political upheaval to build her freediving career. The top woman in Venezuela and a multiple national record holder, Iru grew up posh. Her father owned a commercial fishing business, and they had everything they ever wanted: a modern home by the sea, a chauffeur who could take them to flamenco dance class, even a luxury apartment in Caracas. "We were spoiled girls," she said.

Then her family home was demolished in a devastating landslide. Miraculously, everyone survived, but her father's business was destroyed. All his boats and trucks, and the family house lost. Insurance wasn't an option in Venezuela, so they started over. Where once there had been flamenco class after school, now there was work. The family's last foothold was her grandmother's tiny shop, where she sold *cocadas*, a sugary coconut drink. Iru's mother began selling empanadas, and they expanded the space into a restaurant. Iru and her baby sister worked there after school. Their life was less glamorous, but the family became closer. You could even say happier. They couldn't afford the tuition at their Catholic school any longer, but the nuns arranged a scholarship to keep the girls enrolled.

During high school, Iru and her family lived in Caracas where the schools were better. Chavez was in charge of Venezuela. Crime was high, corruption evident, and the seeds of discontent were already filtering through the streets. But Iru was a kid, and she didn't get caught up in any of that. She was focused on a dream she'd had since she was a little girl. She wanted to scuba dive.

She reached out to Carlos Coste in 2001. He was on his way to becoming the best freediver alive, but at the time he still ran freediving and scuba courses in Caracas. He told Iru she could take a cheap course through the scuba club he founded, which would enable her to dive with the club wherever and whenever they organized a trip. But first she'd have to be accepted, and when she showed up there were ninety-five people to fill twenty-five spots. The organizers put them through an intense training program where they had to run and jump their way through a series of calisthenics, and only the best athletes qualified. Iru was just fourteen and she was small, but she had the strong legs of a gymnast and unlimited desire. She would not be denied.

The scuba training wasn't the typical weekend course either. It involved a physical training regimen and freediving lessons. Her whole life it had been scuba that Iru craved, but she loved the freedom and quiet of apnea even more. The club organized a small pool competition. She was fifteen by then, and being one of a few women and the youngest by far, most treated her like the team pet, but during the pool competition she swam 90 meters on one breath with only small fins. It wasn't world record caliber, but it wasn't far off the national record, and it impressed her coach, who realized she was a budding star.

In 2005, Iru attended her first world championship in Nice. Although she'd competed in pools in Brazil and Cuba, this was her first depth competition and she was the youngest competitor at just eighteen years old. Her clean Constant Weight dive to 56 meters gave her the Venezuelan record and made her the eighth-best woman in the world.

These were the salad days in Venezuelan freediving as athletes were government funded. Not only did the Chavez government cover the costs of their overseas trips to various competitions, but the best divers were given apartments in Caracas and a small stipend to support their training at home. The following year, Iru competed at the world championship again, this time in Egypt. She broke her own national record and placed sixth overall, but college beckoned. After graduation she began competing again, and during the 2013 Caribbean Cup she broke five national records in six days, easily winning the women's draw. But 2014 was a different year. The competition was stiff, and her mind was on Nick—her friend, occasional training partner, and on-and-off crush—not on the podium.

Distractions are the enemy in competitive freediving. It's vital to remain calm, eat and sleep well, and feel peaceful. When focus strays, stress builds and an athlete can become less than whole underwater. That's what happened to Iru. She attempted a 67-meter Constant Weight dive on day one, and perforated her eardrum due to poor equalization. The damage wasn't too bad, but it held her out of day two, and with each lost dive, her hopes to repeat faded.

In the meantime, she joined the cheering section. In ensuing days, Daniel Cordova from Chile, Alejandro Lemus from Mexico City, Carlos Coste, and Sofia Gómez Uribe, a civil engineering student from Medellin, Colombia, scored national records. Each time they did, Iru led the cheers from the bow of the dry boat.

Carlos Coste was particularly popular among Latino divers. The first and only Latin American–born world champion, he won the 2004 world championship in Cyprus when he also became the first athlete to swim past 100 meters on one breath. He defended his world title in Nice in 2005 with a world record Constant Weight dive to 105 meters, but in 2006 tragedy struck, when he was injured during a No Limits training dive in Egypt.

No Limits is dangerous because freedivers, like scuba divers, can get air bubbles in their bloodstream at extreme depths, and the only way to ensure the diver doesn't get decompression sickness, or the bends, is to ascend slow enough for those bubbles to be reabsorbed. If the athlete ascends too quickly, the stray bubbles can become lodged in the ventricle, stopping the heart, or they can clog blood vessels in the brain, which leads to stroke. That's what happened to Carlos.

When he surfaced from 180 meters, his left side was paralyzed. He spent five weeks undergoing hyperbaric treatments in Egypt and Germany, as well as physical therapy which helped him recover some range of motion, but when he returned to Venezuela he had to relearn even basic swim strokes. One year later, in 2007, he placed third at the AIDA World Championships with a Constant Weight dive to 103 meters. In 2009 he won third again with a Constant Weight dive to 110 meters in Dean's Blue Hole, and at the 2011 world championships in Kalamata he earned a silver medal with a Constant Weight dive to 116 meters. Those were remarkable achievements for anyone, regardless of medical history, and when he surfaced after a No Fins dive to 61 meters in Roatan, earning yet another national record, he was greeted by the entire Latin American contingent on the bow of the dry boat, standing and cheering before breaking into song to the tune of Daft Punk's "Get Lucky."

Mi presidente es Maduro
me gusta mucho freediving
(translation: My president is Maduro, and I like freediving a lot)

On May 31, the last day of competition, with the women's title up for grabs, Ashley Chapman earned a song from Iru and the rest. As predicted, it had been a tight battle at the top between Sophie, Christina, and Ashley. The day before, it appeared that Christina gained an advantage. Ashley had to turn early on her 80-meter Constant Weight dive when she felt a slight squeeze in her left ear at 67 meters. She was having equalization problems and didn't want to risk blowing out her eardrum, so she surfaced only to watch Christina nail her 80-meter Constant Weight dive, and extend her lead. Afterward, Ashley, wrapped in her American flag towel, sat beside Sophie and sloshed her feet in a clear and spectacular sea, feeling slightly dejected. "No matter who wins, we'll all be drinking beer together," she said to cheer herself up, "and cold beer, which is even better."

"And maybe smoke one cigarette," replied the Frenchwoman with a smile. Sophie would soon dive to 75 meters, earning her second national record of the tournament and clinching at least bronze. Bronze satisfied Sophie. Ashley wanted to win.

On the last day, she buzzed out to the competition zone on the small panga that ferried the athletes to and from the shore, wearing a stars-and-stripes bikini. She was loose and relaxed, prepared for a Free Immersion dive to 75 meters. According to her and Ren's calculations, if she nailed it, she'd win the competition.

The night before each dive, athletes must announce their target depth and projected dive time. This enables organizers to create a schedule and set the bottom plate, and gives the safety divers an idea of when to go down to meet them at 30 meters on their way back toward the surface. Near the end of the competition, the announcement game becomes a chess match. Numbers are crunched and scores tallied, and with the title in the balance, each athlete has to make an announcement that maximizes their chances to win while hedging against what they think their competitor might do.

Coming into the final day, Christina had hit 80 meters in Constant Weight, 78 meters in Free Immersion, and 45 meters in Constant No Fins. Ashley was close behind in the first two categories, with dives to 75 meters and 70 meters in Constant Weight and Free Immersion, and she had a big lead in the difficult Constant No Fins category, with a dive to 57 meters.

Top competitions are scored one of two ways. The AIDA scoring system awards one point per meter. By that calculation, Christina had the lead with a score of 203. Ashley was on her tail with 202 total points. The Vertical Blue scoring system is slightly different. Each category's winner is awarded 100 points and the rest of the divers in that discipline are scored based on the percentage of the winning depth they've managed to achieve. For instance, in the women's Constant No Fins category, Ashley would be in the lead with 100 points, and with her 45-meter dive, Christina would have earned 79 points. By this calculation, Christina had 279 points and Ashley was the leader with 284 going into the final day.

The trouble was, nobody knew which system the judges were using. A formal announcement was never made at the precompetition meeting. Though one of the judges had mentioned to Christina and Eusebio that they were using the AIDA system. Ashley and Ren, on the other hand, assumed they were using the Vertical Blue system like they had the year before. As a result, both athletes crunched different numbers and both were certain that if they hit their dives, they would clinch victory.

Christina was first up. She'd announced a dive of 50 meters in Constant No Fins, a five-point jump in the AIDA system if she could make it. As far as she was aware, even if Ashley made her 75-meter Free Immersion dive, those extra five points wouldn't be enough to overtake her and Christina would win by a point. In other words, this was the clincher. Or was it?

Christina held the line in her right hand as she breathed calmly, wearing fluid goggles and facing the open sea. Once again, Eusebio hovered close, his left hand on her right shoulder. With ten seconds to go, he backed away. The countdown hit zero, and still she sipped air. Athletes have an additional thirty seconds beyond zero to begin their dive, and within fifteen seconds she was gone.

Everyone, including Ashley, assumed she'd nail it. She reached the bottom plate in just over a minute, grabbed a tag, stuffed it into her hood, and began breast stroking back toward daylight, her eyes closed. Soon she would feel the tropical sun penetrate pellagic blue in bolts and rays. She became buoyant, pierced the surface, and grabbed the line. One problem, she was facing the wrong direction. Where was

Eusebio? Where were the judges? If she'd been too hypoxic, an additional stressor like that might have made a difference between a clean surface protocol and a disqualification. But Christina wasn't depleted. Eusebio shouted instructions. She turned to face him, cleared her face of the nose clip and fluid goggles, made the okay sign, and said, "I am okay," while flashing the tag.

"Keep on breathing," said Eusebio. "Keep on breathing, baby." The white card came. The crowd cheered. Eusebio scooped her into his arms and twirled her in the water. They kissed slowly, celebrating Christina's presumed Caribbean Cup championship.

"Don't pay any attention to that," Ren told Ashley. "We're gonna play our game." Ashley nodded, donned her silver suit, and dipped into the drink.

"Go Conehead, go Conehead!" Sofia Gómez Uribe, the Colombian diver, shouted from the bow of the dry boat. Because of her thick auburn hair, Ashley's wetsuit hood did have a certain cone-like quality. She smiled and waved, and moved to the center of the competition zone. Ren met her there to share a few last words. For a moment they looked like they were about to kiss tenderly, but instead Ashley licked his face with one long, slobbery swipe. Call it a Conehead kiss. The gallery erupted in laughter. Ren smiled and shrugged. The Chapmans weren't exactly Christina and Eusebio.

Because it was the last day, a larger crowd than normal had joined the athletes in the middle of the sea, including several tourists who'd watched the athletes come and go for days, asking questions about their equipment, the competition, and the sport itself. More than fifty people were either on the dry boat or in the water surrounding Ashley as she relaxed on her back, her knees supported by a single foam noodle. Then came the countdown and the lung packing, and soon she was pulling herself down to depth, hoping she could equalize properly this time and claim her first Caribbean Cup championship.

The announcer followed her progress on sonar. At 1:45 she touched down, and by 2:00 she was back at 60 meters, making good progress in what can often be a slow and painstaking pull toward the atmosphere. She reached 50 meters at 2:10; then her progress slowed, but only slightly. She was visible underwater at 2:45, but it took her an additional twenty-five long seconds to pierce the surface. Her work was almost done, and Carla Hanson would lead her the rest of the way.

"Breathe, Ashley, breathe!" Carla yelled. "Nose clip! Signal! Say it!" Ashley followed orders, took her vital hook breaths, cleared her face of gear, made the okay sign, and said those three final words: "I am okay." Her voice was breathy with exhaustion and relief. Iru led a wild cheer from the bow of the boat, as if she too thought Ashley had just won the competition. Iru began the "Get Lucky" chant, and soon everyone was singing.

"Yo soy, North Carolina. Me gusta mucho freediving."

When Christina and Ashley met on the boat soon after, it became clear for the first time that both thought they'd won. There wasn't any prize money at stake, but it was awkward and strange nonetheless. Both had invested time, effort, and competitive fire. When asked earlier in the week, even Kimmo, the lead judge and AIDA president, didn't know how the cup would be scored. He said that would be up to Esteban, the tournament organizer, but if Esteban had made a decision, nobody knew for sure what it was. It would have been neat and tidy if both systems had produced the same winner, like they would in the men's draw, but that was not the case. After some deliberation, there was an unofficial announcement that Ashley had won. Christina was disappointed as she and Ashley came together. "I didn't know the proper scoring system, I guess," she said. "If I had, I would have gone for more. But anyway, it doesn't matter. Congratulations."

"It matters just a little bit," Ashley replied.

However, in a stunning reversal later that night, just before the awards ceremony, Christina was declared the champion, by a single agonizing point, and it was Ashley's turn to mull the obvious. She could have gone for more on that last dive, too. She had plenty left in the tank. Earlier in the day, when she thought she'd won, she'd said, "It sucks because if you win, you want to win clean, not by default." Now she'd lost that way.

"It feels worse having won," Christina said. "I actually feel worse."

"I'm a little sad," Ashley admitted after the medal ceremony. She wanted to win, sure, but with the competition in the rearview, her grief over Nick's death had come rushing back, as well. Barefoot on the beach, in an elegant gown, she sipped that cold beer she'd craved, and stared out to sea as stars spread across the inky night sky. Although Nick had died in Ren's arms, it was Ashley who was having a harder time letting him go. "Sometimes I feel like I have this dark cloud over my head," she said, "and whenever I want an espresso, I think about him."

8

BROOKLYN RISING

Nick gazed over Williamsburg rooftops at sunrise as the prized espresso bubbler he'd smuggled from Cuba gurgled on the gas burner. It let out a last gasp, he poured himself a double shot and sipped caffeine and good fortune. Derek Jeter had hit a game-winning homer to knot the World Series at two games apiece the night before, he lived with the talented love of his life in dear, sweet Brooklyn, and he was just twenty years old. All seemed possible.

As he sipped he counted the drunks and druggies—several of New York's finest among them—staggering out of Kokie's bar on the sidewalk below. Some had burned hours, others days in curtained-off vinyl booths snorting coke cut with powdery additives—baking soda, sugar, creatine, baby laxatives—delivered to them by the waitstaff on the ground floor of his building. He always steered clear of Kokie's but he loved Williamsburg.

It was a neighborhood in the best way. Ethnic and working class, the kind of place his grandparents grew up in. In the early morning he'd bump shoulders with fresh-off-the-boat bubbes—Polish and Chinese—shuffling toward the Tribeca bakery, or perhaps the bagel shop. His bagel shop. Nick was now the apprentice of one, Johnny Bag o' Donuts, who owned the only bagel joint in Williamsburg.

Nick and Esther lived in the North End among Polish immigrants who had moved into the antiquated brick row houses in the early 1990s. South of Broadway, Williamsburg still looked like a war had swept through and wiped away a once thriving industrial city within a city. Antiquated shells of period buildings had long since been gutted and boarded up. When Esther arrived in the mid-1990s, the few open doors were fronts for biker gangs and drug dealers. It was marginally better by the time Nick showed up, and the second wave of the hipster flood was under way, but serviceable cafés, bars, and restaurants could still be counted on one hand. Rents were cheap. Two-bedroom apartments went for $950 a month, lofts for just $1,200.

Cue the steady stream of artists, writers, and slackers. Most would stop by the bagel shop in the morning, before heading into Manhattan for work, and see Nick sweating among boiling vats of dough, shuffling trays of thick, crusty bagels in and out of the oven. He also attended to customers at the counter while Johnny held court by the cash register, often dressed in tight gym shorts and a tank top, surfing Internet porn. If an attractive artsy girl came in for breakfast—and back then the second-wave Williamsburg girls were all artsy and often attractive—Johnny wouldn't let it pass without commentary.

"Hey, Nick, she's checking me out," he'd whisper, in his best Brooklyn patois, channeling his inner Howard Stern. This time he was talking about a tall, long-legged German with golden hair braided into pigtails, dressed like Annie Hall. "Oh man, she's really hot. Ask her if she wants some *cream cheese* with that bagel, eh, Nick. We have the best *cream cheese* in town. Tell her, Nick." Whether she heard Johnny or not, she'd be back. There was literally nowhere else in the neighborhood to get a decent bagel.

Nick didn't take long making Esther's place his home, too. He had a budding chef's collection of cast-iron pots and pans and top-quality knives, the sewing machine, and a trunkload of thrift-store-quality clothes, plus two BMX bicycles and an old radio with a coat-hanger antenna, which he used to listen to Yankees games and NPR on the fire escape. And he had vinyl. By then Nick had begun to move on from the simple sugars of straight edge to the complex palate of jazz. Thelonious Monk was his guru. He'd roll joints late at night, get high, lie on the mismatched hardwood floor, and melt into bop heaven.

His squatter soul remained, which meant he was perpetually driven to create something from nothing. When he noticed how many Lavazza coffee cans were collecting in the corner of his kitchen, he decided to bolt them together. They became legs on a coffee table he built himself from found lumber. Whenever he saw a workable piece of furniture on a lonely street corner, he'd rest it on his handlebars and pedal it home. His best find was an avocado green midcentury modernist armchair. It became his office, his lounge, his base camp.

He didn't just dumpster dive for furnishings. Tribeca Bakery's commercial kitchen was in Williamsburg near the industrial waterfront off Driggs Avenue and each day they used to toss enough bread to feed all the hungry in the city. Nick was down there as often as possible, rooting around in dumpsters with immigrants from Poland and China, and old couples barely making it on Social Security rations. Sometimes Esther would join him on the hunt for free bread.

Other times they'd raid the trash of an old chocolate factory near McCarren Park. In a decade, the park would be revitalized—the pool, repaired and functional; the lawns seeded and trimmed; the area regularly patrolled by cops. But back then it was derelict as hell, a hotbed of drugs and violent crime. Still, they could score a three-month's supply of premium dark chocolate in an hour, so they braved the danger zone.

On their first Christmas together, he and Esther found a five-foot frosted plastic Christmas tree at a Manhattan Salvation Army store for

$1.99, and they made each other's presents. In their happy hippie hut on the corner of 3rd and Berry, Nick and Esther celebrated their way. They ate found bread and homemade gnocchi—a Mevoli specialty—followed by salvaged dark chocolate, and watched snow fall from their rooftop.

New York thrilled him, and it wasn't about the fashionable nightclubs and fabulous restaurants. It was the humanity. The buzz and rumble of turmoil, movement, art, passion, and pain. The knowing that everything was always happening and all at once. The entire spectrum of human emotion and achievement visible on subway cars, street corners, and parks.

He'd ride his BMX over the Williamsburg Bridge and head uptown, all the way to Riverside Park on the Upper West Side. In addition to the green lawns, towering sycamores, and soccer fields, there was a skate park where he could ride rails and drop into a twelve-foot-tall half-pipe, catch air, and float above the Hudson for a few suspended seconds. Or he'd stay closer to home and hammer over the Brooklyn Bridge, then weave beneath the stone and brick pylons on the Manhattan side, where Brooklyn Banks Park attracted all manner of BMX bikers and skaters. Unlike Florida, the cross-cultural shredders of New York came in Benetton colors. Nick loved it. It felt like inclusion.

He'd come home with the requisite bumps, bruises, and gashes, but would barely mention them. He'd just run himself a bath and sink in. Sometimes he'd practice his breath holds, which made Esther nervous. He'd be under for two minutes, then three, then four full minutes before he'd come up gasping, his eyes burning with intensity.

Nick's favorite part of Williamsburg was the waterfront, which back then was a wide-open postindustrial labyrinth of rubble and defunct factories, razor wire and garbage drifts. When Aaron or Sol came to visit, Nick led them through a hole in the fence and onto condemned, turn-of-the-century piers near the old Domino Sugar Factory to take in night views across the East River. Where the twinkling skyline erupted full throttle, accented by the gentle slosh of the river against splintering pylons.

Inspiration was everywhere, and Nick had the urge to channel it. He came to New York for two reasons. He wanted to be with Esther, and he wanted to be an actor. Esther felt he had leading-man looks and talent and made it her mission to help him get there. She was working as a segment producer for MuchMusic, a Canadian MTV-type network, and she'd often get invited to parties packed with producers and directors of the moment. She'd bring Nick along and introduce him around, but he didn't speak the language and didn't care to learn. Most often, he'd fade into the wallpaper.

A natural born DIY-er, Nick wanted them to make their own movies, and he and Esther began to write together. His ideas always included fractured father-son relationships and rebirth. Esther tried to be enthusiastic, but she knew that writing a great script can take years, and financing one can take longer. Plus, they already had a movie in progress, in the form of a plastic tub of DV tapes hibernating in a storage closet. Esther unearthed that *Exist* footage and the more she watched of it, the more she saw the movie materialize. Although they'd shot only one-third of the scenes, there was something to build on. She and Nick decided to write a new version of the film in which Nick, once a side player, would become the lead.

He played a squatter named Top who is at odds with Jake, a black Ivy League–educated activist played by Ben Bartlett. Top squats as a rebellion against mainstream culture, which he thinks will never change. Jake still believes in justice and democracy, but when a police officer is shot during an eviction raid on their squat, Jake is accused of killing him and flees. Jake's sister turns to Top to help find him.

The movie was all consuming, and they shot it for $5 a day, guerilla style, in parks, in their apartment, on the street corner, and on their roof, over five weekends. "My creative life, my sex life, and my love life all crashed into one guy," said Esther. It was exciting, but it was also combustible. They fought—on set, off set, everywhere. Tension mounted, and Nick had a short fuse. He expected a lot from himself and often was his own worst critic. If he forgot a line, or screwed up a scene that had been flowing well, he'd explode in a self-directed tirade. Esther always talked him down. It didn't help that both Esther and Nick had full-time jobs.

Nick had scrapped the bagel shop by then and begun working as a production assistant in New York film and television production. When it came time to edit *Exist,* he'd found himself in the art department of a new, low-budget (read: nonunion) comedy variety show on Comedy Central, hosted by a young, edgy black comedian from the DC suburbs named Dave Chappelle.

With shooting wrapped, Esther churned through editors. Given the different cameras that were used and the various locations, matching shots and camera angles for a consistent edit was a problem, and nobody could seem to make it work until Nick found an unemployed film editor and brought him home.

Nick met Yasunari Rowan in Mullaly Park, the city's only exclusively BMX park. As the number 4 express rumbled overhead, in the shadow of the old Yankee Stadium, they took turns riding rails and catching air in the Bronx, surrounded by the low-rent apartment complexes that rose on the Harlem River bluffs. Yas, twenty-seven at the time, was born and raised on the Lower East Side. He was the melt within the melting pot: a mocha-skinned, blue-eyed black man, a beautiful blend of African American, Irish, and Native American heritage. Yas grew up hanging out with squatters who listened to punk music and skateboarded everywhere. He and Nick had common ground.

They rode together until dark and found out they were neighbors. Yas gave Nick a ride back to Williamsburg in his VW, and on the way, he mentioned he'd been cutting promos for television shows to make ends meet. Nick chatted him up about *Exist* and the squatter activist world they were hoping to bring to life. When they arrived at 3rd and Berry, Nick invited him up to check out the footage. Esther had been ready to give up on the movie again when they walked in. Yas watched a few scenes and experimented with filters, which enabled him to match shots. In a few minutes he'd accomplished more than four previous editors had in a month.

Esther and Yas worked nights, while Nick crafted absurd props for Chappelle's skits. He built a gigantic horse schlong out of gluten one evening. Another week it was a supersized crack rock. When it was time to score the film, Nick called Clayton, his musician friend from Tallahassee. When the film finally premiered, one of the actors, Tunde Adebimpe, the frontman from the up-and-coming band TV on the Radio, played the after-party.

At a time when what passed as American independent cinema was often polished and corporate funded, Esther Bell's little movie, though imperfect and perhaps too earnest, burst with grit and poetry. Nick looked angry and innocent, jumpy yet confident, just like a nervy squatter kid should. There were sex scenes with tall string-bean girls with tattoos, and seeds of disruptive politics. Esther and Nick had come together and accomplished something huge.

Exist was chosen to play the esteemed Rotterdam Film Festival in 2003, and with a good showing, it was possible they might win distribution at the Berlin Film Market the following week. But the process of making and marketing the film had taken its toll on Esther, who had a thyroid condition. She was frequently exhausted and weak, and her sex drive had been sapped. Nick never complained, but he was convinced she'd turned off to him, and he started to drift away. After Rotterdam, she promised to take time off and get healthy.

The festival treated them like rock stars. They were flown out along with six members of their cast and crew and put up in a gorgeous four-star hotel in the city center. This was just the beginning, Esther thought. Their creative partnership and romance would only grow bigger and brighter. Nick was less impressed by the glitz. Still just twenty-one years old, freedom beckoned, but his timing was harsh.

Dressed in a black suit and smoking a spliff, he picked a fight on the evening of their big screening while Esther was doing her hair, getting ready to greet the press. It had dawned on him, he said, that she was driving the relationship, and making all the decisions. He told her he'd had enough. "Okay," she said, "but I'm about to deal with this interview, can we talk about this later?"

"No," he said. "I mean, yeah, but, what I'm trying to say is, I'm not in love with you anymore." Esther was stunned silent. She slipped on her heels, grabbed her handbag, and bolted. Her head spinning, she fumbled through the interview and somehow managed to introduce her film. Nick never showed at the screening. He caught a train to the airport instead.

Esther went on a bender and the rest of the week was a blur. She vaguely recalled Berlin, and couldn't remember boarding her return flight. She did manage to make it home alive, but *Exist* never sold. Their movie lived a brief, hopeful life, and now it was dead. When she entered the apartment Nick was in his chair, smoking and writing in his journal, Monk on the turntable.

"I'll leave," he said. "I'll go."

"Where, Nick? Where will you go?" She stared at him and saw all his youth and beauty, impatience and naiveté. He'd always been a risk, and he'd been a hell of a ride, until he gutted her. Still, she had so much love for him that she felt an urge to protect him. At least here, in this apartment, she knew he'd manage. PA work didn't pay much but rent was cheap, and he was at home on 3rd and Berry. She packed as much as she could fit in one bag, scooped up her cat, and headed to her friend's place. She would soon move to a cabin upstate to get healthy and didn't return to Williamsburg for a year.

In one of his half-filled journals from that time period, Nick wrote an entry while hanging out on the waterfront during a storm:

> *Lounging in the face of a hurricane, pelted by razor rain, six feet steep the waves a wall crashing into me Change has blown in with the wind . . . I feel as though I am finally maturing into the man I was meant to be.*

He threw himself into his work. By the time season two of *Chappelle's Show* was set to shoot, it was a runaway hit, by far the biggest success in Comedy Central's young life, but it was still low budget. Nick worked in the art department, often doing five people's jobs at once. All the skills he'd learned by building the family house with Fred began paying off. He could build, he could paint, and he could rig. All of it with lightning speed. He worked ninety hours a week, commuting on his BMX or new fixed-gear bike. During the first season, they'd hire extras and green comedy actors to dress up as famous people, but by season two, big stars appeared on the show themselves. Susan Sarandon guested one week, Wayne Brady the next. Chappelle did a jaw-dropping Rick James impression, so naturally Rick James appeared.

Once Nick, a union actor, was asked to be in a now dated sketch called "Gay America." It was a *Frontline* (an investigative news program) satire based on the opening of a new public high school exclusively for gay kids in New York City, Harvey Milk High School, which set off a predictable firestorm. Watching the debate play out, Dave and his writing partner imagined a world of gay-only public services, and even a gay chapter of the KKK. Nick worked in the Gay DMV. Campy as hell in a tight tank top, he said, "Your license plate is *so ready,*" as he handed a customer a personalized plate that read: ASS MILK. The sketch didn't make the show's final cut, but pieces of it were unearthed in a compilation episode called "Great Misses," in which Dave showed highlights of a number of sketches deemed too offensive to air. The musical guest was a young and forceful Kanye West. Nick's line got one of the biggest laughs.

The Chappelle crew bonded like family, which happens on set, especially when swept up in a cultural phenomenon. At the time, Dave seemed the second coming of Richard Pryor. His future was easy to imagine. There would be blockbuster movies and sold-out arena shows, and yet he remained unaffected. He hadn't gone Hollywood. He was real. Always.

On weekends, Nick would ride with Yas. They built their own jumps in McCarren Park, and still hit the skate and BMX parks they loved. During breaks on set, Nick would entertain Chappelle's crew by riding up the walls on his BMX. Each week, it seemed, a new restaurant, bar, or club opened in Williamsburg. Kokie's closed, but the space reopened under new ownership and without the shitty coke and crooked cops.

Nick enjoyed late nights but he wasn't into the emerging hipster scene—though he fit the profile. His New York nocturne involved riding the Staten Island Ferry with a cold six-pack, skirting Lady Liberty, and enjoying the waterfront lit up by skyscraper starlight. Most Saturdays he'd ride the PATH train to New Jersey to visit his Grandma Josie and Grandpa Joe and do yard work and other chores they couldn't handle anymore then crash for the night in their guest room.

Before the third season started shooting, Dave Chappelle signed a $50 million deal, and the energy around the show changed. Before, Dave would write 90 percent of the material with his writing partner, but with extra money came more demands and frequent visits from network suits. There was less time to write and the writing staff grew. Nobody knew it yet, but Chappelle was having a crisis of conscience. He was on the precipice of superstardom, about to have it all, and it was more than he wanted.

On the infamous day that Dave Chappelle disappeared and the show was killed, Nick got a text from a girl he knew. She'd just seen Dave at an ATM in Manhattan. He'd taken a fistful of money and bailed without his card. Nick's friend was in line, and stopped him.

Dave was kind but distracted, and he didn't look right. When her text came in, the crew and producers had already been waiting for four hours hoping he'd turn up. Nick had to break the news. That night, after the show was officially canceled, the crew gathered on Nick's rooftop. They drank whiskey and Pilsner Urquell and swapped stories into the wee hours. Dave Chappelle had illuminated the sky like a comet, and they'd been along for the ride.

After *Chappelle's Show,* Nick's best friend on that crew, Morgan Sabia, helped him get in the unions, which enabled Nick to earn $450 a day as a prop master. He worked commercials and a reboot of the children's show *The Electric Company.* Morgan, like Yas, became a big brother to Nick and made it clear that now that they were union guys, Nick had to ditch the ratty thrift-store duds and wear deodorant every day. Nick listened, dutifully swiped his roll-on, and dressed the part. Work was never scarce. Although Larry rarely called to check up on him, Uncle Paul kept tabs, and he was proud. Nick had gone to New York without a pot to piss in, and made it.

Production was just a job, though, and Nick still had a burning passion for acting. He joined Akia Squitieri's Rising Sun Performance Company and starred in a string of small off-Broadway productions. Like Nick, Akia's roots were all New Jersey, and together they would stage classics and debut plays from burgeoning playwrights like John Patrick Bray.

Their best collaboration was *Hell Cab,* which featured Nick as a cab driver enduring a brutal swing shift. Five months of almost daily rehearsals were held in Nick's apartment, and the show ran Thursday through Sunday, from November 2004 to January 2005. As ever, Nick was a perfectionist and his own worst critic, frequently venting his frustration with himself during rehearsals or even after a show. Akia would comfort him, and eventually his brooding would fade.

When they weren't rehearsing, they were cooking and partying. Nick taught the cast how to fold gnocchi, Mevoli style, and frequently produced plates of gourmet cheese and dried fruits, which he'd serve on his coffee table. Often an actor or two might pull a guitar off the turquoise walls, which were also decorated with *Chappelle's Show* souvenirs, including the giant crack rock and ASS MILK license plate. Or they'd get behind the drum kit, which was forever set up beneath a bay of windows in his living room. The only actor who would bow out of the bacchanalia was a young Nepalese immigrant named Saha, who played Nick's rival cabbie in hilarious deadpan style. At one point, Saha confessed that he'd never kissed a girl, been to a party, or sipped a drop of alcohol. Nick and Akia didn't pressure Saha, but quietly hoped he'd come to the wrap party.

"It was a bubble. It was blissful. It was family," said Akia, "and Nick was a huge part of that. His place was our home."

The show was staged at Under St. Marks in the East Village, an old black box theater with a time-nibbled marquee and tagged concrete walls. The tile in the lobby was peeling, the rafters were dusted with cobwebs. It was grungy and lived-in. Nick loved the place, and they were sold out every night, thanks to favorable reviews.

"Mevoli is terrific as the skittish cabbie," Tom Penketh wrote in *Backstage*.

"Mevoli, onstage for virtually the entire play, is superb as the cabbie, creating a very human, very sympathetic character whose travails authentically engage us," wrote Martin Denton on NYTheatre.com.

"He was having his moment," Akia said, "but he was so, so humble and was always about the group." After the Friday shows, half the crew would spend the night in a heap on the floor of his apartment. The next morning they'd wake up, Nick would fire up his espresso bubbler, and they'd all make breakfast, then head back to the theater as a unit. They were living their Brooklyn bohemian dream together.

Toward the end of the run, Larry Mevoli made the trek to New York City to see his son on stage. He came to the show with his stepson, the one who sold Larry that life insurance policy. It was closing night, and Larry brought a load of bananas with him, handing them out to others in the crowd. After the curtain fell, when Nick and the rest of the cast came to the front of the stage to bow, Larry pelted Nick with bananas, and soon everyone in the audience was pelting the actors with mushy fruit. In Larry's eyes it was a sign of respect, and a time-honored theater tradition. It didn't matter that nobody else had ever heard of it or that, in Elizabethan theater tradition, the throwing of flowers was the way you honored a terrific performance.

To those who loved Nick, it was just another strange move from a narcissistic father who managed to make the closing night of his son's best performance about himself. Nick took it in stride. He never said a bad word about his father to any of his New York friends, but the banana stunt cost Larry an invitation to the wrap party.

That night, the entire *Hell Cab* cast and all their closest friends decamped to Nick's to get high, drink Red Stripe, play music, and dance all night long. Even Saha showed up. He sipped, he grooved, and Nick made sure he kissed every girl in the place. Saha's smile bloomed ear to ear. Akia had stocked the fridge with a bottle of fine bubbly to be opened on closing night. As Nick popped the cork and passed the bottle, someone suggested they figure out how many people could fit in his tiny shower. One by one they squeezed in, face to armpit, ass to crotch, until there were seventeen people crammed together in a tile phone booth. Pancaked to soap scum, Akia, Saha and Nick laughed themselves breathless, tangled in a giddy, sweaty knot of humanity.

9

CARIBBEAN CUP 2014
ROATAN, HONDURAS

On day three of the Caribbean Cup, the defending men's champ, Will Trubridge, floated between the yellow ropes that attached the dive platform to the catamaran and delineated the competition zone. He looked serene, his hands folded over his navel, the slosh of the surface current rocking him deeper within. Will was starting to look more comfortable, more in tune. His opening dive, that 72-meter no-fins tribute to Nick, threw him more than expected, so he followed that with another nice and easy one, a Free Immersion dive to 111 meters. Only Will, and maybe Alexey, would consider 111 meters on one breath to be a foregone conclusion.

The surface was whitecapped thanks to a stiff wind that day, and at depth the current was roaring. Will took his position as always, resting and hanging between two safety sausages, as the whitecaps sprayed his face and jostled his body, and a speedboat bore down on the competition zone at high speed. Tournament officials waved their arms, urging the captain to change course and slow down. The captain did veer inside, but he didn't ease the throttle and with a minute to go before his dive, Will was tossed about in the boat's wake. He didn't flinch.

The dive itself wasn't so easy. As he dove past the 80-meter mark, the sonar faded and there was no way to track Will from the surface, but he blipped back on his way up and surfaced with a wobble, lost in a hypoxic haze. It looked like he was about to black out, but Carla's shrill voice blasted through the fog, and she guided him home. Although he'd booked another white card, he didn't look in top form.

The following day Will wore a monofin and was headed back down to 111 meters, this time in Alexey's best discipline. Once again, the dive felt more like a placeholder than an attempt to push the envelope, but if he rocked it, he would have all three major disciplines on his scorecard, with three dives left to improve his position. More important, a white card would put him in first place overall and secure his position on the podium by the end of the competition.

With ten seconds to go before his top time, the announcer counted off the seconds and Will packed his lungs, one gulp of air at a time. After forty packs, he turned, folded forward, and began dolphin kicking to depth. Though conditions were ideal, the sonar feed was iffy again, and Will faded from the screen after crossing the 20-meter mark. Ren adjusted by organizing his safety team to drop based on Will's estimated dive time of 3:15.

"We're going on time," he said. "First safety at 2:30." By then Will was back on the feed at 40 meters and climbing. The safeties met him at 25 meters and followed him as he rocketed to the surface looking strong, far better than the days before. There was no need for Carla to bring him back from the foggy ethers this time. He was clear as a bell, and only slightly breathless. When the white card came, Will was in first place, with a long way to go.

Walid Boudhiaf was next in the zone. After his riveting 102-meter dive on opening day, Walid had taken a day off to replenish before looking to hit 106 meters in Free Immersion, extending his personal best and national record. Like Will, Walid prepared to dive on his back. His left hand gripped the line as the time ticked down, and he packed air with deep gulps and small sips. When it was time, rather than turn over, he pulled himself down with a gentle backbend.

Pull, glide, pull, glide, he hit 20 meters, began freefalling, closed his eyes, and enjoyed the ride. Sonar was lost somewhere after 80 meters, and he became impossible to track, so nobody knew the drama that awaited him at depth. Walid had no idea what was coming either. He was focused on equalizing and listening for his alarm, which would chime as he closed in on 106 meters.

Despite his success on day one, he knew the dive had taken too long, so he increased his neck weight—a horseshoe-like collar made from a bicycle inner tube filled with lead shot and wrapped in duct tape. It worked too well. His freefall was so swift that when the chime came he'd already passed the bottom plate. His lanyard yanked him hard and flipped him upright. He was surprised but stayed calm as that gnawing throb of narcosis reverberated in his brain. He grabbed the Velcro tag, secured it in the hood of his wetsuit, and reached for the line to climb back to depth, but when he pulled, he didn't budge. He tried again. No luck.

He dropped down another meter and was horrified to find his lanyard looped in a knot around the tennis ball, which dangled as a float below the bottom plate. The throb of nitrogen narcosis, a buildup of nitrogen in the blood that can distort perception, grew louder. The bogeymen began invading his thoughts. He was 106 meters away from life and nobody knew what the hell had happened. There was no live video feed, and he knew sonar was iffy at depth. "For the first time, I felt scared," he said later. "The only thing I was thinking of was to tell the people up there to release the counterweight system."

For a moment he thought he might die, and was so narced that he didn't even think about trying to unhook his carabiner from the line instead of wrestling with the knot beneath the plate. If he had, he could have started his ascent sooner, but it was also possible that due to the physical and emotional stress from spending extra time below 100 meters, he might become hypoxic too soon, black out at a level beyond the reach of the safety team, and drift away from the line. If that happened and he was unhooked, the counterbalance wouldn't help, and there would be no saving him.

As narcosis grew and his mind blared with urgency and fear, Walid managed to untie the knot and head toward the surface, still fastened to the line. His contractions came early. His nervous system was on high alert, demanding oxygen, and his intercostal muscles rocked and shuddered, begging for it while he was still at 90 meters. That didn't typically happen to Walid until around 40 meters and he considered it an ominous sign, but when he reached Ren at 30 meters, he was still conscious. Ren, who had been hanging at 30 meters for nearly twenty seconds looking for a sign of life, was relieved to see him. He'd been poised to shake the line, signaling the release of the counterballast, when Walid appeared.

At the surface, Kimmo watched Walid ascend without assistance. He flashed the okay sign, then backed away, clearing space for him to rise. After a dive of 4:05, he came to the surface having already removed his goggles and nose clip. He said the magic words and flashed the okay sign, but he couldn't hold it. After seven seconds his body began to quake. That's what divers refer to as a loss of motor control, or samba. Sometimes athletes emerge from a samba without losing consciousness. Walid blacked out, and fell into the arms of an alert safety team. He was out for only a few seconds, but he came to coughing a river of pink, frothy fluid. Edema. Walid was squeezed. Blood and plasma filled his mouth, larynx, and lungs.

By nature, the mammalian dive reflex sends excess blood and plasma into the lung's blood vessels. On a normal dive, that fluid will recede back to the extremities without leaking into the lungs, but in Walid's case his blood vessels became so engorged, and the extra stress and movement was so intense, he'd suffered a hemorrhage that filled his pulmonary system with edema. When he coughed it all came spewing out.

"That's evidence of a significant lung injury," Kerry said, and it immediately brought back memories of Nick. However, Walid produced much more fluid than Nick had when he died. Kerry placed a continuous positive air pressure mask on Walid to push the fluid out and within an hour, his lungs sounded normal.

Meanwhile, the competition was still on, and Alexey was in the zone, hoping to grab a new national record with a dive to 96 meters without fins. As he moved into position, upright on the line, Esteban Darhanpe was giddy. "Alexey is going to 96 meters, that's just 5 meters from a world record. If everything goes okay, and he feels good in the next two days, maybe we can expect him to attempt a world record here?"

Will was skeptical. "Alexey is 9 meters behind me in no fins," he said, "and the difference between 90 and 100 meters is a lot, but we'll see."

Alexey certainly allowed for the possibility, and he credited his early-season good form to hitting the weights like never before. When he started out in freediving he'd focused on yoga, so he could become more flexible and better relaxed at depth, but the deeper he went he found that weight training provided much-needed power and speed on long swims against negative buoyancy, and that if he maintained a strong pace, he would be less hypoxic at the surface and less dependent on longer breath holds.

Will doesn't carry much muscle mass. At six feet one and 160 pounds, his core is strong, and his long legs and arms well defined, but he's not bulky. He keeps his brown hair cropped, and his diet is nearly vegan, though he supplements his plate with protein he spears himself in the Bahamian reefs.

Alexey is six feet tall and 180 pounds, with the legs of a velodrome cyclist and a ripped upper body. In Roatan, his sandy blond hair was shaggy and receding, and his demeanor placid as a perfect day at sea. He shies away from carbs, but eats all manner of protein, topping off his daily calories by slurping smoothies made from musclehead protein powder, which is always within reach, whether he's home in Moscow, training in Dahab, or competing in Roatan.

In freediving, every gift can be a detriment, and all weaknesses can become strengths. Those with enormous lung volume, like Ashley Chapman, are also more buoyant, which affects oxygen efficiency because they have to work harder to get down. Those with smaller lung capacity drop faster but have less available oxygen to call on during a long dive. In the same way, added bulk translates to higher oxygen demand. Alexey mitigated that with aggressive pool workouts to condition his muscles to withstand hypoxia, so he could rely on his tremendous strength to get to the surface before his oxygen well ran dry. It's all about finding the balance. Will preferred to stay lean and efficient. In 2014, Alexey opted for power, and the prevailing opinion at the Caribbean Cup was that power would soon overcome, and it was only a matter of time before Alexey would eclipse Will in all disciplines.

The countdown began and at t-minus ten seconds, Alexey began packing air. He pursed his lips and sucked it in as if slurping a spaghetti noodle of oxygen molecules he'd need to burn from both ends on a dive he estimated would take 3:45. Packed for the journey, he flipped, resting for a beat on the surface before duck diving and carving the water with his powerful, angular breaststroke. In four strokes he hit 10 meters; after eight he faded from view just below 20 meters and began to freefall.

"Touchdown!" The announcement came at 1:55, and the gallery cheered. The sonar didn't lose him this time and the announcer updated his progress every 10 meters. The hard work had now begun, and though he had made depth, he was running behind time. If he had his monofin, Alexey could expect to ascend at a rate of 1.2 meters per second. With no fins the rate was closer to .8 meters per second. He knew this because his dive computer tracked and graphed every dive, and like Will and other elite divers, those small details enabled Alexey to make the incremental tweaks necessary to squeeze out a few more meters.

Alexey must have been aware of the time crunch because he picked up speed, and at 3:45 he was already at 10 meters. He surfaced just ten seconds late at 3:55, but the hard swim had sapped his reserves. He hooked the line in the wrong direction, away from the judges and toward the dry boat. "*Vichy!*" Marina yelled. "*Alosha, vichy!*" She was telling him to breathe in Russian, and he tried to take his nourishing hook breaths, but on his second inhale, he lost consciousness, falling backward into the water. The judges backed away and the safety team moved in, but they didn't grab him. Sometimes an athlete isn't all the way gone, and can snap back to life without their assistance; as long as an athlete's airway doesn't dip beneath the surface, they are allowed to attempt to complete the protocol in less than fifteen seconds, and earn a white card.

But Alexey was blacked out all the way, and as soon as his face dipped, Ren cradled his head, keeping his airway above the surface. Marina kept yelling, "*Alosha, vichy!*" When an athlete blacks out at the surface, it's as if they are in a shallow sleep, and can often be brought back with words of encouragement as well as a sharp breeze across the eyes. Ren removed Alexey's nose clip and blew while Marina urged him to breathe. In less than ten seconds he was awake and breathing normally.

As Alexey swam over to see the doctor, Will slipped off the platform. Leaning on his monofin, he side-stroked to the dry boat, his record still 9 meters out of Alexey's reach, while the gallery murmured, mulling the latest twist in the competition between two underwater gods.

"I think he's done that depth in training," said Will, grinding one of his homemade vegan protein bars, "but it's a big jump to do it in competition. In no fins there is an exponential curve. In the space of four to five meters it can go from easy to very difficult. It could also just be a bad day. Seeing a blackout can affect you."

Alexey didn't think Walid's problems affected his own performance. He was more concerned about his speed. "Of course, it would be better to have a white card, but all these little problems, they fine-tune your preparation. Every red card gives you valuable information." Still, he'd already taken one comp day off, and now the red card. He had only three dives left and still needed to score in Free Immersion and Constant Weight. Would he move on from no fins, content to have pushed his needle just one meter? "I will rest and see tomorrow," he said, "I don't care about winning the overall. There's not much prize here. If there was a proper cash prize or a car, then maybe, but otherwise I'll just use this comp for training."

Alexey was referencing a famous Static Apnea competition held annually in Dubai in which the winner gets a Range Rover and the runner-up, a Nissan Versa. In the last three years he'd won one Range and two Versas, which he sold in Dubai for over 150,000 euros combined. The Russian was nothing if not pragmatic. He'd dedicated 2013 to extending his Constant Weight record, which he'd set with an infamous dive in Kalamata, Greece, at the AIDA Individual Depth World Championship. 2014 would be the year of Constant No Fins, and one blackout wasn't going to alter his game plan.

That night, Will and Alexey had dinner together. They spoke about training and tactics, and of the rumored medical reforms AIDA was considering in the wake of Nick's death. At the top of a sport or industry, often the only peers available are competitors, so it's natural to eventually become friends.

Their rivalry had not always been so chummy. The most significant flare-up occurred the year before in Kalamata, when Alexey broke the Constant Weight world record with a dive to 128 meters, a mark that brought him a gold medal and made him competitive freediving's deepest man of all time. Much controversy surrounded that dive, but what irked Will was the surface protocol. He and another close rival, Guillaume Néry of France, claimed Alexey flashed the okay sign twice after he'd removed his nose clip. Clearing the face of all equipment signifies the beginning of the safety protocol, and a "double okay" after that is grounds for a red card. On video, he does seem to flash the okay sign once with his left hand and then again with his right, but the judges didn't see it that way. If they had, Will would have won Constant Weight gold. He confronted Alexey, and told him he and Néry were filing a protest.

After a dive is complete, an athlete or athletes can file a protest, which the judges will hear later that afternoon or evening. Those hoping to get a red card reversed usually file them, but at world championship events, things get heated, and athletes do protest one another.

"There are rules but there is also common sense and fair play," Alexey said about the incident. "I did the dive and I wasn't shaking, there was no samba, and I wasn't blacking out. I was clean. I told them if they did some minor thing wrong in the rules and the judges gave them a white card, I would never protest. I told them my opinion and they didn't do it. So there was a little struggle after the dive, but no hard feelings. I was happy they didn't [go forward with the protest] and that's it, but it was a sensitive situation. It was a world record and they were trying to take it away from me."

Then again, Alexey was now in the business of trying to take something away from Will. Despite his failed first attempt, Alexey knew he had 96 meters in him, and if he nailed it the second time, he believed he still had a chance at Will's no fins record.

Alexey's decision to gun for Will's record appeared to be timed perfectly, because Will had been having trouble with his own pet discipline. In the run-up to the Caribbean Cup, Will's training had not been going well. The world record holder, and only diver to reach 100 meters without fins, was struggling with dives beneath 90 meters. It was alarming because swimming without fins had been Will's favorite thing to do ever since he was a boy living on a sailboat.

Will Trubridge was born in North England, but from the time he was two, he, his brother, and his parents cruised the high seas and worked and played in whichever port they docked. Australia, Tortola, Tahiti—wherever they landed, Will and Sam spent most of their time in the water diving for shells. When they moved to the family's native New Zealand after Will turned eight, they carried on living aboard the boat for five more years, spending summers in Vanuatu and New Caledonia. The brothers occasionally got competitive underwater, and Will estimated that he could dive to 15 meters on one breath before he was ten years old.

In 2002, when Will was twenty-two, he abandoned his promising career as a genetic engineer in Auckland—the sterility of lab life bored him—and moved to London to work and travel abroad. One evening, his roommate returned from a trip to Ko Tao, Thailand, and told him about the freedivers he saw there. Will was curious, so he researched the sport online, and what he found intrigued him enough to practice dry breath holds on his bed and do some breath-hold swimming in a local pool, but he didn't manage to impress himself. So he packed his bag and hit the road.

Will spent most of the London winter of 2003 in the Honduran Bay Islands, choosing nearby Utila over Roatan because it was more backpacker friendly. He spent every day in the water, morning and afternoon, often eclipsing forty dives in a day. He seldom used fins because he rarely used them growing up. The breaststroke was his default mechanism and he trusted it. He hitched rides to the offshore dive sites with scuba shops, so he could freedive through soft coral canyons and along walls draped in hard corals that fed schools of Technicolor tropical fish. He dove alone. Nobody watched his back, which was extremely dangerous, but he didn't know any better at the time. "I remember coming up from one dive and feeling this buzz throughout my body and thinking, that was cool. Let's do it again." In reality that was his body sending signals that he should quit for the day or he might black out. Like Nick in those Florida springs, Will got lucky.

He didn't dive with a depth gauge either, until his last day in the islands. As he swam toward the deeper, darker blue that sunlight couldn't penetrate, he passed a handful of scuba divers who regarded him with a mixture of curiosity, alarm, and awe. It got darker and darker and soon he couldn't equalize any further, so he turned and swam for the surface. He took a deep breath and another then looked at the gauge. He'd been to 46 meters without fins, and he'd never been coached. Like Nick Mevoli, Will Trubridge was a natural.

He finally did take a freediving course with the legendary Umberto Pelizzari later that year in Sardinia, and he became one of Pelizzari's star pupils. Never a competitive athlete growing up, always better at chess than sport, Will was on the road to becoming the world's best, and what set him apart was his ability to dive without fins, widely considered the most physically demanding discipline. After the course he stayed on in Sardinia, where he would train by paddling out to depth in a canoe and dropping a mooring in 55 meters of water, but it was never easy. He dodged speedboats and jellyfish constantly and contended with weather and wind swell. Rents were high in Sardinia, and it was difficult to make ends meet at first, but he soon secured a deal to translate Pelizzari's *Manual of Freediving* into English, which kept the coffers full.

In 2004, the same year Pelizzari trained him to be a freedive instructor, Will entered his first competition and hit 55 meters without fins. He surfaced with a mask full of blood. Though he managed a white card, Will had suffered a bad sinus squeeze (when pressure injures tissue in the sinus). It would be his last dive for five months.

As his sinus healed, he spent the ensuing weeks doing apnea walks and other dry exercises to stay fit. It was a frustrating time because he knew the Constant No Fins world record was just 63 meters. He could see it, floating out there, well within reach, if only his body would cooperate. The following year, fully healed, he entered a competition in Sicily and hit 65 meters without fins, but by then the world record needle had moved.

Will had made progress, but he also knew that if he were to ever break a world record, he needed to live somewhere with ample and accessible depth and with reliable conditions year round. In late 2005 he heard whispers about Dean's Blue Hole and set out to find it. Less than eighteen months later, when he dove to 81 meters without fins on April 9, 2007, in Dean's Blue Hole, Will would have his first world record.

Constant No Fins had always been Will's stake in the ground, and if he'd lost that gift, what would become of the rest of his career? Will was no upstart. He was thirty-four, closer to the end of his athletic prime than the beginning, and Alexey, twenty-seven, would only get stronger. But one thing helped Will rest easier as the competition wore on. He'd figured out what was holding him back.

Freedivers can be thrown off by the slightest mechanical error. Bad habits can creep up undetected and become a part of the diver's natural preparation until they are identified and eliminated. Like a pure shooter in basketball rediscovering his three-point stroke, Will considered his preparation minute by minute and remembered that of late he was seeing small stars in his field of vision as he packed air into his lungs, and was no longer feeling an urge to breathe until well after descending to 50 meters. Those two factors led him to believe he was overbreathing during the final minutes before the dive. The breathe up before a dive can be a delicate thing. On the one hand he needed to lower his heart rate and CO_2 level, which helps delay the urge to breathe and can stimulate the Bohr effect, when hemoglobin in the blood naturally binds to more oxygen, enabling muscles to use that oxygen more efficiently on the dive. But if CO2 levels are too low, the athlete won't maximize the dive reflex or Bohr effect, and both are critical to a diver's ability to push his physiological limit.

On day four of the competition, during his next Constant No Fins attempt to 90 meters, Will had no such worries. He sliced through the water with precision and elegance, and came up clean and on time at 3:35, showing no signs of mental fog at the surface. The dive looked easy for him, and Kimmo flashed a white card. Will had lengthened his lead in a competition that hadn't yet lived up to its billing, because Alexey was still fixated on no fins, and it was fair to wonder if this would be much of a competition at all. It didn't take long to get an answer.

Alexey was back in the zone as athletes and fans treaded water and peered below, Will among them. Watching his rival dive, Will hoped to take stock of him, evaluate his preparation, and see how much he had left in the tank in case the white card came and Alexey was that much closer to his record. Alexey was oblivious. Suspended upright, his eyes narrowed on the line, just centimeters from his face. When his top time came, he continued to pack air for twenty seconds before folding forward and swimming toward his elusive goal. He'd been down for nearly three minutes when Will took a breath and swam to 25 meters in his long bi-fins, hoping to catch a glimpse of Alexey's form on his way up. They rose together. This time Alexey was seven seconds faster and oriented toward the judges, calm and under control, the tag peeking out from beneath his golden hood.

"*Vichy,*" Marina said, calmly. "*Vichy.*" Marina beamed with pride, and Alexey almost smiled as he went through the protocol without a glitch.

"A new national record!" The announcer boomed from the platform.

"Beautiful dive, Alexey," one of the safety divers called out.

"That was tough," Alexey said with a smile. "I'm getting tired of that. Maybe I try to win now?" By day's end, Will was in the lead, but the pressure behind him was mounting.

With Alexey setting his sights on Caribbean Cup gold, and Will diving well, there was a good vibe glowing around West Bay, but Walid wasn't thrilled. Kerry had banned him from the remainder of the competition. "I understand that they are being careful, but physically there's nothing wrong with me," he insisted. Walid never considered a ban a possibility after his frightening experience at 106 meters. He took a day off to recuperate plus the official off day, before announcing a 108-meter Free Immersion dive, which was placed on the schedule pending Kerry's clearance.

What makes it so difficult to detect a lung squeeze is that once edema leaves the lungs, which can happen in hours, there is no way to determine if there is indeed an injury. There are no nerves in the lung, so pain isn't a major factor, and only large tears show up on an ultrasound. Three days after his squeeze, Walid had no lingering symptoms, but Kerry wasn't going to clear him. Not after what happened to Nick. She didn't base her decision on science. There wasn't a body of knowledge about lung squeezes and their recovery to work with. Kerry just knew something had to be different. Walid tried to change her mind. "This happens, but my body adapts and it's okay," he said.

"No," Kerry replied, "it's not okay, and if this happens repetitively, that's exactly what happened to Nick." Walid fumed. He didn't like that she made a decision based on Nick rather than his own medical condition, and was furious that Esteban and Kimmo backed her even though there was no AIDA rule in place allowing a doctor to bench an athlete. She hoped he'd take at least a couple of weeks off to heal, but could only control him for the rest of the comp.

On the second to last day of the competition, Will and Alexey traded blows. Alexey began by besting Will in Free Immersion with an easy dive to 112 meters. For the moment he led in two of the three disciplines, with his best discipline, Constant Weight, still to come. Then Will shocked everyone with an announced Constant No Fins dive to 97 meters.

"He hasn't been doing well in training," one safety diver whispered. "He doesn't have it," said another, but everyone wanted to watch him try, because watching Will swim without fins is like watching Usain Bolt run or LeBron James fly. The way his long, slender arms and legs extend and fold into a rhythmic flow of precise right angles, gathering water with their momentum and thrusting him down with superhuman force and effortless glide, is perfection in motion.

At 80 meters, with a dive time of 1:30, he faded from the sonar feed, blipping back during his ascent at 75 meters. He'd been underwater for 2:45. The rest of the ascent went smoothly and on time, and he surfaced at 3:51, grabbing the line and holding himself high above the surface with both hands. Good thing, because as he used his right hand to remove his goggles, he began to slip. Fluid goggles often stick tight to the eye socket and he struggled to remove his, while the shock of his first hook breath stopped him cold. He'd made the okay sign, but struggled to find the air and strength to say the words as he fumbled the tag into the sea.

His lips were blue, he'd stopped breathing, and was about to black out, but Carla was there to catch him. "Breathe!" She shouted. "Keep breathing!" Suddenly the light switched back on, and he said the words, "I'm okay." Then he shook his head and sighed, clearing the cobwebs, his tunnel vision expanding to take in the scene of fifty odd divers and fans watching a master at work. Yes, he'd fumbled the tag, but the judges had seen it and they offered a white card. Will pumped his fist. Alexey had served notice, and Will reminded him he was still the no fins king. He was back in the lead with one dive to go.

The scoring system controversy would have no effect on the men's division. Going into the final day, Will had the top performance in

Constant No Fins with 97 meters and Constant Weight with 111 meters, and was just a meter behind Alexey in Free Immersion. Alexey led that category with 112 meters, and had scored a 96-meter no fins dive. That evening they each crunched numbers to determine a depth and discipline that would give them the crown, and both opted for their monofin. Will announced 116 meters, but this was Alexey's go-to discipline, and he announced a powerhouse dive of 123 meters, just 5 meters off his record.

It was fitting that on the last day of the Caribbean Cup, after the contentious women's race had been settled, Alexey and Will, the sport's two deepest men, would deliver the final dives. The crowd had swelled in the last two days. Tourists rented kayaks to paddle out and watch, while others hopped on the athlete transport *panga*. Close to sixty people were either bunched on the bow of the dry boat or in the water surrounding the competition zone, under an incandescent tropical sun.

At 12:27 p.m. on May 31, Will duck dove and began dolphin kicking toward depth, touching down just under two minutes later. The announcer clocked him as he ascended, and at 3:10, he came back into sight, 20 meters below. He pierced the surface, completed the protocol on time, and afterward hung diagonally off the line with a playful grin. The crowd erupted in cheers. His competition was done. Six white cards in six dives and a gold medal within reach. But was it a gold medal performance? Alexey would have something to say about that.

"Bring in the Russian," Ren shouted as anticipation rippled through the gallery and the bottom plate was moved to 123 meters. Alexey had been pushing the limit in Constant No Fins all tournament long, but this would be his first Constant Weight dive and his first dive of any kind above 112 meters. While the pressure difference between the low 110s and 120s doesn't amount to much, nitrogen narcosis can become a real problem. With every added second of dive time, and every additional meter of depth, more nitrogen builds in the bloodstream, which clouds the brain. Nitrogen narcosis didn't concern Alexey, though, especially when wearing a monofin. He'd been swimming with one since he was sixteen years old.

Alexey was born in Volgograd, Russia, a sprawling city on the Volga River, in the Southern plains, once known as Stalingrad. His mother, Natalia Molchanova, taught him to swim when he was three, and by the time he was five years old he'd set the national age group record in the 800-meter backstroke. Alexey was soon his age-group champion in freestyle and butterfly, as well. Alexey was a swim prodigy, and in Russia, swim prodigies are sent to sports schools where Olympic champions are groomed.

His school was in St. Petersburg, where he switched to fin swimming. Popular in Russia, China, and Brazil and well known throughout Europe, fin swimmers wear monofins and special snorkels, which allow them to skim just beneath the surface, dolphin kicking all the way. It's strange yet elegant and much faster than traditional swimming. For instance, the 50-meter fin swimming world record of 15.06 seconds, set by Russian Pavel Kabanov in July 2014, is nearly six seconds faster than the freestyle 50-meter world record of 20.91 set by Cesar Cielo in Brazil in 2009. William Paul Baldwin of Greece owns the 100-meter fin swimming mark with a time of 34.18 seconds, which is more than 15 seconds faster than Michael Phelps's world record in the 100-meter butterfly.

Alexey made the switch to recapture the joy of swimming, which had begun to wane for him just a bit. It wasn't a calculated move to jump-start a future freedive career, but it worked out that way. As a seventeen-year-old high school graduate, Alexey moved to Moscow, where his mother had begun freediving in earnest. She became his coach once again, and when she went to Cyprus to compete in the 2004 AIDA World Championship, Alexey tagged along. He competed for the first time in 2005, when he was just eighteen years old, and his

82-meter dive in Constant Weight made him the seventh best in the world.

Nine years later, on May 31, 2014, he was trying to defeat the very best and win an overall title against Will Trubridge for the first time. He'd have to hammer his 123-meter dive to do it, something he projected would take 3:45. The sonar followed him to 90 meters and cut out. He'd been underwater for 1:30, and the gallery was held in suspense as the announcer squinted toward the feed, looking for Alexey's fuzzy, digital trail. At 80 meters he was back on line and on the way home; 2:40 had passed. Thirty seconds later he was at 50 meters and the safety divers were on their way down to meet him.

Alexey picked up his pace as the seconds ticked off and he came into view just after hitting 20 meters at 3:35. Five seconds later he was at 10 meters. He took his time from there, gliding the rest of the way and breaking the surface at 3:53. "*Vichy,*" Marina said, "*vichy.*" Just one look and she knew he had it.

He grabbed the line with one hand and removed his yellow nose clip with the other, flashed the okay sign and said, "I'm okay," with a breathy whisper. He removed the tag from his hood, and this time the judges didn't need to huddle to make a decision. Kimmo flashed a white card. Alexey had won.

That night, the athletes gathered one more time on the beautiful beach fronting the boutique, West Bay Resort. A stage was erected, a dance floor laid out, and a DJ was on the decks, ready to spin beats for the eager divers who finally permitted themselves a beer, a rum, and another beer after that. Esteban began the awards ceremony speaking English, but the Latin Quarter wasn't having it. "Espanol!" they demanded gleefully, "Espanol!" They were in Honduras, after all.

In lieu of medals, trophies made of shells, carved by a local artist, were handed out. Carlos Coste, whose 100-meter dive on the final day of the competition earned him a place on the podium, won bronze. Will nabbed silver and Alexey took the top prize. Afterward the three giants of the sport took photos and signed a copy of the event poster, along with the winners from the women's side.

Will was as graceful as ever and there were smiles all around, but whether he acknowledged it or not, he was aware that observers within the sport, and almost all the athletes present, were certain they had witnessed a changing of the guard. With his victory, Alexey, for years Will's heir apparent, had been declared the new king. Or so went the theory. By the bar, on the dance floor, in the barefoot shallows, and even later at a boozy nightclub on the hill, that's what everyone was buzzing about. Will wasn't so sure.

10

DIVE YOURSELF FREE

By 2007, Nick had abandoned making it as a professional actor. He didn't have it in him to endure casting calls, which felt more like cattle calls. Twenty versions of him, all waiting their turn to sound way too enthusiastic about Kraft mac 'n' cheese, or whatever comely cougar he was to bed on *One Life to Live*. He'd still stage the odd play with Akia, but as much as he loved the city, he craved a life infused with much more passion and adventure. That thirst for change, the desire for a new way of living, grew louder with each day. Meanwhile, all around him the ground was literally shifting. Williamsburg was in the midst of metamorphosis.

Real estate money had flooded the riverside. There would be new piers and sea walls. Crumbling factories and warehouses were repurposed and retrofitted into loft complexes. He especially hated the tasteless new build condos, which seemed to be spreading like bacteria. The waterfront, where Nick once roamed free, was fenced off.

In came the dot-commers and lawyers, editors, artists, architects, and young families. The influx, 90 percent of it white, transformed the look and feel of Williamsburg. They came along with an explosion of new bars and restaurants and, gasp, doormen, and rents skyrocketed as high as $4,000 a month. Old heads could moan and groan all they wanted. Bedford Avenue was suddenly the hottest street in the city, and the new Williamsburg even had a soundtrack. Bands like the Yeah Yeah Yeahs, Animal Collective, Interpol, Fischerspooner, and of course, TV on the Radio, were all from Williamsburg, and they helped their neighborhood become a national phenomenon. Tourists flocked to the bar downstairs, which was now called The Levee.

When Nick's friends came through, they'd ask him for restaurant and nightlife recommendations. If Morgan was around, he'd laugh and take over. "Nick didn't know where to go," Morgan said. "He never went out!" Most of the time, Nick would sit in his avocado armchair, stay up late, and watch the world go by through his windows or from his rooftop, smoke cigarettes and spliffs, and listen to a fuzzy feed of NPR or the Yankees game. Or he'd listen to jazz records, write and draw in his journal, and try to figure out what to do next. One night his phone vibrated with a text from his sister at 1 a.m.

Are you awake? Can you talk?

By then Jen was a high-powered wedding planner at the Ritz-Carlton in Orlando. Her husband, Joe, was a pharmaceutical salesman and made good money too. They dressed dapper, voted Republican, and had a nice house in the suburbs. In other words, Jen had become Nick's polar opposite, but they were close, and when Nick answered his phone, Jen was sobbing.

She'd been diagnosed with cervical cancer. The treatment would begin with a conization surgery to excise a piece of her cervix, so the bone could be biopsied. Then, depending on how many cancer cells they found, the second step was likely a hysterectomy. Joe had been oscillating from being a positive force of eternal loving support to crumbling from the sheer terror that the love of his life was dying. Even if she survived, they'd never have children.

Not that she'd ever wanted them. She and Joe loved their life. They went out, they traveled, they had plenty of cash at all times, but now she found herself mourning children she'd never wanted. Joe tried to comfort her, but his words were hollow and there were too damn many of them. She continued to do business and tried to muscle through it. Not long before the diagnosis, however, Ritz-Carlton had begun to require their wedding and event planners to be certified sommeliers. Her exam was a week away, and had been booked before all hell broke loose in her cervix. Now that conization procedure was coming up too, so why the hell was she still studying?

That night, at one in the morning, nothing made sense to her. What was the point of any of it? Joe certainly couldn't figure it out. Her mother, Belinda, was busy projecting worst-case scenarios, and her dad was, well, Larry. He had his own problems. Specifically, his business was in a tailspin. He'd begun leveraging credit, taking out third and fourth mortgages on the house and the store's property in the hopes of saving George's Market. Which is how she ended up bawling into her flashcards, terrified and feeling more alone than ever until she called Nick. "He had this incredible gift," she said. "He wouldn't fill the space with words. He'd let me spill my guts and then he'd comfort me."

"Jen, I love you. You got this," he said. He did not advocate throwing in the towel on the sommelier exam. He didn't advocate any approach at all. He let Jen dictate terms, and asked what she needed from him. And what she needed was to study the damn flash cards. She went through all one hundred of them, dictating the questions and answers to Nick, who wrote them down, then asked them at random.

> What kind of grapes are grown in Bordeaux?
> *(cabernet sauvignon, merlot and sauvignon blanc)*

What is maceration?
(the period of time the grape juice spends in contact with the skins and the seeds)
A kilderkin of beer has how many gallons?
(18)
In the Burgundy region of France, Pouilly-Fuissé has 100 percent of what grapes?
(chardonnay)

He quizzed her until the sun came up, while they joked and laughed about obscure wine trivia, about Larry, the new Williamsburg, and the tragicomedy that is life on earth. When they hung up she was at peace.

A week later their youngest sister, Katie, a high school senior, performed in a marching band competition near Gainesville, Florida. Nick came down for it and Belinda asked Jen to drive up so they could all be together, and to take her mind off things. She'd just had the conization biopsy and the surgeon had determined the cancer was too invasive for caution. She was told a hysterectomy was the only safe course of action. Jen was cranky, in pain, and too uncomfortable to sit on the hard bleachers with her parents, so she and Joe drifted to the concession stand. They were standing in line when Nick turned up.

"I ran to him, and he came towards me, and gave me the biggest hug of my life," Jen said. "He just held me for like ten minutes, and told me I was going to be okay. The love and the support and whatever I needed that I couldn't quite get from Joe at that time, he gave to me in that moment. And then we were watching Katie, and I was just standing there, and he put his arms around me from behind, and laid his head on my shoulder, and held me. There were no words. No words. But through his actions and his hug alone, it spoke a thousand words. He gave me that love and assurance. It was the most healing hug I've ever experienced in my life. It was this unconditional, amazing thing that helped me get through everything I had to get through. He was my rock."

What Jen had to go through was a slalom course of prognoses and second opinions, prayer circles, healing sessions, and perhaps, a medical miracle. She never did have her hysterectomy and was soon cancer free. Within two years, Jen and Joe welcomed a baby daughter named Elizabeth into the world, and Nick became an uncle.

Around that time, Nick started attending services at a Catholic church two blocks from his apartment called Our Lady of Consolation. Lit by wrought-iron chandeliers crowned with candle-shaped lightbulbs, the room was filled with the melodic groan of a pipe organ, and perhaps twenty regulars seated among the thirty-odd rows of pews. Nick, the only young man in the nearly empty historic church, dressed for mass in an ill-fitting suit and thrift-store tie, and prayed with great intensity. A nineteen-year-old, platinum blonde, Polish American girl couldn't help but notice him. He noticed her, too, and often tried to get her attention with a nod and a smile when he stepped to the altar for the sacrament. She ignored him every time. Her life was falling apart and the last thing she needed was a new friend.

For a while church became Nick's antidote to a life that felt increasingly shallow and directionless. He'd begun working on *Gossip Girl* in 2009, another hit, but one he didn't enjoy. Glamour and glitz still weren't for him, and neither was the gathering hipster storm that engulfed Williamsburg. Nick's apartment was his cave. His refuge.

He'd made several trips to the Czech Republic in his twenties, and his love of old Europe permeated his apartment. He stocked his fridge with vodka, kielbasa, and slivovitz, and fed the birds with stale bread on his fire escape. The apartment itself fit the bill. The ceiling tiles were warped, the floors splintering. The stove wouldn't ignite without a jiggle on the gas line. There were six different locks on the front door, each with its own key. One weekend when Sol and Aaron were visiting, they woke up on Sunday morning only to see Nick walk out the door in his oversized blue suit with a bible under his arm. In the context of the Williamsburg zeitgeist, Nick was still a rebel. This time, that meant going old world. He stopped dating. His moral ground was shifting. He was becoming an anarchist monk.

And none of it helped. Work didn't make him happy. Church didn't fill the void completely. Lobster season was still on his radar, and he'd hang with the *Bonzo* crew every year, but it wasn't enough. He needed a mission. Then late one night in the fall of 2011, four years after Jen's cancer scare, he stumbled upon a Yahoo group called New York Area Freedivers. It was a forum for local spearfishermen and recreational freedivers, and to his delight he learned that they periodically went diving in an abandoned quarry in Bethlehem, Pennsylvania.

Dutch Springs is a private half-mile-wide lake nestled along a green ribbon of low-lying hills, ancient oak trees, and historic wooden homes. Once a working quarry, in 1972 it was filled with water and became a mecca for scuba divers who came to explore a sunken chopper and Cessna, a school bus, an army truck, and other vintage man-made wrecks. New York Area Freedivers hit Dutch as well, and Nick asked if he could join them.

The next weekend he caught a ride from an attractive, athletic Long Island schoolteacher named Kelly Russell. She pulled up to his corner and honked her horn. Nick waved and hustled her way. He was tall and lean, and now had shoulder-length hair. He was dressed in rolled up jeans and flip-flops and had an apple in his mouth. "He was beautiful," Kelly said.

Among the eight divers who would regularly join the group at Dutch was Meir Taub, an IT consultant in his late thirties who had been diving with the group since 2004. His interest in freediving was sparked by a friendly challenge to swim the length of a 25-yard pool underwater at a Vermont ski resort. He'd barely made 10 yards and couldn't hold his breath for more than 30 seconds. When he got home he searched the web and found out about a guy named Martin

Stepanek who held the world record in Static Apnea at the time at 8:06. Meir decided to take a course from Stepanek and his partner, Kirk Krack, in Florida. The whole experience was full of physiology, technique, and adventure and Meir was hooked.

By the time Nick showed up at Dutch Springs, Meir was one of the longest-tenured divers in the group, and he took it upon himself to watch newcomers and gauge their sense of safety. Nick knew nothing of their golden rule: one up, one down (when a diver always has a buddy watching him on the surface). He'd come along to dive at his own pace.

The group warmed up and started diving on a line attached to a buoy that went to a small depression in the lake—its deepest point, 32 meters below. Nick was bored waiting his turn, so he rocketed down to the muddy bottom and lay there looking up at the shimmering silver surface illuminated by the Indian summer sun, blowing bubble rings at Kelly, who was about to dive the line. He swam and popped up behind her and made her laugh, distracting her from her breathe up. She loved it, but it wasn't exactly protocol. Meir watched from the corner of his eye, none too pleased.

Soon they ditched the line and began exploring the lake together, but instead of diving safely and waiting for one another on the surface, Nick called out "Follow me! Follow me!" It was impossible for Kelly to resist, and not just because Nick was cute, but because she saw something in him she hadn't seen in any of the other divers. She saw a palpable joy. "The others were very technical, but he was very natural," Kelly said. "It was almost like he merged with the water. It was pure poetry. He was very, very fluid. It was just so intuitive with him. It was second nature. The others were working, and he wasn't working at all."

Together they dove the chopper and the plane, soared over an old army truck, and lingered in the big yellow school bus, where Nick walked down the aisle pretending to be the driver and wagging his finger at imaginary kids. When the day was done, the divers gathered at nearby Wegman's, a natural food store with a café and deli where they would refuel and talk diving. Nick's antics had annoyed Meir, who saw them as reckless.

"So Nick, how long have you been diving?" he asked.

"My whole life, I guess," he said.

"Have you ever taken a freediving class?" Meir asked. Nick glanced at Kelly.

"No. No class. I've just always been able to do it. It's easy for me."

"Right. Well, you need some training." Nick couldn't believe what he was hearing. Nick hadn't been too impressed by Meir's dives, and it ticked him off that this guy, who couldn't hold a candle to him underwater, had the nerve to suggest training. "I put my life in your hands and you put your life in my hands when we do this," Meir continued. "You have to understand the seriousness of that and you need to get trained so you know how to react appropriately in the event of an emergency."

Meir suggested a course taught by a teacher in Fort Lauderdale named Ted Harty, an American record holder in Dynamic, a pool discipline. Nick researched the class online. He liked that Ted had a record and some impressive depth numbers, too. Then he read that students of his Level II class could dive to 100 feet and hold their breath for three minutes by the time they were through. Nick laughed. He could already do those things. Hell, he'd gotten his breath hold to over four minutes without any instruction at all.

He stared out into the Brooklyn night from his armchair. The window leading to his fire escape was cracked, and a chill in the air announced coming change. It was already late October. Leaves were turning gold and red. Dutch Springs would soon be closed until April. The dive season was almost over, and he'd only just begun. If he took the class he could at least go deep again. Spearfishing and lobster diving were fun, but he'd enjoyed the feeling of diving for diving's sake, and Meir didn't seem like such a bad guy. He was a little conservative, but he wasn't saying don't come back, he was saying take this course and let's keep diving together. Nick considered his schedule. He'd be in Florida for the holidays. Why not fit in a class?

Born in Atlanta, Ted Harty was running a successful scuba shop on Marathon Key when he took his first freediving class in 2008. It ruined him for tanks. He'd always been competitive and the idea of measurable performances in freediving appealed to him. In his first class he held his breath for 2:45 and hit 75 feet, but, like Nick, he wanted more. After taking the course he also noticed for the first time how loud scuba divers were. He could hear their bubbles churning from around the corner, while he would glide down and hang with the fish before the bubbles scared them all away. When Kirk Krack offered Performance Freediving's first-ever instructor program, Ted enrolled, and became one of PFI's first certified instructors.

Ted could see Nick's obvious talent right away, but he also noticed inefficiencies in his technique. He wasn't as relaxed as he could be on his pull-downs, and if he relaxed his stomach and worked his kick cycles a bit better, he could conserve oxygen on his deep dives. Unfortunately, weather marred the course, so while they did the necessary pool work, and Nick managed to reach 30 meters (100 feet) on their only day of open-water training, the other two open-water days were canceled. Still, after being bored by it in Dutch Springs, Nick had become gripped by the challenge of line diving, and what he had learned in the classroom blew his mind. He never knew how dangerous he'd been. He was such a natural, he'd never calculated his surface and bottom times, and frequently dove alone. He hadn't known about the mammalian dive reflex or how increased depth meant rising partial pressure of oxygen in the blood, or that it was possible to dive to 100 meters on one breath. That number stuck in his mind, from then on.

Also embedded within the course were references to freediving competitions, specifically Deja Blue, organized by Kirk and scheduled for the following April in the Cayman Islands. Nick was intrigued. Before the comp there would be weeks of training and ample opportunity to push his personal best in all six freediving disciplines. Nick hadn't competed since he'd left the BMX world, and he was hungry for it. He told Ted he was interested in coming to Deja Blue, and if possible, he'd love to get some tips so he could train while back in Brooklyn. Ted offered to coach him, for a fee.

After the course Nick flew to Orlando to spend Christmas at Jen's house, where her newborn Alexandra, Nick's goddaughter, had lured their whole family south from Tallahassee. Inspired by his course, he cued up YouTube videos of freedivers while he rolled his famous gnocchi in the kitchen. His three sisters and stepfather, Fred, crowded around his laptop to watch. Belinda took a passing glance, poured herself a glass of wine, and retreated to the family room sofa. The videos were ethereal and thrilling, but Jen, Fred, and Belinda were concerned.

"Are you sure this is safe for your lungs?" Fred asked. "How well do you understand the physiology? What are the risks?"

"There's nothing to worry about," Nick said. "They taught us the physiology and it's a lot less risky than driving your car to work. Statistically speaking."

"You know he's gonna do what he wants to do," Belinda said, "and if he wants to kill himself and drive his mother crazy, let him do it!" Jen watched as her mother poured herself another glass. She was a nervous drinker and Jen could tell Nick's new obsession frightened her. Later that night she took her brother aside.

"So this freediving thing, it's something you really love to do?

"Yes," he said. Jen smiled.

"Just . . . please be safe," she said. Nick nodded. "Promise?" He nodded again. "Okay, because you know we love you."

"I do," he said. As they stood staring at one another in the hallway, a hungry Alexandra began wailing for her mother. Jen rolled her eyes.

"Good, I'm gonna go breast-feed now." She hugged him tight and walked off.

Nick stayed in the dimly lit hall and watched from around the corner, as his family joked in the living room. While Jen picked up her ravenous baby and headed for privacy, he lingered, enjoying the scene. Belinda caught him staring and smiled. She'd never fully comprehend him, and was weary of trying to protect or influence him, but she loved him with every cell in her body. Nick knew that, and he cared deeply for his family, too, but he also understood that from then on he'd have to shelter them from the truth. If he was going to succeed as a competitive freediver, he was going to have to push himself and take risks they wouldn't like or understand.

Nick returned home after Christmas and trained every possible moment—if nothing else to get that Blake Lively out of his mind as quickly as possible. He quit smoking cold turkey, and dropped his weed habit too. Alcohol was also verboten. Ted prescribed a series of diaphragm and lung stretches, which were to be done each morning. At night he performed a regimen of dry apnea walks, where after a two-minute breathe up, Nick would sit and hold his breath until the contractions rattled his ribs, which usually occurred in the second or third minute. That was his cue to stand and walk as far as he could on one breath, holding a gashed tennis ball in his hand, which he'd drop when he reached his limit. Then he'd walk back to the chair, breathe up for two more minutes, hold his breath again, pick up the tennis ball, and walk it even farther on. His apartment wasn't big enough for apnea walks, so he did them on the street. When that got too easy, he began doing apnea lunges.

"Everything about freediving is tolerating extremes," Ted told him during one of their early Skype sessions. "You have to tolerate low levels of oxygen, you have to tolerate high levels of CO2, and you have to tolerate high levels of lactic acid." The lunges set fire to Nick's quads, filling them with the cramping burn of lactic acid. All of it was painful.

There were pool workouts too. He began training two blocks away at the Metropolitan Pool, a historic brick bathhouse recently converted into one of Brooklyn's fine public gym facilities. A classic natatorium built in the Art Deco style, it had tarnished bronze tiles that climbed toward a peaked glass roof. The pool's grout could have used a scrub, but it was Nick's kind of place. He would share the dressing room with old Polish men and Hasidic Jews, serious Speedo swimmers, and the elderly looking to maintain range of motion in their silvering years. He'd begin by practicing Static Apnea on the side of the pool, then dive to the bottom and lie flat below the swimmers who puttered and glided back and forth on the surface. Then he'd do one or two laps at a time on one breath. All of it worried the lifeguards, who were on alert whenever Nick turned up.

One night while he was doing an apnea walk, he came across a group of drunken students who watched him stroll, tennis ball in hand, while his diaphragm and chest heaved. He was walking over 90 meters at a time by then and was trying to get to 100 meters. "That dude is really creepy," one of them said, loud enough for Nick to hear. Nick smiled and made the last 10 meters before hook breathing, seated on the sidewalk. He shared that story with Ted in an email, and also mentioned an interest in going for his first depth record. He'd looked it up and the American record in Constant Weight was 90 meters, held by Robert King. Nick hadn't even passed 30 meters, but something told him that 91 was within reach.

Ted appreciated Nick's confidence, but he also knew that breath hold alone doesn't get a man deep. Equalizing becomes increasingly tricky the deeper one dives, and Nick had a lot to prove before Ted would take a statement like that seriously. First things first, Ted told him. Come back down to Fort Lauderdale, and finish your Level II training. Two weeks later, Nick landed in Florida.

Ted has an open-door policy for PFI alumni to join his students on open-water dives, and when Nick posted to the New York Area

Freedivers forum that he was headed back to Fort Lauderdale, Meir decided to come along. They weren't yet close, but Nick, ever frugal, wanted to share a hotel room. Meir agreed, but there was a catch; Nick would be arriving late at night and Meir, a light sleeper, insisted that he enter quietly so Meir could be rested for the dives.

When Meir woke up that morning, he found Nick sleeping in the entryway. There were two beds in the room, but he'd been so concerned about disturbing Meir that he opted to sleep on the floor, fully clothed. Meir felt like an asshole. Nick laughed it off. "I like sleeping on the floor," he said with a yawn when he woke to a puzzled Meir peering down at him. Later that day, after a pool session, Nick was trying to figure out the Fort Lauderdale bus schedules so he could hit church the following morning.

"Nonsense," Meir said. He hadn't pegged Nick as religious, but growing up Orthodox Jewish imbued him with respect for those who believed. "I'd be happy to drive you to church." Two days later, he did just that, and waited outside for Nick until the service was over.

Ted owned a thirty-five-foot boat, which he used to motor his students out to blue water from the Fort Lauderdale marina. Once clear of the shallows, Ted set a float in the drink and dropped a line from there with a weighted bottom plate, which he adjusted to their target depths. By the end of day three, Nick had no trouble tapping the plate at 40 meters. When he returned to Brooklyn he wrote about his experience on the East Coast Divers forum. His post was riddled with typos and misspellings, yet brimmed with excitement and wonder.

> Hands down one of the BEST EXPERIENCES OF MY LIFE. As I drifted down in sink faze Ted's words echoed, "If you have the proper head position you should be able to see the surface." I tucked a bit more and the surface world revealed to me upside down was rippling with wind cresting waves rocking my buddies in its pitch and roll near the floats and here

> dives Ted to meet me at depth with a GoPro in one hand and his ever watchful eyes on me. And as the first time passing my previous bench mark of 30meters I could feel the weight of water really start to press in on my rib cage, again Ted's words came to mind, "like a Pilsbury dough boy, soft." Refering to the stomach and diaphgm, I relaxed and allowed it to be pressed in by the pressure, grouper calling up another mouth fill to equalize . . . From day one in his class I knew the way I would dive would never be the same and since then it has evolved in such a positive way that I couldn't be happier with the results. I have taken Ted on as my private coach training for the last three weeks and I have seen my performances increase significantly in that time. Goals that I set day dreaming at work turn into reality when I get in the pool or ocean . . .

Around that same time, Nick shared his desire to chase King's record with Meir and Kelly. Kelly was a believer, but Meir was more skeptical. He'd seen Nick dive to 40 meters, but Meir was in IT. He was more pragmatist than dreamer, and the data said that Nick would have to accumulate a lot more experience as a competitive freediver before he could snatch a record like that. It was February 2012, and the first time Nick had ever dived along a line was the previous October. Nobody, no matter their talent, could get to 90 meters that fast.

One night Kelly and Meir were gossiping about Nick's quest online. Kelly understood Meir's point, but her intuition told her that Nick was special. If anybody could get there, he could. She suggested a wager. Lunch at Wegman's. The next day, Meir called Nick and confessed that he had a betting interest in his record attempt. "Look man, I don't think you'll get there this fast," he said, "but I'd hate myself if I didn't do my best to help you try. From now on, I'm your training partner. Whatever you need, and whenever you need it, I'm your guy."

By then Nick had bought a monofin and melted the foot pockets for a snug fit. He'd built his own neck weight, and he bought a custom freediving wetsuit made to measure too, but the Metropolitan Pool wouldn't let him practice Static any longer and they insisted he only swim one length at the most on a single breath. Meir, who lived in Flatbush, knew of a pool at a Hebrew Educational Society Rec Center much deeper in Brooklyn at the end of the L train line in Canarsie. That's where Nick trained.

Most days he'd catch an early train from the Bedford station and nestle between snoozing passengers heading home from Manhattan after their graveyard shifts. After a few stops, the L climbed out of the underground and onto elevated rails above Broadway Junction. From there it was all rooftop views of antiquated stone and brick relics, iron bridges, onion-domed Orthodox churches, and stained-glass subway stop windows. This was old Brooklyn, the way it had always been, and Nick liked watching it rumble by.

The pool was only four lanes wide but Meir and Nick were soon on a first-name basis with the lifeguards, who always let them have a lane of their own. Meir would lean on a kickboard, and safety from above as Nick did a series of breath-hold lap swims. He'd do 25 yards at a pop, then 50 and 75, with a two-minute break in between, and those were warm-ups. After that he would relax completely and try to hit 100 yards and eventually 125, on a single breath.

In between pool workouts he amped up the dry apnea work. He'd do his stretches and run through what freedivers call training tables: a series of breath holds designed to build tolerance for hypoxia and high levels of CO2. He was still doing the apnea walks and lunges, too, and he'd climb the stairs in his building while holding his breath, or go for a jog, and alternate between breathing normally and holding his breath for thirty-second intervals. Sometimes he'd push himself to a "brownout." He wasn't ashamed. Many a pair of underpants had been soiled on the road to freediving fame. He augmented it all with a strict alkaline diet.

Ted scheduled the work, and Nick reported back via email or Skype. Each week he would ask for more drills, hoping to increase his workload. Ted told him to relax and take his time. "I'm a competitive freediver, and I would never train that hard," Ted told him, but Nick wouldn't listen. He always wanted more.

At the end of March, Meir, Nick, and Ted reunited at Dean's Blue Hole to train before heading to the Caymans. Nick showed up on the island with two bags full of dive gear, seventeen Clif Bars he'd smuggled from Craft Services at work, one shirt, and a single pair of shorts. While some found the darkness of the hole foreboding, Nick took to it without hesitation. It felt good to get out of the pool and dive deep again. It felt natural.

Between dives, Ted told him it's an athlete's breath hold and ability to equalize that dictate how deep he can go. Robert King's American record in Constant Weight at 90 meters would require a three-minute active breath hold, which meant that Nick would have to work up to close to a six-minute Static to have a legitimate shot. But six-minute Static breath holds aren't rare at the elite level, and by the time Nick landed in Long Island, he was almost there. What nobody knew—not Ted, Meir, or Nick—was whether he'd be able to equalize to such a depth. To do that he'd have to master the three-stage mouthfill, aka the Frenzel-Fattah technique, which was once taught only to experienced and elite freedivers. By 2012, it was shared far and wide by the majority of instructors to new students without hesitation. Although the prevalence of lung squeezes had started to rise at competitions as a result, sidelining competitors for a day or two, few athletes, if any, considered them life-and-death dangerous.

Ted started Nick off slowly and did his best to temper his perspective. "I'm not saying you can't break the record, but it is a totally unreasonable expectation," he said as they sat on the edge of the platform, staring into inky blue, watching wisps of white sand fall over the edge of the bluffs below.

"Nice pep talk. You're supposed to be coaching me," Nick said.

"I'm just saying it's unreasonable," Ted said as he lowered the plate to 50 meters. Over the next four days, Ted kept dropping the plate with every dive, and Nick kept tapping it, always pushing Ted to drop it farther than he wanted. When Ted wanted to drop the plate five meters, Nick pushed for ten. When Ted thought two or three would do, Nick asked for at least five. By the end of the trip word had started to filter to other divers around the hole that there was a new American kid in the mix who was no joke. Among those in the area were Ashley and Ren Chapman. Ashley was training for her upcoming attempt on the women's Constant No Fins world record, and though they wouldn't officially meet until the Cayman Islands, they noticed Nick.

Nick loved everything about Long Island. Its rustic simplicity, its wooden churches, its bathtub-warm turquoise waters, and the offshore reefs teeming with lobster. After training he'd dive for lobster, just like he did on Marathon Key. This was the life he was meant to be living, he thought. He was in his element, but he'd started to sour on Ted, confessing to Meir at their last dinner on the island that he suspected Ted might be intentionally hamstringing him. "Think about it," Nick said, while sipping a Kalik. "He's a competitor. He doesn't want me to get the record because he wants it for himself."

Ted claims he was always supportive, though he'd become alarmed by Nick's approach. "Nick was excited. He crushed it, and I supported him," Ted said. "I wanted him to do well, but the more time I spent with him the more I realized that he just doesn't listen." Ted was trying to slow Nick down, because he knew that if he didn't have his mechanics together he might get a lung squeeze, which would limit what he could do in the Caymans. Meir squeezed in Dean's Blue Hole, and had to stop diving because of it, so Ted's wasn't a remote concern. That's why he asked Nick to repeat dives at 50, 55, and 60 meters, before he dropped the plate farther. As Kirk had always emphasized, Ted felt Nick should own each depth before making the next jump. Nick was impatient because he was a natural, and every dive only emphasized that point. He could hear his uncle's words echo in his brain. He was *born for this shit,* and all he wanted was to go deeper.

Nick hit 70 meters on their last day in the hole, yet Ted still didn't believe Nick would get the record. As depths increase, each new meter is exponentially more difficult than the last, and 21 meters was a hell of a gap to jump in just a few weeks.

11

DEJA BLUE

Kerry Hollowell and Steve Benson were rookie freedivers when they landed on Grand Cayman in April 2012. Most people know of the Caymans as a glitzy tax shelter where the streets are tidy and the preppy droves, golf bags over their shoulders and portfolios in hand, trade stock tips over Manhattans at mega resorts or while browsing Georgetown's exclusive boutiques. Kerry and Steve were not headed in their direction. When Kirk Krack, the brain behind Deja Blue, picked them up in his rented minivan, they skirted snooty Georgetown and headed north along the coast to low-watt West Bay, where the white sand shimmers and the sea beckons.

Kirk gushed about the beauty of the Caymans and the upcoming schedule, which included two weeks of training in the pool and the deep blue, and a full week of competition. "We have a great setup, guys. We can do depth in the morning when it's calm and pool sessions at night. Plus, no other comp has the level of safety protocols that we have." Kirk knew that Kerry was a doctor and Steve a physician's assistant. "Our head of safety is John Shedd. He's been an ER doc for twenty-five years. You can feel comfortable pushing your limits here. What are your PBs [personal bests]?"

Kerry and Steve were giddy, if a little nervous. Deja Blue was their first competition and they'd arrived on a whim after Steve hit an incredible seven-minute breath hold during the Static portion of their intermediate freediving course they took from the Chapmans. That was a world-class breath hold, and Ashley and Ren took note. Part of building the sport is finding raw talent and flipping a new freediver from would-be hobbyist to serious competitor, which is what they were hoping to do with Steve at Deja Blue. Kerry was simply along for the ride.

Steve grew up running, hiking, and mountain biking in northern Colorado, and had been scuba diving and spearfishing for years. Kerry was new to the underwater world, but was arguably an even better athlete. She had been a track star in high school and at NC State. Both were tall, fit, competitive, and intelligent, and when Ren told them about Deja Blue and how close Steve was to the American Static record, they knew they had to give it a shot. Aside from Steve's outrageous static number, however, their personal bests weren't too impressive.

"I've got 40 meters in Constant Weight," Steve told Kirk. "She hit 35 meters, I think."

"We're really new," Kerry said, with a shy smile.

"Right, Ren told me about you two," said Kirk as he swerved into the driveway at Coconut Bay Condos, an understated collection of townhomes and cottages, painted with pastels and surrounding a pool and Jacuzzi, right on the beach. It wasn't fancy, and was nothing like what Kerry had imagined Grand Cayman to be, but it was perfect. "Don't worry, we'll get you deeper than you ever thought possible."

Kerry nodded, stepped out of the minivan, and saw Nick Mevoli for the first time. He was shirtless, sitting on his patio, reading a book and having an espresso. Despite his lifelong athleticism he'd always looked more regular guy than elite jock. On the street, nobody would ever guess what he could do on a bike or underwater and how much pain he could tolerate, which is why he never failed to surprise, whether it was the Tally crew, a Havana lifeguard, or the production hacks he submarined with his stunts. On Grand Cayman, he looked the part. Thanks to months of training, eliminating smokes and booze, and shifting his diet, the weight had peeled off him. He was superlean, tan, and muscular; his eyes were bright; and his long hair fell around his shoulders. He was thirty years old, and in his prime.

He set down his coffee, came over, and gave them both a hug. All around they could see athletes milling about the pool and lazing on lounges. Nick threw on his threadbare chambray. There were holes in the denim and he left it unbuttoned as he helped move their gear into the condo next door. Steve and Kerry didn't know it yet, but that was the only outfit he'd wear for the entire trip.

That night they had dinner at Nick's place. He made curry, dipping into his portable potpourri of spices he'd smuggled in from Brooklyn. He got Kerry to chop the tomatoes and Steve to put on the rice. On the stove was Nick's espresso bubbler—he'd made sure to bring that too, and a can of Lavazza espresso beans. His computer was open, tuned to NPR, and his dive gear was scattered on the floor of the living room. Nick had been in the midst of building another neck weight and a new pair of fluid goggles. He'd been around for only a couple days, but the place felt lived in. To Kerry and Steve, it felt like home.

The three new friends shared their stories and bonded over the fact that Nick and Steve were both going for records. Nick had seen the Chapmans around, but they hadn't met officially. He'd heard Ashley was gunning for a world record, so he kept his distance. He didn't want to disturb her.

The next day, training began. There were fourteen competitors, all of them connected to PFI, and everyone traveled between the competition pool, the boat dock, and the condo complex in the same minivan.

Though they called themselves the Water Tribe, tribal relations weren't always perfect. Ted and Nick continued to clash. Nick wanted to dive 75 meters on the first day of training. Ted suggested starting with 70 meters. When Nick wanted to push the plate to 85 meters, Ted would only drop it to 80. To make matters worse, Ted was hitting all the same depths as Nick. Nick was starting to think roles had reversed and that *he* was helping *Ted* to break Rob's record, and paying for the privilege besides.

"You shouldn't go this deep so casually. You can get squeezed," Ted said for the umpteenth time.

"Stop trying to protect me and just coach me."

"Trust me, you need reps. Competition dives are a different animal. You have to get a few under your belt, and build up to the record."

"I have been building up. I feel good. I'm fresh and I'm ready. I don't want to wait for the end of a week of serious diving. Isn't Ashley Chapman going for her world record on day one?"

Ted and Nick did their best to keep their growing rift private, and often Ted could be heard touting Nick. He told the Chapmans that his athlete was prepared to do some big things at the competition. Privately, however, he was worried, and reacted by focusing on his own preparation. If Nick wouldn't listen, Ted wouldn't bother to try. Ted hit 80 meters, then 85 in the run-up to the competition. Nick watched and privately fumed. He didn't let their conflict cloud his perspective, however. He was there to enjoy himself and it was easy when he was rocking his training dives, cooking with new friends, doing yoga every day, and enjoying island life.

On May 3, the day before the competition began, photographer Logan Mock-Bunting arrived on the scene to shoot the competition for CNN. Logan had done his training with PFI and knew the Chapmans, so when he arrived he sought out Ren. In addition to helping Ashley prepare for her record attempt, Ren was part of the safety team, and had been spotting divers on training days in the pool and at depth. Logan asked him if he'd noticed anything or anyone interesting. "There's this one guy who does this tightrope thing on the warm-up line, which is pretty cool," Ren said. "You'll definitely want to get pictures of that."

Logan had been a late arrival to the competition, and his housing assignment was shuffled. That night Nick, Kerry, and Steve and a few others had been up chatting about deep equalization techniques—brain food for the dive geek—when Logan knocked. "Seems I'm supposed to crash with you guys," he said. Nick had been rooming with another diver, who took the downstairs bedroom. Nick's room was upstairs, but instead of feeling put off by a new face and shared quarters the day before his first competitive dive, or haggling with his roommate about who would sleep where, Nick made a unilateral decision.

"Welcome," he said. "You'll stay upstairs with me." Nick grabbed one of Logan's camera bags and led him upstairs, where he pulled one of two twin mattresses from a frame and dragged it to the window. The other twin was already made up, right next to Nick's abandoned frame. "You take that bed."

"Sorry about this," Logan said.

"No big deal. I always have random friends staying at my place in Brooklyn. There are probably three people there now."

"Right, well, I've been known to snore a little bit. So, sorry, again." Nick laughed, and patted Logan on the shoulder.

"Good, you'll blend in with the geckos. Come on down when you're ready, we have plenty of food." Nick headed downstairs as Logan shook his head and laughed to himself. He'd just met the tightrope walker and didn't know it.

The next day, under a patchwork of low-hanging clouds stitched with seams of blue sky, the Water Tribe motored a half mile offshore and set up the Deja Blue competition zone. Unlike Vertical Blue and the Caribbean Cup, Deja Blue didn't operate from a platform. Its dive rig, built from a Tinkertoy-like carbon fiber frame, was tied to a dry boat that drifted in the mellow current. The dry boat was where athletes would hang out before and after their dives.

The rig had six lines in total—two competition lines, each hung from a red float, and four warm-up lines on the periphery. During Deja Blue, athletes dive from the deepest depth to shallowest, but world records always take precedence regardless of depth, so on the morning of day one, Ashley was up first. There was one other diver in the water, however. Nick was on a warm-up line, dressed in his silver hooded wetsuit, about 25 meters below. Ashley's attempt was still 15 minutes away, so Logan kicked over and dove down, just as Nick began tightrope walking up the line. Logan was practically laughing into his viewfinder as he finned closer to get the perfect wide angle.

Dive lines are vertical, and Nick had spread his arms wide and gone horizontal, clutching the line between his big and first toe, gently using his hands to help propel him up the line one step at a time. It takes tremendous core strength to use only the smallest hand motion and clenched toes to stay face up at that depth. But if it took work, it certainly didn't show in Logan's artful images, where Nick, in a field of deep blue, looks to be tiptoeing a line that disappears to nowhere. Later when Logan asked him about his tightrope motivation, Nick said, "I do it to remind myself that this should be fun, that this is something I enjoy doing. It relaxes me."

By the time Ashley floated toward the competition line ready to dive to 63 meters without fins, Nick was on the surface to watch an American woman attempt to take the Constant No Fins world record for the first time. She wore a charcoal-gray wetsuit with an American flag stamped on the left shoulder and her name on the back, a pair of blue fluid goggles, and an orange neck weight.

Though she had completed four straight, clean 65-meter dives in training, there was no guarantee that Ashley would nab the record at 63 meters. For one thing, this was her first world record attempt, plus Ashley hadn't slept well, and when they had to delay the dive for a few minutes because of problems with the bottom plate camera, her routine had been trashed. She was nervous when Grant Graves, the lead judge of the event, clipped her to the line, her neck cradled in an inflated horseshoe pillow and her knees resting on a foam noodle. Nerves can be troubling to a freediver because they lead to anxious thoughts. Like muscles, thoughts too demand oxygen, which is one more reason why it's critical for competitive freedivers to relax deeply and maintain a clear mind before and during a deep dive. Ashley told herself that she would be just fine. Ren was close by, and he would have her back, no matter what.

Just after the countdown hit zero, ten seconds late but still well within the rules, she flipped onto her stomach, paused for a moment, folded over, and started to swim. Her first six strokes were strong, without much glide in between. When she hit the 10-meter mark, she began gliding for two seconds between strokes, bringing down her heart rate and becoming as efficient as possible. From there she became negatively buoyant and it was time to freefall. Visibility was exceptional and behind her the surface looked a light blue as she fell toward the plate. When her dive computer chimed, she opened her eyes and saw the plate. She grabbed the line, pulled herself close, snagged a tag, then let go to begin swimming up. It would be a slow, steady climb back to life.

Ren was the first safety to meet her at 30 meters. He flashed three fingers so she knew where she was. The mind can race in a myriad of fruitless directions when underwater for two minutes or more, and the sight of her husband helped chase all bad vibes away. Five strokes later, at 20 meters, he flashed two fingers. Now a second safety was with them. Ten seconds later she was 10 meters from the surface, and she took her time floating up.

She breached with blue lips, a sure sign of oxygen deprivation, took three hook breaths, and removed her nose clip, then went back to the nose a second time, as if her brain had skipped a beat. Precious seconds ticked away. She had only fifteen seconds to complete protocol and it was obvious she was bumping against hypoxia, confounded by that lag between the time a diver takes her first fresh breath on the surface and when that nourishing oxygen reaches and saturates her brain. Ashley's fog cleared just in time, and with five seconds to go, she removed her goggles and flashed the okay sign. "I'm okay," she said, breathless.

"Tag?" Grant asked. She pulled it from her hood and presented it, her lips still blue, her lungs still heaving, but with each passing second she became more grounded. Her color was coming back and her eyes remained fixed on Grant, alert and waiting. When he offered the white card, everyone cheered. The athletes on the boat, the organizers, the safety divers, and even the judges clapped. Ren kissed his wife and the Water Tribe splashed her with water. Natalia Molchanova had owned the sport since busting onto the scene in 2005, and Ashley Chapman had surpassed her by diving deeper without fins than any woman in the history of the world.

If athletes have one gripe about Deja Blue, it's that there isn't enough depth to attract more world-class talent. Will and Alexey would never compete there because the deepest point is just 92 meters. It's a family competition for the PFI diaspora, and only Ashley Chapman was truly elite among them. Nick and Ted Harty were still under the radar, and even if one of them got his 91-meter record, the US men would still be a fair distance behind the world's best divers. In other words, internationally, Ted and Nick were anonymous, but at Deja Blue, they were big hitters. The fact that they were teacher and student, going for virtually the same depth, at the same exact time, only augmented the drama.

As the countdown hit zero, they both disappeared beneath the rippling surface. Ted was headed to 85 meters. Nick was going for 86. Three minutes later they reappeared, seconds apart. Both had tags in their hand. Both earned white cards, but Nick's dive was cleaner. A few minutes after reaching the surface he was barely breathing heavy, while Ted coughed and spit bits of blood into his palm. Ted was on oxygen for several minutes before his breathing normalized. Nick had no need for O2, and he knew he had more in him.

By the numbers the two competitors were virtually tied, but ironically, after all his worrying, it was Ted who got squeezed. His lungs were shot, and from Nick's perspective, so was his credibility. The next morning, Nick was back on the line with Robert King's American Constant Weight record in sight, and the entire Water Tribe was on hand to witness his attempt to 91 meters.

There was a cloud cover, which made it easier to relax. Tropical sun has a way of steaming up a wetsuit, and Nick was in his silver hooded number, his left hand on the red float, and his neck supported by one of those inflatable horseshoe pillows some travelers bring on airplanes. The countdown reached zero and Nick didn't hesitate. His lungs packed to the limit, he flipped and kicked below, his light blue and black monofin propelling him deep, his arms stretched overhead, and his nose clip ratcheted tight. After about seven swipes with his fin, he eased the throttle, still kicking until he reached 25 meters. Visibility was 40 meters that day and the sea was a field of perfect blue. At 50 meters he knew he was past the point of no return, and said a prayer. "It was then," he'd write in a blog post for usfreediving.org, "that I completely let go."

Mechanically the dive was a mess. He wasn't streamlined, and his lanyard tugged him sideways, creating drag with his monofin. He was almost perpendicular, falling face first instead of head down when he approached the bottom plate, and his chin was jutted as he stared toward the tags. None of it was textbook, and the atmospheric pressure was so strong—we're talking 10 ATM, or 10 tons per square foot—he could feel a tickle in his trachea, which was squeezed by the extreme force. It took him a few seconds to snag the tag before he turned and kicked hard toward the light.

The safety divers met him at 30 meters and again at 20, but he stared through them, his arms still stretched overhead, focusing on one kick at a time. Kirk was among the safeties and he flashed two fingers so Nick knew where he was. At 10 meters, Ren flashed one finger and Nick let his arms fall to his sides. With two more kicks he was at the surface, exhaling along the way. He grabbed the red buoy, took his hook breaths, removed his nose clip, and then his goggles. He flashed the okay sign, and said those three magic words to make it official. Then he produced the tag. Grant Graves flashed a white card.

"It felt like he was down forever," Kerry Hollowell said, "and when he came up everyone just erupted. We were all so happy, and he was ecstatic. It was beautiful."

There were high fives all around. Ren threw his fist in the air. Everyone wanted a picture with him. If there was any lingering bad blood between Nick and Ted, it certainly doesn't appear that way in Logan's photographs, where coach and athlete are shoulder deep in blue water, their arms thrown over one another. Nick had set a goal, and though they'd clashed and competed toward the end, Ted had helped him get there. Back in New York, Meir owed Kelly lunch.

For the rest of the day, Nick had visitors. Everyone wanted to congratulate the new American beast in the water. Although 91 meters wasn't exactly elite, his feat made the rounds through the various freedive interweb communities, including Deeper Blue, and even the top divers were impressed that an unknown could get from 30 to 91 meters in just a few months. Nobody had ever heard of that before. It meant that he was a comer.

Nick made sure to give Ted Harty plenty of credit in his blog post, and he let Meir know what happened in a Facebook chat. A longtime Facebook holdout, Nick's devotion to a sport with international reach and critical Facebook forums made it impossible to spurn Zuckerberg any longer, but he never gloated about his success on Facebook. Francesca Koe Owings, one of the leaders within the US Freediving

Association, did that for him, posting his picture alongside Iru Balic, who had also set a national record with a 42-meter dive in Free Immersion that day. After she took the picture, Francesca chatted Nick up about making the US team for the world championship later that summer. His record dive was a good start, but he'd need a decent showing in the pool to insure his selection. Later that afternoon, Ashley knocked on his door.

He had his computer locked into NPR, as usual, and his espresso bubbler was steaming up a fresh pot on the stove. Ashley had never had much affinity for coffee, but she liked the look of that stained and tarnished relic on his stovetop, and she loved NPR, so after they'd exchanged congratulations, they sat and listened, sipped espresso, and talked. Nick was quiet at first. She found him almost aloof, but not in an elitist way. He seemed a tortured soul, but she enjoyed his company. Their afternoon espresso and NPR summits became a regular thing.

Later that night, Nick competed in the pool, hitting 83 meters in Dynamic No Fins. He was frustrated by his performance. He'd hoped to make it to 100 meters, and when he didn't, he let out an enraged rant—the kind Meir had witnessed several times in the pool back in Brooklyn. But Meir always laughed it off, and the lifeguards accepted his apologies without fail. New Yorkers take that kind of thing better than most freedivers, however, and shooting off a geyser of self-directed expletives during a freedive competition is kind of like unleashing a profanity-laced tirade in yoga class. It's just not done.

The very next evening he was back in the pool for a Dynamic dive. Again he'd swim for distance, this time with his monofin. He was going for Ted's American record of 170 meters. In Dynamic, the swim doesn't get interesting until the athlete makes the turn at 100 meters, and the suspense builds. Ted watched, uneasy, as Nick double kicked and glided in rhythm, made the turn at 125 meters, and had his record in sight, just two lengths away.

When Nick approached 150 meters, however, the pain had become unbearable. Pressure wasn't a factor but contractions were. Lactic acid burned and threatened to seize his quads and calves. He managed to make the turn at 150 meters but he couldn't hold out much longer and came up. He stabilized himself on the pool ledge and went through the protocol. For a rookie, 156 meters was an incredible feat. Just 14 meters off the national record, his performance intrigued the US team all the more, but Nick wasn't impressed. After the white card came he cursed at himself, his eyes on fire. Disappointment wasn't the word. Nick was pissed, never mind that he was on track to win the entire competition.

By then it had become apparent to his new friends that there were two Nicks. The one out of the water lived free and easy. He was generous and kind, but something about being strapped into a competitive environment turned a key, and opened a door to his soul.

As a child Nick had spent hours on the curb wondering if his father would pick him up that day, and when his dad skipped visits it was only human for Nick to wonder if his father even cared about him at all, if he loved him, if he was worth a damn. Nick never went to therapy and rarely talked about those days, but when he dove with the *Bonzo* crew, soared on his BMX bike, took the stage, or suited up to freedive with records on the line, he had a place to put all that darkness, like so many athletes, performers, and adventurers before him. Each athletic success became proof that he did matter. That he was worth something. The trouble was, the feeling always faded. For Nick, self-worth was ephemeral.

Still, having an outlet enabled him to channel his fury and live with generosity and warmth. In the Caymans Nick hosted dinners and made coffee for all comers. He was a social vortex who didn't have to speak to own a room. That's the guy who intrigued both Ashley and Iru, who made friends with anyone and everyone. Of course, although Nick was a remarkable athlete, he didn't land every jump, grab every lobster, or rock every dive. Nobody could, and whenever that happened to Nick, some reptilian part of his brain took over, and he'd snap into a self-directed tirade. The storm would soon pass and he would land back in his body with a smile on his face, but that didn't make it healthy. Or sustainable.

"Seeing him hit 91 was absolutely amazing, and he was a fantastic person," said Kirk Krack. "I really liked Nick, but I didn't like him as a competitor. He was exorcising demons from his past and using freediving to do that. Out of the water he was an amazing heartfelt soul, but he was Jekyll and Hyde."

Nick went for another record on day four of the competition, this time in Free Immersion. He'd announced a depth of 88 meters. The way Nick rationalized it, he'd just hit 91 meters, and since Free Immersion is considered the easiest discipline, 88 meters seemed like a safe bet. Never mind that he had never pulled down to a depth below 40 meters in his life. Not everyone was optimistic about the outcome. Furious, Ted found Nick and told him he was dangerous, that his ego was getting the better of him, and that he'd hurt himself, but Nick was tired of listening to Ted moan and groan. When he went for 85 meters on the first day, Nick could see the conflict of interest plain as day.

Ted insists his intentions were always pure, and it wasn't just Ted who was worried. All of the experienced competitors were concerned. They thought Nick wasn't respecting the sport or the sea enough. "Don't do that," Ashley told him that night, "that's stupid." He wasn't hearing it, and she didn't have time to try and convince him. The next morning she'd be back in the water, too, hoping to extend her world record.

Kirk didn't hear about Nick's announcement until the morning of his dive. The biggest problem was that Nick had no idea how long it would take for him to complete it. Although Free Immersion is considered an easier way to get to depth, it also takes longer than Constant

Weight dives. Kirk took Nick aside, along with Dr. Shedd, the head of safety. "We don't think you're looking at this in the proper light," Kirk told him. "Just because you went to 91 meters kicking, doesn't mean you can do 88 in Free Immersion. They are completely different disciplines."

Nick held his ground, and there was nothing in the AIDA rules preventing him from making a leap from 40 meters to 88 in any discipline. Kirk and Shedd devised a special safety plan. Shedd would drop to 35 meters to act as a spotter, and alert the rest of the safety divers of Nick's condition so they could be prepared should he need assistance. Kirk would kick down too, shoot the dive with his GoPro, and be on hand in case of an emergency.

If the mercurial run-up to his dive wore on Nick, it didn't affect his warm-up. He pulled down to 25 meters and walked the tightrope just as he'd done on the dives before, surfacing in time to watch Ashley extend her world record, to 65 meters. This time around she was far less nervous, and her dive was rock solid. Her lips weren't blue and there was no hesitation when she surfaced. She did her three hook breaths and went through the protocol with ease, holding the tag high. When the white card came she pumped her fist three times while her Water Tribe went wild. Ashley would have won the overall competition if she'd gone for it, but she had come to Cayman for one purpose, to grab a world record and then spend the rest of the week putting as much distance between herself and Natalia as she could. After her second white card, she had four meters on the Russian and planned to add two more with a 67-meter dive on the last day.

Natalia had enjoyed a dominant career, but Ashley was twenty-eight and coming into her own. She and Ren figured that after a strong week at Deja Blue, the record would be hers for a long time. They didn't know that in a few hours, Natalia would hit the water in Dahab's Blue Hole in Egypt. She and Alexey were hosting the Russian championships in their preferred training ground. Natalia had been watching Ashley's progress the whole time. It was her fiftieth birthday, and she knew exactly what she wanted.

Ashley was still on oxygen, replenishing her supply, like a running back might after a long touchdown run, while Nick was breathing up on the line. He'd gotten to 91 meters with questionable mechanics, and what got him there was letting go and trusting in his innate ability to dive, to do what came natural to him. This time it didn't work out nearly as well. It took only four pulls to get to 10 meters, and another three before he was at 20 meters, where he tucked his chin, placed his arms at his sides, and became streamlined for the sink phase; 88 meters was still a long way down.

Freedivers don't breathe underwater, so they don't succumb to nitrogen narcosis as often as scuba divers. But just as the partial pressure of oxygen rises in a diver's bloodstream to keep him conscious, so does the nitrogen percentage, and that can feel downright psychedelic. If an athlete maintains focus, he may not notice, or might relax into the high. If he has any doubt, however, that narcosis can reverberate in the brain and turn negative thoughts into a tidal wave, which can sap oxygen stores and turn a peaceful dive into a bad trip. That's exactly what happened to Nick. He wrote about it in his post for Freediveblog.com:

> I felt extremely vulnerable [at 88 meters] without anything on my feet. My mind got the better of my body and my emotions took over. I panicked and raced to the surface instead of relaxing and accepting the vulnerability. I burned through all my reserves . . .

If only he'd let the thoughts pass and pulled up slowly and confidently, he might have made it. Instead, he rushed, and with each stressful pull and panicked thought, oxygen burned. Three minutes into the dive, as he approached Shedd, he signaled that he was in distress, but Shedd didn't recognize the signal. Kirk did, and quickly relayed it to the next safety down, Robert Lee. Lee swam to Nick, who blacked out in his arms at 30 meters. "It was the most horrible blackout I'd ever seen," said Shedd.

Lee secured Nick's airway by placing one hand over his nose and the other under the chin and began kicking up. Two more safeties, including Ren, kicked down to 20 meters and helped Lee swim Nick to the surface. At the surface Nick remained out for fifteen seconds, while the safeties called his name, blew across his eyes, and tapped his cheek. No luck.

"He didn't come around right away so we started doing ventilations," Shedd said. "I did two or three ventilations and he woke up with this dead, thousand-mile stare, and then blood just started spewing."

Deep-water blackouts are uncommon in freediving and they are almost always accompanied by pulmonary edema, and sometimes pulmonary hemorrhage. When Nick came to, he coughed up pink froth. The blood and plasma, which was shunted to his core and engorged his alveolar capillaries (blood vessels in his lungs) thanks to the mammalian dive reflex, had leaked into his air sacs, like water from leaky pipes. Shedd placed an oxygen mask over his nose and mouth, and that positive pressure helped move the fluid from his lungs back into the bloodstream. He recovered quickly, occasionally removing the mask to spit globs of red blood into the rippling blue.

There was a fifteen-minute delay in the competition while the safety team took care of Nick, and another fifteen to give them time to rest, but a whole day of diving lay ahead, and the competition went on. Kerry was next on the line and had been in the water preparing to dive when this happened. "There was a lot of blood," she said, and it shook her up. Her dive was stressful. Fear had crept in and followed her deep. The stress sapped her oxygen stores and she blacked out at the surface. So did the next diver. The one after that turned early.

Shedd disqualified Nick for the remainder of the depth competition. But that didn't stop him from going back to the doctor every day, professing how much better he felt, and asking for one more open-water dive. Shedd wouldn't budge. Nick also approached Kerry for her opinion. "I told him to take a break, but he wanted an exact time [when his lungs would be healed], and I couldn't give it to him. There was no data, but I kept pushing that bleeding from your lungs is serious."

"He had something driving him," Steve said.

"He saw what he could do and he wanted to be the best," added Kerry.

Ted felt terrible about the incident. "I should have jumped up and down and said, 'No, no, no! He's not doing that dive," he told Ashley after Nick died, but in the immediate aftermath, part of him also thought it would humble Nick. Perhaps he wouldn't feel so invincible and be more inclined to listen. Still, nobody thought Nick was in mortal danger.

"We just thought he was young and aggressive and didn't know any better," said Ren. "We never thought death was a possibility. It had never happened in twenty-two years of competitions. That's why we have a doctor there, that's why we have a medic there, that's why there's a whole team of safety divers."

"You can't lie to the water," Grant Graves told him in the aftermath. "Whatever you are going through in your life, whatever issues you are dealing with will come out in the water." Nick hinted that he'd learned something from his ordeal in his blog post, and wrote about his conversation with Grant.

> I was really angry with myself for being so reckless and arrogant . . . You can't lie to water, a hard lesson to learn.

Later that afternoon, Ashley was in celebration mode. She'd had a dream, set a goal, and acheived it; now she wanted to share it with her family. She called home to spread the word. "This record has been around since 2008," she told her father. "And guess what? I broke it twice." She told him the whole story, while her mom and sister chimed in with questions. Afterward she strolled out to the pool, feeling fulfilled. She spotted Ren, Ted, and a few other divers sitting under a gazebo in the shade looking glum, so she walked over to spread her cheer.

"Natalia broke your record," Ren said flatly.

"No she didn't," Ashley said, smiling, thinking he was joking, but their expressions hadn't changed.

"Ashley, Natalia broke your record. She's competing in Dahab right now," Ren said. Natalia had held the record for four years and Ashley held it for just over seventy-two hours. Ted logged on to find out the depth.

"She hit 66 meters," he said. Fine. It was true, but there was still hope. The competition in Dahab was scheduled to end on the same day as Deja Blue, so Ashley and Ren decided to wait and watch Natalia's announcements. If Ashley could beat her on the last dive of the comp, her record would last longer than three days.

Though Shedd benched Nick from the depth competition, he was still allowed in the pool, and competed in Static the night after his injury. "Since he wouldn't be exposing his lungs to pressure in the pool, theoretically it should have been safe to compete in Static," Kerry reasoned. "But there was no data to back that up." Such was the medical wilderness in the freediving world.

Nick's Static dives mattered because he needed to hit at least five minutes to make the US national team. He came up with plenty left in the tank at 5:36. Despite his injury, on balance it had been a splendid first competition for him. He'd earned an American record and a spot on the US team bound for Nice later that summer, along with Ashley and Ted Harty.

Steve Benson got his national record too, with an astounding static of 7:43, but the competition didn't end happily for Ashley. She'd originally planned to dive three times and push the depth two meters at a time, but the day before her final dive she checked Natalia's announcement, and noticed Natalia was planning a dive to 68 meters. Ashley announced 69 meters. "Instead of sticking to my plan," she said, "I played her game and blacked out." It wasn't a scary episode. She was only out for a few seconds, but that was enough. Natalia never did dive that day. Once she knew Ashley red carded, there was no need.

All freediving competitions end with a blowout party, and Deja Blue was no exception. After eating mindfully and going to sleep early for weeks, the athletes stayed up all night long. Nick started it off by mixing a round of drinks for Ashley and Iru by the pool. While he was in the kitchen, Ashley teased Iru. "He's cute. Don't you think he's cute?" she asked.

"Of course he's cute. Come on, Ash." Iru had enjoyed Nick right away. She'd come to his dinners, cooking Venezuelan specialties like *tostones* and *arepas,* which Nick loved. And she'd do yoga with him some mornings, too. She'd just gotten out of a long-term relationship and allowed her mind to wander in Nick's direction, especially when he flirted with her in the kitchen.

"You guys should hook up," Ashley said. "I'm serious."

"We'll see," Iru said, giggling.

Nick enjoyed Iru's beautiful smile, thick brown hair, and curves. She didn't think he was classically good looking, but she found him sexy, and funny too. She'd laugh hardest when he tried to speak Spanish because he sounded closer to a *telenovela* actor than a native speaker. Still, he was charming, and though he wasn't an especially good dancer, he tried very hard.

Drinks flowed, they got tipsy, salsa music blared, and eventually the party stormed the pool. Everybody was wet when Iru breathed up and swam underwater among the bare naked legs. One length became two, which became three, and Nick was worried, so he stopped her, and lifted her into his arms. They made eye contact and he kissed her sweetly. "Kiss me more," she said. Iru enjoyed his sweet kisses but she wanted passion. She wanted a magic carpet ride.

While the Water Tribe partied on, Logan's images posted to CNN .com. Included among them were photos of Ashley's and Nick's triumphs, his tightrope walk, and his underwater blackout. Although Nick had checked in with his mother and sister, so they knew he was safe, he never told them how to track the competition. He didn't want them to know when he was diving or how deep, and he certainly never told them what had happened on the day he went to 88 meters, but it didn't take long for someone to bring it to their attention. Fred, Belinda, Jen, Kristine, and Katie all saw the images in a matter of hours.

"It concerned us all," Kristine said. "That's the first time I realized that something bad could happen."

12

DIVE BUM CHRONICLES

Nila Girl carved the water and the Caribbean trade winds filled her sails. Nick stood on the bow, his eyes closed, the sun on his face, the wind billowing his long hair. Ren was at the helm smiling and laughing, Ashley's arm around him. The day after Deja Blue wrapped, Ashley asked Iru and Nick to join them on their cruise to Florida. Iru couldn't make it. Besides, her would-be-romance with Nick had ended with a thud. He was too passive, and when she tried to get aggressive, he became uncomfortable and she felt rejected.

"He's too much like a woman," she told Ashley, jilted, which made Ashley even more curious about her strange new friend. She'd known him for only a few weeks and she'd seen so many sides. He was part brooding intellect, part petulant bad boy, part elite athlete, and part nurturing host; she was stoked when he trashed his return ticket from Grand Cayman to come along.

It took two days to sail from Grand Cayman to Cuba. When the sun was up, the sea was that perfect deep blue. They were visited by dolphin pods and trolled for skipjack tuna, and at night they took shifts at the helm so everyone could sleep. It wasn't long before Ashley and Nick began taking their shifts together. Nick told her about his broken-home childhood and Ashley told him about her father who was a heavy drinker. How she'd get nervous on her walk home from school, wondering if he'd been drinking again, if he'd be slurring his words, especially if she was bringing a friend home to play. If her fears were realized, and she became upset or burst into tears, he'd lash out at her to grow up. Lucky for Ashley, she had a superstar mom who never failed to tell her how beautiful and intelligent she was. By the time she got to college she felt she could do anything. Ashley wondered if Nick's mother filled the void the same way when his father drifted away. "Did your mom ever do that for you?" she asked. "Tell you how handsome and smart you were? Make you feel more special than the other kids?" He turned to her, lingering on her eyes, enjoying their closeness for a long beat.

"No," he said, and turned away.

It was after dark by the time they saw the Cuban shore twinkle on the horizon at Cabo San Antonio. It was late, so they anchored for the night without checking in. The wind had dwindled to doldrums, it was 95 degrees and steaming, and they dove in to cool off. Still dripping, Ren and Nick grabbed guitars and started jamming, while Ashley drummed along on an empty five-gallon water bottle. Nick lit a joint, took two drags, and passed it along. Ren and Nick had scored before shoving off from Grand Cayman, and Nick had insisted on tying their stash at the top of the mast to beat Cuban customs. After the joint had made the rounds a couple of times, Nick was high enough for paranoia to set in. When a bright light bobbing offshore caught his eye, he stopped playing guitar, stood up, and pointed.

"Look at that. They see us. They're coming our way!"

"Who is?" Ren said. Ren craned his neck and took a last drag.

"Cuban customs."

"I don't think so, man. I'm pretty sure that's just a light."

"What if you're wrong? We've got that stuff! We gotta get rid of it! I'm not doing time in a Cuban prison!" Within seconds, Nick had scaled the mast without a harness. Ashley and Ren watched in wonder as he liberated the stash, held it between his teeth, climbed down, and dumped it overboard. They stood next to him as he tossed it into the black water.

"Feel better?" Ren asked.

"Yeah, I'm fine now." Nick was right, customs did come out to say hello. It was one guy in a rowboat and a lantern. He rowed out to say that they couldn't enter Cuba in San Antonio, and that they had to head up to Marina de Hemingway, just outside of Havana, to check in. He was friendly, not the least bit suspicious, and didn't speak English. Nick dusted off his *telenovela* Spanish, which did the job. The next day they slipped out to the open sea through the reef, where they dove for conch, then chopped and marinated it in chili and lime for a light lunch. Nick grabbed a couple of lobsters too, which they steamed up for dinner as they cruised to Hemingway, landing at 4 a.m.

Nick and Ashley shared the swing shift. Again they talked all night, mostly about the meaning of dreams, one of Nick's favorite subjects. They also drifted toward God. He told her about his renewed faith and was surprised to find out that she'd been going to bible study, and after years of not believing was proud to call herself a Christian. Ren, on the other hand, was still an atheist.

Marina de Hemingway was stifling hot and buzzing with mosquitoes, so they spent their days wandering the Cuban streets, Nick's español just effective enough to get them into trouble. One day they met a young cigar roller who moonlighted as a taxi driver. He took them to a bordello where they could hear some Cuban *son*. Two days later, the same driver borrowed his buddy's Russian jalopy and gave them a tour through the lush mountains of Piñar Del Rio. They drove through the jade-green limestone hills, carved by a wide river, which snaked past acres of tobacco, their broad leaves billowing in the wind. They bought a bottle of Havana Club, queso, and guava paste from the side of the road. The queso had bugs in it. "Just more flavor," Nick said as he downed a slice of cheese slathered in sugary guava. The Chapmans followed his lead.

That night they crashed in a *casa particular,* and the next morning they rode horses through the mountains to a swimming hole in the river, which led to a cave. The freedivers did their thing, held their breath and explored. It was an epic road trip and the perfect Cuban farewell.

They left Cuba on a Sunday, which was a point of contention because Nick and Ashley wanted to attend services at a local church. Captain Ren turned a deaf ear to the Lord, though he'd be baptized within a year, and pointed out a weather window they had to make. Ashley and Nick shared one last night, shoulder to shoulder, at the helm of *Nila Girl* as they sailed toward Fort Lauderdale. Nick's eyelids were heavy and he nodded off.

"You should lie down," she said. "Get some sleep."

"No," he told her, "I want to soak up every moment we have out here."

That's when Ashley knew for sure that Nick had feelings for her, and if the situation were different, if Ren didn't exist, if they lived in some parallel universe, then maybe she could see the two of them together. But she wasn't that kind of dreamer. She lived in the real world with a wonderful husband whom she loved and adored and was devoted to. Nick knew that, which is why he never made a pass. He didn't whisper so much as one suggestive comment. He would bottle it up, tuck his feelings away, and take the pain. He always did have tremendous pain tolerance. They would be friends, he said to himself, all three of them. Forever.

Nick was back on the *Gossip Girl* set within days of his arrival, and the rest of his time was spent in the pool, training for Dynamic or climbing stairs, jogging and doing burpees while holding his breath. Morgan occasionally came by to roust him from his lair. It didn't surprise him when he found out Nick got the record. He knew Nick was a stud athlete.

"What are you gonna be? A pro freediver?" Morgan asked. Nick had picked up a sponsor. A company called Destalt was invested in Team USA and was helping Nick with gear and travel expenses for their upcoming trip to Nice. The head of Destalt took to calling Ashley and Nick "America's Pink and Blue." Nick liked that. In his mind it connected them all the more. "You have a job that pays 150 grand a year, and you're switching to a gig that pays what?"

"Nothing," Nick deadpanned.

"Exactly, your new job pays nothing."

"It's not a job, Uncle Morgan," Nick said, "it's a lifestyle." He laughed along with his friend, but as funny as it sounded, it was also true. He was tired of selling his hours and wasting his days. He wanted to be on the edge again, to live madly and completely like his heroes from Kerouac's Beat novels. Morgan could see how much it meant to him, but it made him sad, because eventually they'd get to the part where Aquaman kisses Gotham goodbye.

One night when Nick was on his way to the Metropolitan Pool to do laps he saw the young, blonde girl from church walking home. He didn't know Denny's story yet, but he knew she was in pain. She couldn't walk without leaning against a fence or the wall, and each step took intense focus.

Three years earlier she'd been a star high school swimmer from Philly who had just enrolled in art school in New York to study photography, but in 2010 something changed. She felt numbness and pain in her extremities. Her vision blurred. She would become exhausted after walking a few steps, and each one was excruciating. Nobody believed her. Her mother, her aunt, her friends—everyone told her it was psychosomatic until the end of the year, when she could barely stand unassisted. That's when she was diagnosed with MS, a crippling autoimmune disease. She fought it the best she could, and the water was the one place where she could still move normally. There was no pain when she swam, so she'd hit the pool as often as possible. When she was exhausted, however, her vision was the first to go. As Nick approached her that night, all she could see were white lines and a hazy image coming close.

"Can I help you?" he asked. Breathless, she narrowed her eyes and tried to make him out. Most people ignored her on the New York streets. Long past embarrassment, she'd crawled home from the subway once and not a single person had offered to help. "It's Nick, from church," he said. "Let me walk you home."

She nodded. He took her arm and her backpack, and led her down the sidewalk one gentle step at a time. "I pushed myself too hard at the gym," she said. "That's why I'm walking like this. I did laps, then hit the treadmill. Overdid it." She wasn't lying, but inside she was laughing at herself. She had hit the treadmill and it was tremendously difficult to go half a mile an hour for ten minutes. She sounded ridiculous. "I used to be a competitive swimmer," she continued. "I could probably beat you."

"You probably could," he said. She braced for the inevitable question: "What happened to you?" She'd encountered a few good Samaritans over the previous two years and they always made her explain herself, which was a different kind of torture. Nick never brought it up. It took them twenty minutes to walk less than a block, and when they arrived at her front stoop, her vision had clarified a bit. Nick pointed kitty-corner to his apartment. "We're neighbors." He smiled. She checked her watch.

"The pool's closing in ten minutes. I made you miss your swim."

"I'll go tomorrow," he said. Denny nodded. Nick crossed the street, then looked back. "See you in church!"

TRAINING CAMP FOR Team USA was held at Dean's Blue Hole, and on his way south Nick stopped in Marathon Key for lobster season with the *Bonzo* crew. Paul and his friends were getting older, and though the *Bonzo* was still on the water, they had a more updated boat too, *Bonzo's Buddy*. They'd also had children, and Nick became the resident dive instructor and life coach for the next *Bonzo* generation. Over the years, he'd taught them how to duck dive, equalize, catch lobster, and clean fish. Everything Paul taught him, he passed along and then some. Paul couldn't get over what a gifted and kind teacher Nick was. As impatient as he could be with himself, he was a saint with the kids, and they adored him. When Nick took Paul's daughter, Ashley, out on the reef for the first time, she was scared, but she took his hand, and soon they'd gone deeper than she ever had been before. The years went on, and whether he was protesting, acting, or working on set, Nick rarely missed a lobster season, and the older Ashley and the other children got, the more he taught them.

By 2012, those kids had begun to carry some of the weight, especially on scouting days, which was good, because the original *Bonzo* crew had slowed down and Nick had become the workhorse. One afternoon the weather gods unleashed six-foot seas on the lobstermen, toying with both *Bonzo* and *Bonzo's Buddy*. They were at Seven Mile Bridge and the current was charging hard. The sea was whitecapped and the sun was going down when Nick dropped into Grouper Gorge with a spindly speargun. On board, the crew was restless. They craved both a shower and beer. Paul blasted the horn, and called out to Nick to hurry up.

"Relax!" Nick shot back. "You need me more than I need you!"

Paul smirked proudly as he leaned over to Scotty. "Fuck, you know what? He's right, the little bastard."

"What did you say?!" Nick yelled.

"I said you're a little bastard!"

"Fuck off!" The *Bonzo* crew exploded with laughter. They weren't as touchy as the freedivers and they liked watching Nick dive angry. He took a peak inhalation and went back down. He was underwater for over three minutes and came up with a 35-pound amberjack dead on his spear. Paul was in awe. Anybody who has fished for amberjack knows how hard they fight and how much force it takes to subdue even smaller specimens. At that size, and with that tiny spear Nick had to stone it right behind the eye. If he'd hit it in the tail or gills, the thing would have taken off with the spear and the gun.

That evening, as the sun set and most of the *Bonzo* crew were on dry land, Nick and Paul went back out on the boat to have a beer. "Tell me what's going on with you," Paul said, streaks of orange fading in the western sky. He knew Nick had a habit of brooding, and Paul had both the strength and sensitivity to get to the heart of any difficulty without intruding. "I can tell. Something's eating you. What is it?"

"I'm in love. I met someone, and she could be the one." Nick told Paul about Ashley Chapman. He gushed about her athletic ability, her beauty, and their conversations.

"That's great, Nick! That's really great, man! What's the trouble?"

"I can't have her. She's married. Her husband is a great guy, and I'm fucked." Paul knew what unrequited love felt like. Before he'd married his wife, Terri, he'd fallen for a different girl, but the timing was off. Paul had offered advice when Nick was troubled countless times, but that night he had no answer. He just put his arm around his nephew and opened another beer for him. There was nothing else to say.

TEAM USA SHARED a house on Long Island near the Blue Hole. Ashley was the women's captain, Ted Harty was the men's captain, and Ren was the coach. In team world championship events, each athlete on every team competes in three disciplines: Static, Dynamic, and Constant Weight, Nick's specialty. Their scores are tallied together and the highest-scoring team wins. But there's a catch. Competitors get but one attempt in each category and a single red card can shatter a team's gold medal dreams, which is why athletes often take fewer chances at team worlds than they might in an individual competition. Nick's goal was to get to 100 meters at Dean's Blue Hole before leaving for France. He didn't mind taking chances, and wanted to make a splash on the sport's biggest stage.

It had been months since any of them had done intensive depth training, so they lowered the plate little by little, from 50 to 55, then to 60 meters. Nick was still impatient. Worse, he didn't listen when Ashley and Ren tried to explain the facts of life. Prudent divers—even those with triple digits on their resume—know they must venture down little by little to acclimatize to the pressure before they can hit the rocket boosters and push the limit, in the same way that the most experienced mountaineers on Everest must spend time at base camp each season before heading to the summit. Nick resented being subject to the laws of physics like a mortal and Ted was done trying to tame him. If he hadn't learned his lesson at Deja Blue, then the sea would have to teach him. Again. Nick took control of the plate. He lowered it from 60 meters to 75, a huge jump.

"That's unheard of," Ren warned him. Nick ignored Ren, breathed up, and dropped down. He didn't black out at depth or at the surface, and it wasn't nearly the same kind of episode that he'd had at Deja Blue, but he came up coughing and breathless, spitting thick gobs of blood. He'd injured himself and was furious. He swam to the beach, threw down his monofin, and stormed off. While he sulked, Ashley, Ren, and Ted decided it was time to rein him in.

All the greats flew into Nice for the 2012 Team World Championship and during the opening ceremony, the athletes grouped by country affiliation, dressed in national team T-shirts or track suits, carried their national flags, and paraded along the waterfront. Nick loved everything about it. At home, he was just a no-name athlete in an obscure niche sport, but here were athletes from thirty countries, and some—like Goran Colak of Croatia, Guillaume Néry of France, Natalia Molchanova and her son, Alexey, from Russia—were well known back home. It proved to Nick that his sport had some stature, and representing his country among them gave him pride. So would donning his stars and stripes wetsuit, and hammering a deep dive. He felt fully recovered from his squeeze and was ready to ramp up in the training days ahead.

Ted, Ren, and Ashley had other ideas. They held an intervention and told him they weren't going to let him hurt himself worse and damage the team's prospects. They gave America's best male diver the team player speech and told him that they'd be making his announcement on his behalf. They even had a number in mind.

"I didn't fucking come all the way over here to do a 65-meter dive," Nick said.

"No, you came here to be part of a team," Ted replied. Nick was pissed, but he had to accept their decision or quit, and he wasn't a quitter.

On the first day of competition, Ashley dove to 75 meters, just 2 meters behind the leader, Misuzu Hirai Okamoto of Japan, and Nick nailed his dive easily. If he had been patient and managed to hit 100 meters in training, perhaps he would have been tied with Alexey, who dove to 100 meters, for the third-best depth. That's how tantalizingly close he was to the top athletes in the sport, and he'd been diving along a line for less than a year. But instead of appreciating the possibilities before him, he was embarrassed and upset that he wasn't allowed to compete to his potential. He threw his computer and lanyard on the floor of the dry boat and sulked, infuriating Ashley.

Aside from Ashley's performance, it was a forgettable tournament for the Americans, who finished in the middle of the pack in both the men's and women's standings. Nick made one more run at Ted's Dynamic record on the last day of the comp, but blacked out after a 156-meter swim. The Croatians, led by the world's best pool diver, Goran Colak, won the men's draw, and the Japanese women took gold.

Nick's best day in France took place away from the water. Iru Balic had turned up to compete as a one-woman Team Venezuela and at the closing party, they found each other. They danced, drank, and talked. She told him he had to get his emotions under control if he wanted to be a successful athlete. Ashley had told her about his tantrum after his 65-meter dive. "You are a really nice person, but when you do those things it all goes away, because the only thing we see is Nick being childish."

"I know," he said. "I'll do better." Nick stared into her eyes. He had this way of looking at her that made her feel completely transparent. She'd had a tough competition too, partly because she had family drama at home—her parents were on the verge of breaking up, and she couldn't concentrate. He listened and showed her some of his own childhood scars.

Once again they connected. After the party, Ren, Ashley, Nick, and Iru slept it off, on the floor of the Team USA condo, and the next day Iru and Nick took a long walk through Monte Carlo. It was one of those spectacular afternoons bursting with magic and color, all the beauty and harmony in the world at their fingertips. They strolled through gleaming plazas, past high-dollar fashion boutiques, and snapped playful photos with parked Ferraris and Maseratis, pretending they were rich and famous, too.

They drifted up and over rolling coastal hills, pausing in silence to absorb the bobbing boats and a series of deep blue bays. She confessed that she had felt rejected by him in the Cayman Islands and that she was embarrassed. He held her in his arms. "There's nothing to be embarrassed about. We're friends and we kissed. It's normal," he said. For him it was. Not for her, but she let it go. It was time to forgive and be forgiven.

Soon they realized they were lost, so they caught the first bus they found, with no idea where it would lead. They didn't care. They reveled in the wonder and randomness of life, and as if to prove their point, the bus stopped at the doorstep of a perfect cove, with soaring cliffs on either side and a placid blue bay between. They hopped off and ambled into a beach club called L'Eden, grabbed a table, sipped mojitos, and took a long swim. The sunset was marbled fire with purple aftershocks yielding to a navy night sky.

It was a warm night and they walked themselves dry deep into the hills, where they found a candlelit Italian bistro. He had a thousand chances to kiss her, before dinner, during, and after, but he never tried. Neither did she. Everything had felt so perfect, the energy so full of magnetic calm, she didn't want to do anything to ruin what had been one of the best days of her life. She got her magic carpet ride, after all. They wound up back at the Team USA condo, each taking up position on the L-shaped couch, where they slept with their foreheads touching.

When she woke up the next morning, he was gone.

It was November, on Long Island, when they saw each other next. Vertical Blue 2012 was on and it was a special year for Will Trubridge's signature tournament. Alexey Molchanov threw down a world record dive of 127 meters in Constant Weight, Will did the same with a Free Immersion dive to 121 meters, and he won the tournament with an impressive Constant No Fins dive to 97 meters, while Alexey managed just 80 meters without fins. Still only twenty-five, he knew then that he'd have to do better than that to be considered the best diver on earth.

Ashley got her world record back too, when she dove to 67 meters in Constant No Fins, and came in second overall. Rob King took third among the men behind Alexey and Will when he grabbed his national record back from Nick with a clean 94-meter Constant Weight dive.

Nick was reduced to a spectator early on. He'd heard his record was in danger and attempted 95 meters on his first dive of the competition, hoping to extend it beyond Rob's reach. When he got to 90 meters he ran out of his mouthfill and couldn't equalize any deeper, but instead of turning early, he pushed to the plate. At 92 meters his eardrum ruptured. The pain was excruciating and the anxiety of vertigo finally caused him to turn around. He came up and unleashed one of his classic tantrums. By then, few paid him any mind when he exploded. They knew the routine and gave him space. Besides, this time he had a reason to be pissed at himself. One bad decision ended his tournament.

In his blog post from the previous May, "How I Got to 91 Meters," he'd written:

> The most important tool in this sport, and the hardest part to train, is your brain. Emotions can be a great detriment to a freediver and one has to learn how to control and focus them into a positive energy.
>
> Water is acceptance of the unknown, of demons, of emotions, of letting go and allowing your self to flow freely with it. Never lie to the water because you are only lying to yourself.

It had been six months since his first squeeze, and he was still pushing past where his body wanted to go. He was still lying to the water.

Iru did well. She hit 70 meters in Constant Weight, set a new national record, and placed sixth overall, but she and many of Nick's dive buddies were upset that he sulked, then disappeared from the herd after he got injured. They saw it as selfish and didn't understand why he couldn't hang and support his friends. When he did venture to the hole, it was during off hours, to test his ear, gently trying to equalize, hoping to get one more dive in before the competition was done. It didn't happen, but contrary to popular freediver opinion, he hadn't let his disappointment in the water overwhelm him. He loved being on Long Island. In many ways he'd never felt more free.

He stayed at the rectory of the St. Peter and St. Paul Catholic

Church in Clarence Town to save money. Set on a hilltop, the white plaster church is a stunner. From either of the two double-barrel bell towers Nick could see the vast estuary to the southwest, the Clarence Town harbor, and the barrier islands, which shelter the island's east coast from the Atlantic. Inside, the church stayed cool, thanks to thick walls. The sanctuary had an arced ceiling, polished cement floors, and a bare-bones altar. It was a pure, simple, healing hall.

Nick had been to services there with Ashley when they prepared for the world championship, and befriended the priest, Father Doug Grant. Before they left for Nice, Father Doug told him should he ever return, he could stay in the rectory: a prim, tiled house with wood-paneled ceilings and a shaded front porch blessed with the same sweeping views as the church. When he wasn't busy mopping the floor of the church or helping repair the roof of the bazaar grounds, damaged by a recent hurricane, he'd spend his time on that porch, discussing world peace, religion, love, and the meaning of obscure Beatles lyrics with the American priest, and marveling at the island's beauty.

Set in the Bermuda Triangle and intersected by the Tropic of Cancer, Long Island has a homesteader history. Its various hamlets are named after founding families, like the Deans, Hamiltons, and Cartwrights. The island's tiny museum in Deadman's Cay, which also has the main airport, offers mockups of old settlers' houses, along with the glass buoys, basketry, and fishing nets integral for their survival. Older residents fondly recall the gravy train days when Diamond Crystal—the famous salt company—sourced a fair chunk of its sea salt from Long Island. From 1962 to 1984, Diamond Crystal turned the island into a company town. A generation of parents raised their children on those paychecks, but after the company left the island with a gaping economic hole, nothing and nobody filled the void.

Some folks started their own businesses. Young people headed for Nassau, where they could still find work. Others spiraled into poverty and resorted to subsistence living. Families on the Caribbean side chopped sponges from the sandy bottom and dried them on laundry lines, then exported them to Nassau with their children. Many hunted pigeon and crabs in the mangroves. In other words, the hard homestead times were back, and it was especially difficult for the elderly. That's where Father Doug stepped in.

Dispatched to the Bahamas from Providence, New Hampshire, by the archdiocese, Father Doug didn't care much for church rules or standard protocol. He'd spend most of his hours in the community, passing out cigars, chewing the fat, and getting to know families. The local people had a term for Father Doug's smoke sessions. They called them Puffing with Padre, and when the padre came across a family that needed a few dollars to make ends meet, he'd hand them money from his own pocket. If they needed help repairing their house, he'd roll up his sleeves and swing a hammer.

"He was real," Sean Cartwright said. A lifelong resident of the island, Sean sells conch salad for a living and he and his wife, Lauryn, are the main food vendors at Vertical Blue. "He was always cool with us. He connected so well with everybody."

So did Nick, and the islanders felt that too. They'd often see him driving the church's brown pickup truck to the island's poorer southern reaches, where he would fetch seniors, and take them to the bank so they could cash their pension checks and go grocery shopping. On Thursdays, he'd take them to Denmore's for a family-style lunch that the church covered. He adored the long drives, which gave him time to examine the island's beauty at close range. He stopped to glimpse flamingo flocks in sunrise salt ponds, and explored countless empty white-sand beaches and offshore keys. On calm days he'd drive to the Caribbean side and watch the water and sky blend into one magnificent color over a rippled blanket of white sand.

He took note of property lines defined by stone pile fences, older homes with collapsed roofs in the midst of a wild bush reclamation process, and newer cinder block constructs framed up and waiting for a phase two that would never come. He saw wild pigs scramble in the bush and hardscrabble goats graze weeds in vacant lots, while their goatherders contemplated in the shade. Mesemerized, he'd watch storms blow in from nowhere on blue-sky mornings, drench the island with a nourishing gale, then fade away. Good thing. Most residents relied on captured rainwater to cook, clean, and live.

Nick loved everything about Long Island—the pastel-brushed clapboard houses, the tiny stucco abodes, the way drivers would raise a finger in salute as you passed them on the ribbon road. He adored the islanders' melodic singsong patois and the countless churches, at least two for every persuasion. There were Baptists, Anglicans, Greek Orthodox, and Seventh-Day Adventists. But his favorite was on that hill in Clarence Town—the perfect place to while away an afternoon and let his dust settle, his heart open, and his consciousness expand.

The year 2012 had started with promise and achievement. Nick had emerged from obscurity and nabbed an American record. He'd represented his country, made new friends, and traveled the world. He was disappointed in the way it ended. He would have liked to compete to his full potential in Nice and at Vertical Blue, but within days of his injury another medical emergency helped put Nick's in perspective. A Spanish diver, Antonio Garcia Abilleira, suffered a pneumothorax, or collapsed lung, while stretching and packing his lungs, preparing for his dive.

In the medical response to both Nick's and Abilleira's injuries, it was revealed that the competition doctor had arrived on remote and rural Long Island without much medical gear. Nick messaged with Meir about it on November 22 in a thread that would prove prophetic:

> **Nick:** Medical team had good doctors but no equipment! Kinda bullshit. They didn't even have a blood ox monitor, I have one of those. The guy came with a stethoscope.

> **Meir:** They should have at a minimum intubation kit, O2, pulseox, aed . . .
>
> **Nick:** That is the problem with this comp. I guess you just have to stay healthy.

Seeing another athlete airlifted to Nassau with a collapsed lung made an impression on Nick, and he also understood that, were it not for his broken eardrum, his Long Island experience wouldn't have felt so rich. He'd lost an opportunity to compete, but gained a chance to contribute. On December 2, the morning he flew away, he left a note in the church's visitors log:

> *God has blessed this land, for sure. Thank you to all the people of Long Island. You have opened my heart and set it free in ways I never thought possible. . . .*
>
> *Nick Mevoli, Brooklyn, NY, USA*

Soon, a new year would dawn. Nick would allow his body to heal, then rededicate himself to training. He wrote down his goals and shared them with precious few. By year's end he hoped to break every national depth record on the books, hit 100 meters, and grab one or two pool records too: 2013 was a fresh slate. All dreams were possible.

13

SARDINIA, ITALY: 2014 AIDA TEAM WORLD CHAMPIONSHIP

Gray storm clouds huddled on the horizon as the sun dawned on Alexey Molchanov, who waited on the small pier for his ride. His head freshly shaved, he rolled into plow pose, his feet kicked overhead toward his outstretched arms, hoping to get loose. Always a hard worker, Alexey is no early riser. At home in Moscow, he wakes when he pleases, then eats and works nonstop—in the gym, the pool, the classroom, and finally on his computer until the wee hours. Days off don't hold much appeal, but a good night's sleep is essential. Still, he seemed to relish that September morning light as he readied his body and mind to go deep once more. This time he was headed to 120 meters, hoping to move Mother Russia into contention for a gold medal at the AIDA Team World Championship.

When the speedboat arrived, Alexey hopped in along with Mike Board. The competition zone was five miles away from Hotel Setar in Cagliari, where the majority of athletes were staying, and two miles offshore. Upon arrival they'd find a flotilla of six boats—some sleek and fast, others lumbering and built for a cruise, along with two buoys stretched out in blue water for about 100 meters from end to end. There would be two competition lines running simultaneously, a vast safety team—including divers on underwater scooters and an ER doc, two teams of judges, several photographers, dozens of athletes, and team coaches. Worlds, whether a team competition like this one, which was held on even years, or individual worlds, held on odd years, were always the biggest competitions of the year.

Alexey yawned, as if it were just an ordinary workday, and this, his standard commute. Mike had a bit more on his mind. He'd follow Alexey with a dive to 98 meters. The next deepest man in the competition and the leader of the UK team, his dive wouldn't affect the standings much. That wasn't his concern. The UK wasn't a contender for the podium. He was worried about something much more fundamental—his lungs.

Nearly a month earlier, on August 30, he had a squeeze while competing in a small competition in Kalamata, and after arriving in Sardinia he suffered another small squeeze during training. Now it was competition day, and he wondered how his body would respond. None of his squeezes were major events, like Nick's or Walid's. There were only specks of blood in his saliva, and he didn't feel injured, congested, or constricted. But by the time the athletes gathered on Sardinia, nobody knew how dangerous it was to dive with a squeeze. Athletes like Mike were still waiting to hear what exactly had happened to Nick, and were left to wonder if they were in danger of suffering a similar fate.

Sardegna, or Sardinia as most know it, is rugged and parched. Its vast plains are brown, its valleys in need of a good rain, but the olive orchards and vineyards never disappoint and neither does its spectacular coastline, best viewed from the open water. As Mike and Alexey disembarked onto one of two dry boats dedicated to the athletes, they glimpsed layers of mountains to the south—some steep and peaked as suddenly as shark fins, others gently sloped. Those up close looked veined and detailed, and it appeared that the Mediterranean had taken bites out of the crumbling cliffs, forming secluded bays fringed with white sand. To the west the island arced along a slender sandbar backed by a maze of estuaries and salt flats until the landmass bunched together again in yet another jigsaw of purple mountains tucked beneath a blanket of cottony clouds.

In Sardinia, the day began with the deepest diver, and about twenty-five people surrounded Alexey, dressed in a black wetsuit with red sleeves, as he hung off the line in the purpling blue. On his feet was a Molchanova monofin, which he designed and sells to freedivers all over the world, and his wetsuit was a Molchanova too. In freediving, most elite athletes hope to be sponsored. Others buy their gear. Alexey and his mother, Natalia Molchanova, built a brand. The surface rippled with current, and the wind had blown away any threat of rain as he moved toward peak inhalation. It took him over half a minute to sip and pack the air he'd need, before he slipped below.

Diving in thermal waters offers unique challenges, and at 21 meters the divers would have to penetrate a thermocline, when warmer surface currents comingle with a colder upwelling. Thermoclines are the boundary line, and there was a twenty-degree difference between the surface side and depth. When the athletes passed through, it felt as if they'd stuffed their head into an icy cooler. It was enough to shock their system and temporarily blur their vision. Think of watching a car move through steam rising from a tarmac. That same blurred effect occurs with underwater thermoclines. The cold penetrated their bones, tempted their minds to race and bodies to tense just in time for the freefall, when staying loose was critical.

Alexey shouldn't have had a problem. He and the rest of the Russian team had been training in the Mediterranean, off the coast of Croatia, for weeks. His announced dive time was 3:40, and he was on schedule all the way down, hitting 60 meters at one minute. That's when he faded from sonar. The seconds and minutes ticked by and nobody knew where he was. He was still off the grid as two minutes became three. At three and a half minutes he was still blank, which was disconcerting because it was clear enough to see down to the thermocline, and yet he was still invisible. The safety divers had been deployed, and were waiting for Alexey at 30 meters. They were trained to shake the line and signal the surface safety to deploy the counterbalance if Alexey was in trouble, and each passing second increased the likelihood of such an outcome.

Even if he did make it back on his own, a dive that stretches into overtime only increases the likelihood of hypoxia and the chance of blackout. One more blackout would doom the Russian men. On the first day of the tournament, during the Static comp, Russia's very first diver, Aleksandr "Sasha" Kostyshen received a red card when he muffed the surface protocol, giving the okay sign twice, after a Static dive of 6:37.

Coming into the competition the Russian men figured to battle it out with the defending champs from Croatia for the title, but in team events, one red card can doom even a team as gifted as Russia. Especially since two of the Croatians went over seven minutes in Static and their leader, the world's best pool diver, Goran Colak, clocked 9:13. Unless Croatia slipped up, Russia was in trouble, and they were finished if Alexey blacked out. If he nailed the 120-meter dive, on the other hand, Russia would still be in position for a medal, and it would at least put some pressure on Croatia to keep diving clean.

At 3:40 Alexey came into view. His elegant dolphin kicks effortlessly carved the water as he rose up, and at 3:57 he pierced the surface with a smile. He aced the surface protocol, fished the tag from his hood, and elicited several "bravos" from the gallery, including one from the only boat captain in a bikini who happened to be in command of the slickest boat at sea. Everybody loves a winner, but this was a team event. Alexey couldn't win gold by himself.

Set amid a rocky notch of peninsulas and hills east of the tidal flats that lead to Cagliari, the Hotel Setar is a brutalist construct of a three-star resort that won't be winning any design awards. But hosting competitions like this is generally a money loser, and Setar had the price point. It also had a 25-meter pool, which would host the pool disciplines, and a nearby marina where divers could be shuttled to the open water competition zone.

Plus, the design of a hotel doesn't much matter when the Mediterranean sun is shining and freedivers from fourteen countries are mingling and competing against one another. The opening ceremony found teams decked out in custom gear. The Croatians and Russians wore bespoke red polo shirts. Team Japan had slick track suits with that blood-red sun on the back. The Danish team took group photos holding their flag. Because there are more competitive freedivers in Europe than on any other continent, AIDA's world championship events are almost always held in the EU, which makes it difficult for teams from Latin America to attend. Ditto for the Australians and Kiwis. There would be no Team Venezuela or Will Trubridge's Team New Zealand this time around.

The biggest stars were Alexey and Natalia, and Goran Colak, who traveled to Sardinia in a chartered minivan with the Croatian team—the only squad to bring its own masseuse. They'd need him, after a ferry schedule change had extended what was supposed to be a sixteen-hour road and boat trip into a thirty-hour ordeal. Goran could have passed on the van ride and met his teammates in Sardinia if he'd wanted. Hell, he could have flown first class. For the last two years he'd defeated Alexey in the Static competition hosted by the prince of Dubai, called the Fazza Freediving Championship, winning the Range Rover, while Alexey took home the Nissan Versa. Both times Goran sold the Range and pocketed over 100,000 euros. He'd also broken his own Dynamic world record the year before in Belgrade with a swim of 281 meters. In Croatia, each freediving world record and gold medal comes with a cash bonus from the Ministry of Sports. Goran has stockpiled golds. The Michael Phelps of pool apnea, he's the only freediver ever to win the individual world title in each of the three pool disciplines, and he won them all in the same year. Overall he's won five individual gold medals, two silvers, and one bronze, has made a six-figure annual salary for years, and his only job is to train.

Most athletes are self-funded, however, and though several countries subsidized their athletes' trip to Sardinia, the majority were either freediving instructors, like Mike, or well-paid professionals, like Kerry Hollowell. They were extremely fit but not exactly young. The vast majority were over thirty, some over forty. Among them were engineers, architects, and marine biologists as well as landscapers and roofers. One of the English freedivers worked for the left-wing ocean conservation group Sea Shepherd. Alexey and Natalia ran their own freediving business in Moscow, a thousand kilometers from the sea.

Then fifty-two, Natalia Molchanova was the Martina Navratilova of freediving. An ageless wonder, she'd proven impossible to beat for nearly a decade. Her quiet nature and Eastern bloc heritage, like Navratilova at the peak of her powers, often led to her being misperceived as cold and calculating, when in reality she was the open-hearted Zen poet of her sport. Better yet, the Mother Superior. Her fellow athletes called her the Queen, because she kicked everyone's ass, and did it with love.

Natalia was born in Ufa, a southern Russian city founded as a sixteenth-century fort on orders from Ivan the Terrible and set on the banks of three different rivers. It was there that she first fell in love with swimming. She swam breaststroke competitively through school, competing at the highest levels until she met her future husband, another athlete, at a swim meet when she was just twenty years old. After university, like all Soviet students, the couple was obligated to teach in small towns to pay the country back for their free education. The Molchanovs were stationed in Marx, a little town near Engels.

Three years later her husband got a job in a Volgograd shipyard, and Natalia soon had two kids. Alexey was her youngest. She swam with him in her arms when he was still an infant and by the time he was just three years old, he was swimming for distance. Once a year they would travel to the Black Sea to dive for mussels. By then Natalia had become a swim coach and a teacher, and life was good. They even managed to weather the storm of the Soviet collapse. "It was hard," said Alexey, who was five years old at the time. "I remember there was no food in the shops, no clothes or shoes in the stores, but we managed." Mostly because Natalia hustled to make sure the family's basic needs were met.

In 2001, when Alexey was thirteen and Natalia was thirty-nine, they weathered another storm. Alexey's father had met another woman—another Natalia—and fallen in love. She was twenty years old. Natalia had given everything to this man, and now he'd traded her in for a new model, like she was disposable. The separation was tough on Alexey, but it also bound him closer to his mother, who soon left Volgograd and settled in Moscow. A year later, in 2002, she read about freediving in a magazine, and it sounded healing. She looked for somewhere to learn, but there were no freediving schools in Moscow. So she started one herself.

Natalia read all she could about the sport, and launched a freediving program at Moscow's Russian State University of Physical Education, Sport, Youth and Tourism, one of the old Soviet-era sports universities, which used to churn out Olympic champions. She eventually became an associate professor there. By 2003 she had already snagged a Russian record and tied the world record in Dynamic with a swim of 155 meters. In the ocean she was still relatively shallow, though. Her personal best was a mere 45 meters.

The next year she began collecting world records in the pool, but pool diving wasn't what she loved the most. "Compared to the ocean, the pool is like running on a treadmill versus running in the forest," she said. She'd always bring Alexey to competitions, and the two of them would train for depth in Dahab, which remains a vital training center for the Russian Freediving Federation thanks to ample depth and the four-hour nonstop flights to Moscow. Of all her many early freedives there, she can recall one special journey, in Dahab's Blue Hole, that fundamentally shifted her relationship to her sport.

There is a famous underwater red rock arch in Dahab, which is more like a 25-meter long tunnel, and is an extreme challenge to swim through. When a diver submerges to 53 meters, swims the length of that tunnel and makes it back to the surface unscathed, they know they are among the elite. "I have a big experience inside when I go through the arch," Natalia said. And her "big experience" led to an epiphany that true power in freediving comes from a deep relaxation that feels like surrender. She tried to explain: "Freediving is not only sport, it's a way to understand who we are. When we go down if we don't think, we understand we are whole. We are one with world. When we think we are separate. On surface it is natural to think and we have many information inside. We need to reset sometimes, freediving helps do that."

None of the young men in Dahab could keep up with her that day. They hadn't the courage or ability to make it through. Few athletes worldwide had the chops back then, or do now, but she was so relaxed it was easy, and when she breached the surface she knew she would try for the world record at the 2005 world championship. She achieved it with a Constant Weight dive of 86 meters. Thus began Natalia's period of complete domination through total surrender.

In 2012, when she took back the Constant No Fins record from Ashley, she did it on her fiftieth birthday, for herself but also as a lesson to older athletes everywhere. "Many people, when they reach fifty, they think life is over," she said. "I want to show them, there is more they can do." In 2013, at fifty-one, she broke all six world records, and her Constant Weight mark of 101 meters made her the only woman to swim below 100 meters in the sport's history.

As Natalia began to dominate, Alexey also progressed, and like his mother, he set his first world record in the pool in 2008 with a Dynamic swim of 250 meters. He had trouble with persistent blackouts in Constant Weight in his early years, so he slowed his progression and stopped making big jumps in depth; by 2011 his patience paid off when he had a shot at winning the Constant Weight world championship. Unfortunately, he'd trained too hard in the lead-up and lost motor control at the surface after his dive to 118 meters. If he'd had a clean surface protocol, he would have won the title. Instead, Guillaume Néry of France took gold. The next year, in 2012, Alexey broke his first depth world record with a Constant Weight dive to 125 meters in Sharm el-Sheikh, Egypt.

Although Natalia always had faith in Alexey's ability, she often felt tortured watching him dive, as time ticked on, suspense set in, and her son remained cloaked in blue. "Many times I'm nervous," she said. The most stressful moment came on Alexey's world record 128 meter dive in 2013. Less than a week before, he'd had a deep-water blackout and a bad lung squeeze. She begged him to quit the competition. "He don't listen me. I'm nervous, of course, but I must not show it. I nervous only inside. Outside I'm quiet because it's important for Alosha [her pet name for Alexey]."

Although they'd been among the best in the sport for years, Natalia never considered either of them to be professional athletes. "I am not professional sportsman," she said. "I have not money from sport. I haven't sponsor. Me and Alosha work as teachers. We are instructors. We work." There's never been any doubt about that. In fact, Alexey is arguably the hardest-working man in freediving.

He and his mother ran the Russian Freediving Federation out of the same Moscow university where Natalia had worked for years.

Its marble halls are lined with sports memorabilia from yesteryear: wooden skis, snowshoes, tennis rackets, and basketball jerseys. A new exhibit recognizes Russian medal winners from the Sochi Olympics, and in the water sports wing, several of Natalia's trophies, photographs, and books are on display.

Natalia had written a handful of instructional manuals, which she and Alexey used in their freediving classes, as well as a volume of poetry. She also lectured at the university, and commuted from her simple but comfortable one-bedroom high-rise apartment on a motorized kick scooter. Unlike her son, who drove his souped-up Honda Accord on Moscow's three-ring roads like a Bangkok cabbie on speed, she was always too timid to drive. They lived less than a block away from one another in a neighborhood of midcentury high-rises. Hers was a bit more chic than his apartment, which was cramped, with wood floors and a smallish kitchen and living area. His mattress rested on the bedroom floor. Spent protein-powder barrels were lined up in a hedgerow on his dresser. Not that he clocked much time there. He's usually on the road competing or training in Dahab.

When in town, he could be found by his mother's side at the university's vast, yet aging natatorium, where they ran their freediving school and the Russian Freediving Federation out of their office behind two black-bottomed, Olympic-sized pools. Next door to the office was their storeroom, stocked with over a hundred monofins that Alexey designed, beta tested, and had manufactured in Siberia for customers in Russia and overseas.

Nobody built the sport like Alexey and Natalia, whose sixty-odd instructors each taught a dozen or more students every week at four different pools scattered around the city. They held training camps in Dahab and Bali, and Natalia and Alexey still taught newcomers, who crammed their office two dozen at a time, relishing the chance to learn from the very best. They should. They might as well have been learning how to serve from Roger Federer and Serena Williams.

While Natalia was a born teacher, her son preferred to focus on the business side. He stayed busy fielding orders or stocking dive shops in Egypt and across Russia with Molchanova gear. He also handled the money, collecting soggy and wrinkled checks from new faces in class. Each one made his eyes twinkle. Alexey may have been born into socialism, but he'd become a shameless capitalist who took business calls at all hours from his Bluetooth earpiece and emailed students, customers, and suppliers deep into the night.

In some ways mother and son were similar. Both had muscular lower halves, their thighs and calves bulging, and were stoked with an inner competitive fire. But while Alexey was gregarious, Natalia was shy. He loved buying new tech, and wore designer jeans and bespoke sandals from Italy. She couldn't have cared less about shopping. He did all the driving, of course, and could be bombastic, talking about new records to break and competitions to win. She rarely discussed competitive goals, instead waxing wistfully about how nice it would be if Alexey would just forget about all of this world record business, settle down, and have a family like his sister.

When Natalia talked about freediving, it was always about the soul of the sport. "In training, is very important to dive for pleasure inside. To feel pleasure. In training, I never push," she said. "It's big problem to be fanatic sportsman, and think about only result. Life is not only sport. Life is more. So if we concentrate on the result and become fanatic, we don't feel our body and we push our body. The biggest problem with freedivers now is they hurry. They go too deep too fast. That is the problem with Nicholas. In all other sports they start young and there are levels. You start at the first level and go up. But freedivers are adults, and they don't want to start at the beginning level. They think, I'm strong, I can do, but no. This is what Nicholas did."

Alexey agreed. When he started out, it was common for competitive freedivers to build to 80 meters over the course of eight years. "It took me two years to get to 80 meters, and that was already fast," he said. Natalia believed that because she and Alexey took their time, their bodies were better adapted to depth. She hypothesized that their blood vessels and rib cage were more flexible, which allowed them to withstand intense barometric pressure.

"I think Nicholas started very quickly," Natalia said. "He was talented sportsman of course, but his body was not ready for big depth because the body needs adaptation. [Eighteen months] is very big speed for 100 meters. His blood vessel don't adapt. He was not flexible because he hadn't time."

Alexey and Natalia obviously weren't afraid of pushing their limits. They trained in the pool and the gym for two hours almost every day, and they never trained alone because their popular freediving school delivered a talent pool stocked with training partners to their doorstep. The best of them tried out for the national team in July 2012, when Alexey and Natalia hosted team trials at the university.

Alexey's longtime girlfriend, Marina, made the cut, though they had recently split. Marianna Krupnitskaya, a recent college grad, posted an impressive Dynamic dive, earning a spot. So did Andrey Matveenko, Alexey's weightlifting buddy. Once tall and scrawny, he'd put on thirty pounds of muscle in the past two years and become Russia's second-deepest man. His progress got Alexey's attention, and the two began weight training together.

Sasha, the diver who red carded in Sardinia, already booked his spot when he beat Goran at a recent pool comp with a Dynamic dive of 265 meters, breaking Alexey's national record along the way. Seeing his record broken didn't concern Alexey, because thanks to Sasha, the Russian men had a team capable of winning gold for the first time, or so he thought.

After trials, Natalia gathered the group at the pool's edge, a stopwatch dangling from her neck. She praised the newbies who came out to experience a competitive environment for the first time and talked about safe ways of approaching and moving beyond limits. Her greatness and her softness made her a leader easy to follow.

Sometimes she led by example—like when she dove to 93 meters in Sardinia, making her the third-deepest diver in the entire tournament, men included. Like Alexey, she prepared by breathing up vertically on the line, dressed in the Russian women's custom gold wetsuits. As time ticked down, she stretched her neck in one direction, then the next, arched her back, and expanded her chest. With twenty seconds to go she began packing air, sipping forty packs before putting her face in the water and kicking down. Her descent was a little slow, but she surfaced at 3:29, right on time. As she hooked the line, she let out a sunny laugh, the tag dangling from her finger like a toy ring. No wonder they called her the Queen. With another white card secured, after a strong showing in Static on day one, the Russian women were in control.

Other times she took a more active leadership role. Like when Sasha red carded. According to Natalia, he didn't slip into the water with a clean mind. The problem: Marianna and Sasha, who had a live-in girlfriend, started to hook up during their training camp in Croatia. But Sasha would bring that same girlfriend, one of Moscow's best pole dancers, with him to Sardinia. He was caught between two women. It was not going well.

But Russia caught a break when Croatian Bruno Segvic, who had hit 100 meters in training, blacked out after a 92-meter dive. He fell backward and thrashed in the water before going limp for ten seconds. Though it certainly looked dramatic, it was a simple loss of motor control and a brief blackout, but it changed everything. Thanks to Alexey's heroic 120-meter dive and Andrey's 90-meter jaunt right afterward, the Russian men were back in the mix for gold as long as Sasha nailed his 81-meter dive. If he slipped up again, however, they could kiss even bronze goodbye.

Natalia shadowed Sasha as he floated to the line, looking for redemption. She whispered in his ear, reminding him to focus on "deconcentration," one of Natalia's fundamental principles of freediving. When the diver relaxes deeply, and lets the world as it is fade into white noise until all that matters is one breath, one stroke at a time. But he can't get too loose or too soft. He must stay in the moment and allow his training, his habits, and muscle memory to take over.

As the countdown began, Sasha looked over to Natalia, who beamed with motherly pride, love, and confidence, as if she were communicating the vital truth that his problems didn't exist in the water. Nothing existed except Sasha and the line. He relaxed his shoulders, packed fifty sips of air, inflated his lungs to the zenith, adjusted his mask, and went down. His pace was swift. Within twenty seconds he'd passed 25 meters. Thirty seconds later he was at 60 meters and dropping fast. Once at the bottom he turned and kicked back hard. Two minutes after his dive had begun he was already past 50 meters, swimming toward blades of Mediterranean sun that pierced the blue like a sundial. All was well in his world when he rose up, grabbed the line, and aced the surface protocol. He coughed a bit, but there was no blood and no drama, other than that love triangle awaiting him on shore.

Love problems didn't interfere with Marianna or Marina, who had spent a month in tears after Alexey left her, but pulled herself together to represent her country. Both nailed their Constant Weight dives and the Russian women continued to build their lead over Team Japan, looking for their third straight gold behind Tomoka Fukuda, Hanako Hirose, and Misuzu Okamoto. Mike's dive seemed to go reasonably well, though he was penalized a couple of points for not letting go of the line before dipping his face in the water, but afterward he coughed, spit in his hand, and found specks of blood. He washed his palm in the sea, and spat again. More blood. Not too much, but it was there.

Nick, age 3, suited up and ready to dive into his family pool, takes time for a photo op with Uncle Paul. *Courtesy Paul Mevoli*. RIGHT: A teenaged Nick hugs his mother, Belinda Rudzik, in his grandparents' garden in South Plainfield, New Jersey. *Courtesy Katie Rudzik*. BELOW: From left, Aaron Suko, Soliman Lawrence, and Nick Mevoli at the Cloisters museum in Washington Heights, New York City, March 2006. *Courtesy Aaron Suko*

The DVD cover and poster art for *Exist*, starring Nick Mevoli and directed by Esther Bell. *Courtesy Esther Bell*

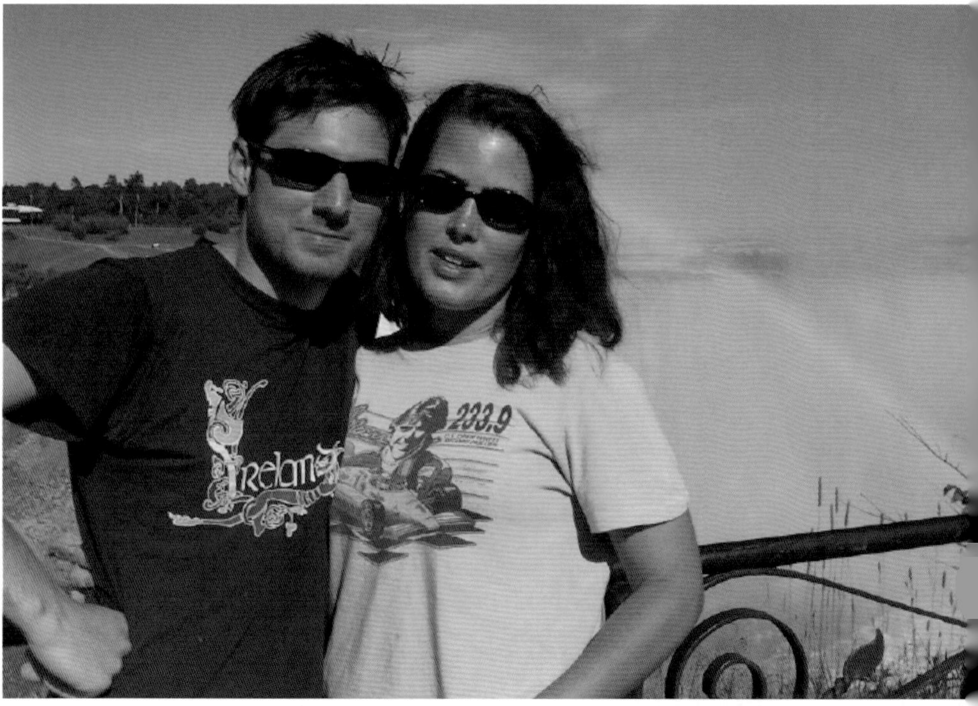

Nick and Esther pose above Niagara Falls in July 2003. *Courtesy Esther Bell*

Nick and the US Freediving Team join the parade of athletes on their march through the streets of Nice, France, during the opening ceremony of the 2012 AIDA Team World Championship. *Courtesy Ren Chapman*

Nick and Jen, with their father, Larry Mevoli, enjoy the sunset on St. Petersburg Beach in August 2011 while Jen is pregnant with Nick's goddaughter, Alexandra. *Courtesy Katie Rudzik*

After a prolonged hunt at Seven Mile Bridge off Marathon Key, Nick surfaces with the biggest fish he ever caught, a 35-pound amberjack. *Courtesy Paul Mevoli*

With Slovenian champion Samo Jeranko in the background, Will Trubridge flashes a grin after scoring a white card with his 120-meter Free Immersion dive at the 2014 edition of Vertical Blue. After a rocky start and a failed world-record bid in Constant No Fins, that dive placed him back in the hunt for gold. *Photo credit: Daan Verhoeven*

Russia's Natalia Molchanova, the greatest female freediver of all time and one of the very best of all time regardless of gender, waves to an adoring crowd after breaking the women's world record in Dynamic Apnea with a swim of 237 meters at the 2014 AIDA Team World Championship in Sardinia, Italy. *Photo credit: Daan Verhoeven*. RIGHT: Natalia Molchanova glides down to 96 meters at the 2014 AIDA Team World Championship, where she led the Russian women to the gold medal. Natalia remains the only woman ever to eclipse 100 meters in any of the competitive freediving disciplines. *Photo credit: Daan Verhoeven*

Alexey Molchanov completes the surface protocol and flashes the tag he fetched from the bottom plate after a dive to 123 meters in Constant Weight, while fans and athletes look on. With that dive, Alexey secured overall Caribbean Cup gold and defeated Will Trubridge for an overall title for the first time in his career. *Photo credit: Lia Barrett*. RIGHT: Former Royal Marine and England's best freediver Michael Board on the beach in Sardinia, where he competed for Great Britain at the 2014 AIDA Team World Championship. *Photo credit: Daan Verhoeven*

Kerry Hollowell poses with her monofin on the beach in Roatan, Honduras, where she competed in the 2015 edition of the Caribbean Cup. *Photo credit: Lia Barrett*. RIGHT: Ashley Chapman celebrates after breaking Natalia Molchanova's world record in the Constant No Fins discipline at the 2012 edition of Deja Blue in the Cayman Islands. Natalia would take the record back within days, but Ashley's mark still stands as the American record.
Photo credit: Logan Mock Bunting

From left, Ren Chapman, Ashley Chapman, and Nick enjoy stogies and rum on their road trip through Pinar Del Rio, Cuba, in 2012. *Courtesy Ren Chapman.* RIGHT: Nick and Iru make arepas for all comers in Nick's makeshift DIY kitchen during the 2013 AIDA Individual Depth World Championship. *Courtesy Iru Balic*

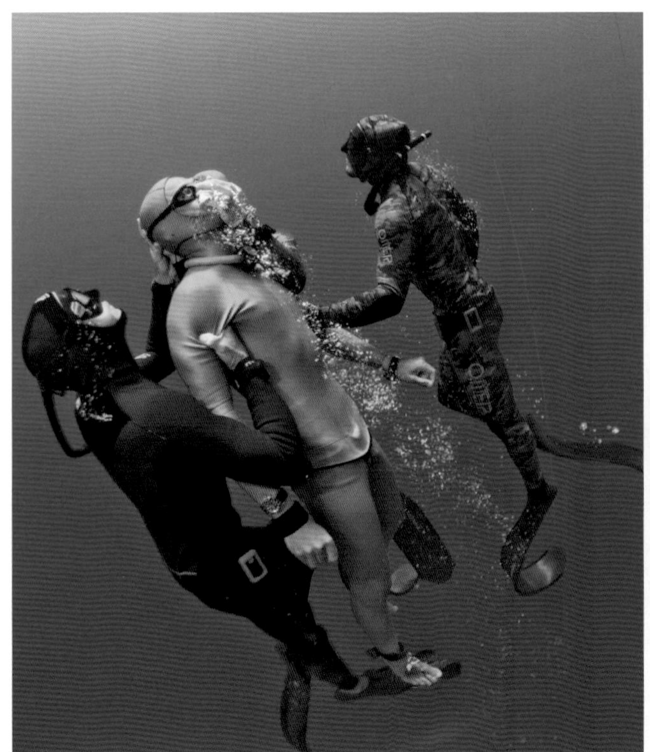

Safety divers assist Nick to the surface after a deepwater blackout during his failed Free Immersion attempt at Deja Blue 2012.
Photo credit: Logan Mock Bunting

On May 27, 2013, Nick kicks down toward an American record of 100 meters and back on a single breath, in Constant Weight at the Caribbean Cup in Roatan, Honduras, just thirteen months after his very first competition. Nobody in the history of the sport reached that milestone in such a short time. *Photo credit: Lia Barrett*. RIGHT: After the white card comes, Nick lets loose. *Photo credit: Logan Mock Bunting*. BELOW: Fifteen-time world-record holder William Trubridge in his element at Dean's Blue Hole. *Photo credit: Daan Verhoeven*

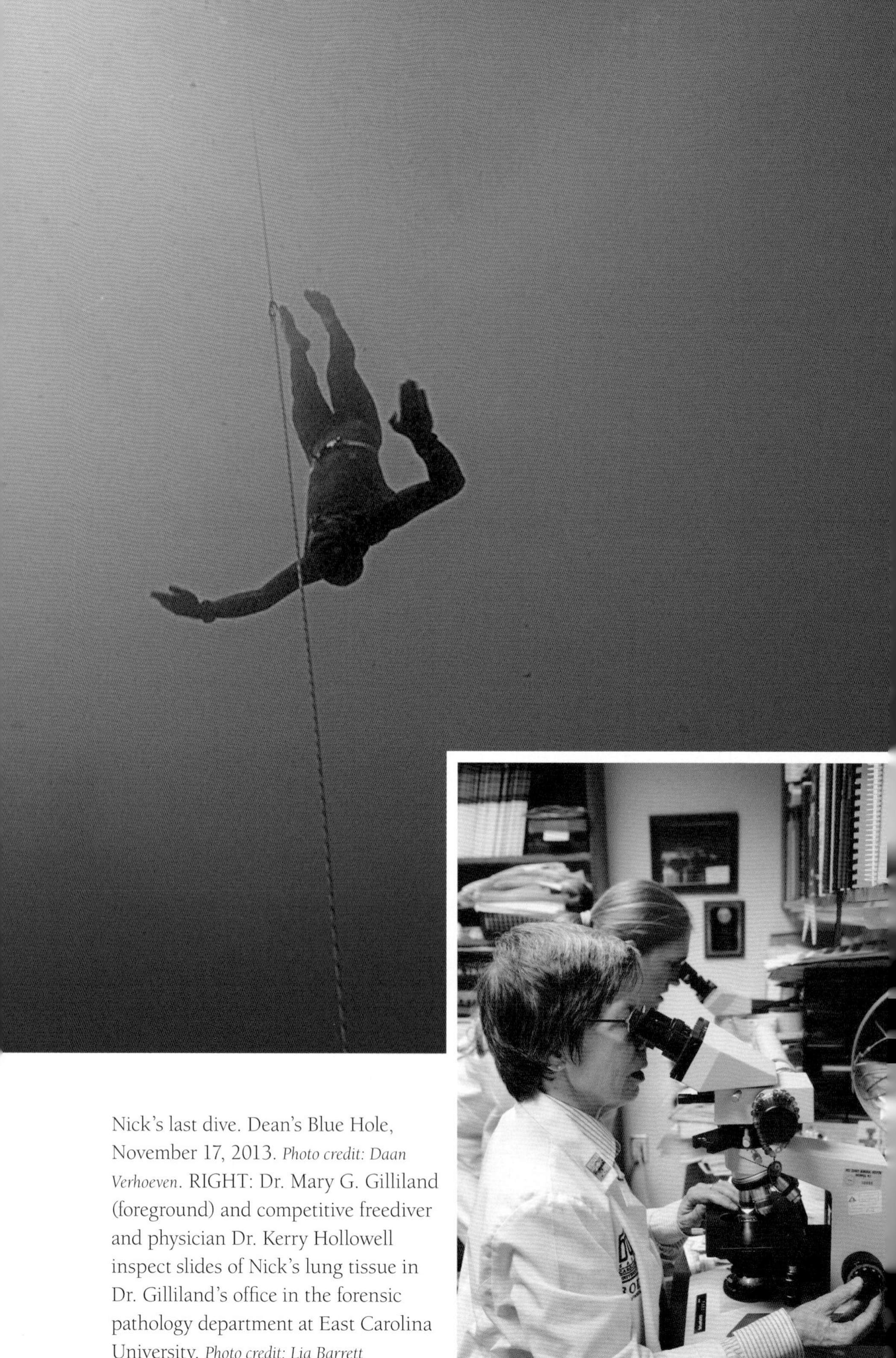

Nick's last dive. Dean's Blue Hole, November 17, 2013. *Photo credit: Daan Verhoeven*. RIGHT: Dr. Mary G. Gilliland (foreground) and competitive freediver and physician Dr. Kerry Hollowell inspect slides of Nick's lung tissue in Dr. Gilliland's office in the forensic pathology department at East Carolina University. *Photo credit: Lia Barrett*

Before he'd hopped the boat to the competition zone, he talked about diving with a small lung squeeze. "With the experience I've had, and what I've seen, you'd think I'd be very cautious." Yet even though his team had no chance of winning, he couldn't stay out of the water. "The attraction is the competition, the athletic accomplishment," he explained, "because there is nothing that nice about doing a competition dive until you're coming up with a tag in your hand."

He wasn't the only diver to check his palm that day. Kerry Hollowell was in Sardinia leading Team USA. On the men's side were Steve; Kyle Gion, a gifted twenty-year-old Brown University student from Honolulu who held the American record in Dynamic; and Kurt Chambers, a freedive instructor and photographer from Kona who coined his own hashtag: #girlsgonefreediving, which he posts along with shameless booty shots of beautiful ladies in g-strings and monofins on his Instagram account (@chambersbelow, for the curious). In 2015 Kurt would break the American record in Free Immersion. Ashleigh Baird, an architect turned dive bum from Florida, and Mandy Sumner, a Honolulu geologist, rounded out the women's team.

After hemming and hawing for weeks, Ashley Chapman decided not to represent Team USA. She didn't think they had a chance of winning a medal, and she and Ren were too busy fixing up their new boat and raising Ani to uproot for a month of training and competition. Francesca Koe Owings, Team USA's coach and lead organizer, couldn't make it either.

Kerry could have used their support. She'd had a miserable week. She and Steve had split up on the flight over after a long training camp in Kona, and the breakup rocked her world. Her mind was scrambled as she struggled to fill the Team USA leadership void. Even her training was shit. Worse, she'd suffered a minor lung squeeze a week before the competition. Still, the American women were hanging tough in fourth place, with an outside shot at bronze, when Kerry clipped onto the line. She made a strong dive to 60 meters, flashed the tag and completed a clean protocol after surfacing. As she swam over to the oxygen bottle to recover, she felt relieved for the first time in weeks. Sitting on the bow of the dry boat, she breathed deep, and enjoyed the pure healing of 100 percent oxygen and the nourishing view of the Sardinian coastline shining in the sun. Then she coughed twice and spit into her palm. Blood.

The event physician in Sardinia was Diego Olivari, an ER doc with a master's in hyperbaric medicine. Big as a bear, with an ever-present smile, he was also an avid scuba diver, and while in the area for the competition, he started taking freediving classes. Unlike doctors at other events, when an athlete blacked out in Sardinia, he didn't wait for the safety divers to bring them around. He'd pounce and blast a shot of 100 percent oxygen into their mouth from a tank he slung over one shoulder.

Kerry had discussed Nick's case with Olivari, as doctors do, and he came in with an understanding of freedive physiology. She also showed him the blood in her palm. "It looks dry," he said. "It's an old injury. It isn't fresh." Kerry agreed, and if they were right, it meant she didn't reinjure herself on the dive, but that she still had remnants of her minor squeeze the week before rattling around her lungs.

Mike Board felt something new had happened on his dive, so he made an appointment with Olivari later that day to have an ultrasound done, partly out of concern, but also out of curiosity. Up until then, event doctors had been using a stethoscope to listen to the lungs and determine if the diver was squeezed, but Olivari believed he could detect edema with ultrasound. He met Mike in his de facto exam area: an empty banquet room on the fourth floor of the hotel. Mike removed his shirt, and Olivari scanned his chest with a transducer to take a sonic picture of his lungs.

On the shadowy image, it looked like rays of light were streaming down, which Olivari called a ULC, or underwater lung comet. ULCs, he said, are caused by blood, which is blocking the light from his transducer. "You have a little edema," he told Mike. "This is the first symptom of a serious injury for the lung, but it's not bad. Just a little bit." For an injury like Mike's, Olivari said that breathing 100 percent oxygen, 5 meters underwater, would dry up the edema in ten minutes. He sent Mike to the pool.

He went on to explain that while ultrasound could also reveal a large rupture in the lung, smaller tears would be impossible to detect. Unfortunately, even major squeeze events during a freediving competition are believed to cause only small wounds, and it was a series of such injuries, Kerry had begun to suspect, that may have led to Nick's death. In other words, Olivari's innovation was exciting, because at least there was a way to detect edema, but his diagnosis was also incomplete. There was no way of knowing based on Mike's ultrasound if, or how badly, his tissue had been damaged.

Mike was happy to have at least some confirmation that he had been only slightly squeezed, and the next day, another ultrasound showed his lungs were clear. When it came to Nick, however, Mike was still in the dark and he was growing frustrated with AIDA, which had initially blamed Nick's death on his reckless diving history and followed that up with nothing at all. Nearly a year after his death, athletes were still diving blind. Yes, new rules had been voted on, but they wouldn't be implemented until January 2015, so in the wake of the sport's biggest tragedy, nothing had changed.

Much of that lack of responsiveness comes down to time and money. AIDA's eleven board members are all volunteers, most with demanding, full-time jobs, and it's as disparate an organization as one can find. AIDA is a federation, made up of thirty-five national freediving associations that form a General Assembly. Any individual who belongs to one of the national associations can nominate a rule change or board member, and the General Assembly votes on the rule or candidate in question—one country, one vote. The board is elected every two years, and meets via Skype once a month, while rule changes are put up for a vote as suggestions arise throughout the year. The only time everyone is in the same room at the same time is during world championship events, when the General Assembly meets. But Eurocentric AIDA isn't just the governing body of a sport. It is also a certifying organization that puts out freediving curriculum and certifies recreational freedivers and instructors, placing them in direct competition with many of its members.

Put it all together and you have a multicultural organization staffed with mostly well-meaning folks dedicated to their sport, but one with built-in blind spots, thought gaps, and conflicts of interest. Over its nearly quarter century in operation there has been a ballot box–stuffing scandal, and an embezzlement of over 200,000 Swiss francs by the organization's treasurer and former president. Yet despite competitive freediving's inherent risk, AIDA had never been confronted with an athlete's death until Nick's, and, to some athletes, the organization's response was underwhelming.

"Last month in Kalamata there was an athlete getting squeezed repeatedly, but because the rules hadn't changed, the doctor did not disqualify him," Mike said. In the end Mike and photographer Daan Verhoeven, another witness to Nick's death, convinced him to stop diving. "But the fact is he didn't have the knowledge to make that decision himself, so I'm a little upset that I'm having to chase around for information nearly a year later."

Mike didn't know that Kerry, who also had an ultrasound done by Olivari that showed no edema at all, had spent the past ten months meeting with dive doctors and consulting with emergency medical professionals. She was even working with a forensic pathologist at East Carolina University on a secondary autopsy that she hoped would reveal what happened to Nick, once and for all. What she would soon find would provide needed clarity, and just might change the sport.

The final competition day at team worlds was held at the Hotel

Setar pool, which is dug into its concrete pad overlooking the Mediterranean. The 25-meter pool was corded off into two competition lanes, one on either end, with empty lanes between. A gentle breeze billowed a banner plastered with the face of Umberto Pelizzari, the freediving legend and national hero, who was hawking Omer freediving computers, and the national flags from all the competing countries, which were draped from the railing of the hotel's painfully average restaurant.

The athletes gathered on a patch of lawn, where they suited up and relaxed as they awaited their top times. Goran Colak was still steaming about his countryman's slipup in the open water. "If we all just did 75 meters, we would have been so far ahead of everybody we could have had one of our guys not dive today," he said. "But he did 95 meters the day before and he wasn't even breathing hard. I'd seen him do 100 meters, so I said, okay, do 92. Actually, it was my fault. I should have known better. This was his first big competition, and it was just nerves, I guess. The Russians gave us a gift and we gave it back with interest."

Still, Croatia was very much in contention, and if Goran could pull off a swim close to his personal best, which was the world record, they might eke out another gold. Going into the final day, Croatia was in second place, eight points behind Denmark and eighteen points ahead of Russia, but Denmark wasn't as strong in the pool and they would need their rivals to earn a couple of red cards to hold them off.

While in the depth competition athletes earned one point per meter; in the pool they earned one point for every two meters. In other words, Croatia had a 36-meter head start on Russia when Goran slipped into liquid, slow and calm, and clipped his neck weight into place. In Dynamic, athletes must stay beneath the surface, and the only way to do that without fighting buoyancy is to be weighted. He stretched his left arm overhead, then his right, loosening up, his eyes focused into the light blue water. All around the pool, more than a hundred spectators gathered close to watch the world's best at work.

He sipped and packed air audibly, dipped below, and pushed off. His long, elegant dolphin kicks were calm and rhythmic. Kick, glide, kick, glide. A safety diver on a kickboard trailed him the whole way. In Dynamic, suspense sets in as the athlete closes in on his or her limit, and by the time Goran touched the end of the pool after 200 meters the entire gallery was fixated, everyone standing yet perfectly silent, as if on the eighteenth green of the Masters. He touched the wall at 225 meters and turned again. How long would he go, how far could he push? One more lap. When he reached 250 meters he came up suddenly. A crush of photographers and judges formed a tight semicircle to watch Goran ace the protocol. Croatia was back in gold medal position.

Alexey was one of the few not to pay attention to Goran's dive because he was preparing for his own in one of the warm-up lanes. As Goran smiled and shook hands on the pool deck, Alexey, this time dressed in a clean black wetsuit, with no sponsors or Team Russia logos, was ready to go. Calm as a bodhisattva, he breathed up facing forward, his eyes closed, his yellow nose clip locked in place. With ten seconds to go he took his peak inhalation, packed more air on top of that, secured his neck weight, and kicked away, gliding through the blue, smooth as butter.

His technique was slightly different. He did a double dolphin kick before his glide, which was a beat longer than Goran's. That's how he learned to do it as a young gun fin swimmer in St. Petersburg, and he hadn't changed. Goran stood on the side of the pool watching, as Alexey tapped to 200 meters, his form still holding. Could he pass Goran's 250 meters and gain points? If so, Russia would be in terrific position. Alexey turned at 225 meters, but couldn't hold out much longer. He came up and leaned his elbows on the side of the pool at 234 meters. Hypoxic, his protocol was wobbly, and he could barely choke out those three important words, "I am okay," as the judges leaned in and the cameras clicked. But it was clean enough for a white card. Russia was now in second place, twenty-six points, or 52 meters, behind Croatia.

Alexey climbed out of the pool to accept congratulations from Goran. Coming into the competition, these were the two men everybody wanted to see. Goran had been dominant in the pool for years, but his obligations frequently precluded him from entering depth competitions, something he wanted to do more frequently. Already a 100-meter diver, with his breath hold it stood to reason that should he decide to focus on depth, he could be one of the world's best. As it was, he and Alexey, who rarely enters pool competitions, seldom compete against one another unless they're in Dubai holding their breath for pink slips. And like many world-class athletes, they appreciated this opportunity to go head to head, and talk some trash.

"I beat you," Goran said. He'd been tallying his and Alexey's points, hoping to edge out his friend for unofficial, man of the comp honors. Two years ago, when Croatia won gold, Alexey won their head to head. "I needed 9 meters and I got 16, so I beat you by 3½ points."

"But my Static doesn't count, it was shit," griped Alexey.

"Yeah, like my depth counts. I can do 102 meters. I was taking it easy."

"I was taking it super easy."

"Yeah, I saw how easy you were taking it," Goran snarked, referencing Alexey's difficult protocol. Alexey shook it off, but it didn't end there.

"If both of your guys do 200 and both my guys do 230, that will be fun," Alexey said.

"Yes, but they need to do 230."

"They can do 260."

"You can do 268," Goran said.

Point Goran, but bragging rights would only go to the gold medalists, and Sasha was diving next. After fumbling his Static dive, he'd kept Marianna at a distance, and his focus was on the competition.

Russia's best man in the pool, he was dressed in an all-red bodysuit, his neck weight wrapped in duct tape. Favoring a simple one kick, glide rhythm like Goran, he moved more quickly than the others. Of course, in this distance race, slower can be better if it means a more efficient use of oxygen. Still, he got to 225 meters with nary a ripple in form, and as he closed in on 250, he came close to the side, rising just before he hit the wall. His protocol was perfect. He wasn't even breathing hard after swimming 247 meters on one breath.

"That's why he's on the team," said Marina, who ran to congratulate him. Alexey gave him a bear hug, then rushed over to Goran to goose him a bit. After clawing back from a nightmare start, Sasha had moved the Russian men into first place. Goran could offer only a thin smile. It was going to be close.

Andrey, Russia's last man in the water, needed 213 meters to get to the magic 460 number Alexey thought would win gold. He came close, clocking in with a dive of 209 meters, which put Russia in the clubhouse with 802 points. Goran's guys would need to swim a collective 404 meters to catch them.

Bruno was the first to go, and like Sasha, he craved redemption. Goran knelt beside him as he breathed up, whispering last-minute tips and helping him relax. Anything over 210 meters would put them in a terrific position, but Bruno didn't look relaxed at all. He looked intense, and after just a few packs, he pushed off with a dodgy entry, splashing Goran in the face with his monofin. He kicked with force and his glide was smooth, but his speed picked up as he approached 175 meters, as if he were fighting to get to 200. When he got there he blew right past it, rising at 215 meters and delivering a clean protocol. The swim was strong but he received a yellow card and a 10-meter penalty for piercing the surface with his fin in the middle of the pool.

With the penalty, Croatia's last man, Bozidar Potani, needed a 200-meter swim to win gold. The shortest of the three men on the squad, his head was shaved smooth, and he exhaled audibly, hoping to bubble off all the pressure and deliver one more clean dive for his country. He could not. His form was solid until he hit 150 meters, then things went wobbly. He'd been too slow, perhaps attempting to relax too much, and never found his sweet spot, that perfect balance where speed and relaxation meet and oxygen efficiency peaks. He slowed down even more as he approached the 175-meter turn but couldn't make it that far. He moved to the side of the pool, in trouble. His arms buckled as he attempted to lift his head out of the water. He tried to rise up again, and again he buckled, his chin nearly bashing the pool ledge. His eyes were open but he wasn't all there. The judges called that a mechanical blackout, and he received a red card. The Russian men won gold, and the Russian women were in prime position to make it a double.

Russia's gold-suited women had been the best in every discipline, though Team Japan wasn't far behind. In the weeks before the comp, Marina had been heartbroken, trying to piece her life back together. She'd even thought of quitting freediving altogether. Then just before coming to Sardinia she booked a job as an underwater stunt double on *Point Break 2*, shooting scenes in Tahiti with champion big wave surfer Mark Healey, who's also a terrific spearfisherman. That gig reignited her love for freediving, and every one of her dives in Sardinia had been so enjoyable, she wasn't leaving the sport anytime soon. Her Dynamic swim of 205 meters was elegant, and better than any American man has ever achieved. As she got out of the pool she was surrounded by photographers, a position she's quite used to. She indulged them as long as they clicked.

Geeky cute, Marianna, with her thick ringlets of strawberry-blonde hair and rosy cheeks, also had a roller-coaster ride in Sardinia. She knew Sasha was spoken for when they started hooking up in Croatia, but she thought she'd fallen for him. Thanks to her iron will, she didn't let heartbreak follow her into the water, and she glided to an easy 155-meter white card.

Natalia, of course, stole the show. Thanks to her teammates, when she slipped into the water, she needed to swim just 30 meters on one breath to defeat the Japanese and win gold, but she had other plans. With a crowd rapt in anticipation, in a country that reveres its free-diving stars, Natalia began to glide beneath the surface, using the double kick technique, same as her son. After four laps and 100 meters, everybody assumed she'd rise and claim Russian gold at any moment, but she kept swimming.

Back in Moscow she said, "For me, I have not good results in training. Only in competition. I like to train but I don't like to swim long-distance Dynamic because many discomfort. So I train with pleasure, very easy, like a dance. There is no gravity, and my body is happy to move with music inside. But in competition, if I feel I have power, and I have potential to go for a record, why not?"

Though Kyle Gion, the American record holder, was swimming on the far side of the pool, he may as well have been swimming alone. Every spectator hovered over the near side, watching Natalia double kick and glide with power and grace. She was in a zone. Kyle rose at 175 meters. Natalia kept swimming. Now even Kyle was watching.

When she hit 200 meters, a murmur filtered through the crowd. The women's Dynamic record was 234 meters. When would she stop? Was she pushing too far? Would she falter? Could the Japanese win after all? At 225 meters she touched and turned, gliding closer to yet another record. She rose up about halfway down. With her elbows on the pool ledge and the Mediterranean spread out before her, she completed the cleanest of protocols. The white card flashed and the crowd went wild, cheering and clapping for minutes on end. The Russian men and women had both won gold, and Natalia had claimed one more world record with a Dynamic swim of 237 meters. She waved, beaming as the photographers surrounded her, calling her name. She was the best woman in the tournament by far, and she'd scored better than any man other than Goran and Alexey.

Kerry had been watching with her teammate and good friend, Ashleigh Baird. "She's abnormal," deadpanned Ashleigh, still clapping.

"Or she's just an awesome athlete," Kerry said.

The Russians threw a wild party that night in the hotel bar. After weeks of training and teetotaling, the freedivers were cleared to drink, and drink heavily. Even Alexey got lit, and why not? Though it had been Natalia's tournament, it was Alexey's year, at least so far. He beat Will in Roatan, took down Goran's Team Croatia on the world championship stage, and had Vertical Blue in his sights, but for now, he was going to enjoy his party.

The night did get wild. Athletes binged, some purged, several swapped hotel rooms, others roamed the streets or crashed on lobby sofas. As for Marianna, she was done with Sasha, and so was his girlfriend, at least for a little while. He would look for her most of the night, come up empty, and spend the rest in bed, alone.

In the wee hours, Mike bellied up to the bar with American alternate Jonathan Lata to discuss Nick Mevoli. Lata, who never knew Nick, was taking a hardline position that he'd caused his own demise—that because he dove for numbers and either ignored or simply refused to heed warnings, it was all Nick's fault when his body finally gave in. Lata, a talented spearfisherman and big-wave surfer from Maui, was by no means alone in holding that position, but Mike wasn't having it. He had competed alongside Nick and knew what the herd mentality was in 2013, because he'd shared it.

"I dive for numbers," Mike said, "and I think all of us here, we all dive for numbers. And the thing is, Nick didn't know he could die. He didn't know that was even possible. None of us did."

14

KERRY HOLLOWELL INVESTIGATES

It was a somber trip home from Sardinia for Kerry and Steve. After three flights they finally landed at Raleigh-Durham International and shared a ride back to Greenville, where they parted ways. She packed a few things, said goodbye to Steve's precocious thirteen-year-old daughter, whom she'd helped raise from the time she was six, and drove off to the house she'd owned since before they started dating. She'd held on to it as an investment, and her renter had recently moved out, so it was a convenient place to land.

Steve and Kerry met in medical school and then reconnected in the hospital halls when Kerry was a surgical resident and Steve already a physician's assistant in the surgery department. He found her attractive, but was married at the time. When he and his wife split, he became a full-time single dad of two girls. Kerry was single too, but when they'd cross paths on a local mountain biking trail or in the OR, he never asked her out. She didn't know about the divorce and their chance meetings were always too rushed for him to explain himself. He kept hoping for the right moment to arise.

Being a thirty- or forty-something atheist, single intellectual in Greenville, North Carolina, is not the ideal life predicament. Hell, it's hard just being single in Greenville. Sure, the Research Triangle is ninety minutes away, but that's still a long drive, and not an option for a working single parent or a surgical resident. Hard up and looking for love, both registered on Match.com. Steve found Kerry within a few clicks. They chatted online that night, and he told her he was newly single and felt a little lost. They decided to meet for dinner, where they shared their stories and talked for hours, ticking mental boxes: smart, funny, well read, athletic, attractive, and yes, atheist. By the time dinner was over, they both knew.

Within a few weeks, Kerry had moved into the house that Steve was remodeling himself. He built and installed the custom cabinetry in the kitchen, and the treehouse in the backyard. Kerry never considered that she had a maternal instinct, but now she was part of a family. She clashed with the older daughter, already a teenager, but grew close to his youngest. They shared happy years, and many interests. They rode mountain bikes, blended morning smoothies, and started freediving together. Toward the end they'd even adopted an orphaned baby squirrel. For days, Kerry warmed her in her sports bra and fed her almond butter by hand. As Nutnut grew older she would spend most of her time outside, but she'd still scurry onto their shoulders as they fed her whole nuts at the dinner table.

There were hard times, too. In 2009, during her last year of residency, Kerry was in San Diego for a medical conference while Steve was visiting his brother in Colorado. It had been a wonderful trip. Her whole life, Kerry had felt like an oddball. Tomboy and bookworm don't go over well in Greenville, much less in Edenton, North Carolina, where she grew up hunting and fishing, often better than the boys. She was also faster than most of them. She lettered in basketball, tennis, track, and cross-country, and snagged a track scholarship to NC State, where she ran the 1,500. Her personal best time of 4:32 came in the Atlantic Coast Conference finals. But while mingling with women docs from across the country in San Diego, she realized that, just like her, most were fit, tough, fun women who'd achieved big things and were capable of more. Her world opened that week. She felt more comfortable than ever in her own skin, and toward the end of the conference, she went to dinner with a group of her new friends. When their cab arrived at the restaurant, the driver stopped in a no parking zone, close to a corner. Kerry was engaged in conversation, glanced over her shoulder, saw it was clear, and opened the door.

If the other car had come around the corner right then, it would have taken the door off and only given Kerry the fright of her life. Sadly, there was time enough for her to stand directly in its path. She saw headlights and jumped on her taxi's trunk to dodge it, but the car hit her legs, spun her in the air, and dropped her in the street. The cabbie rushed to her aid but his car was still in gear, and when he took his foot off the brake, it rolled over both her legs. Unconscious, she was rushed to the hospital with a scalp laceration that would require thirty staples and a compound fracture of the tibia and fibula in her left leg. Incredibly, her right leg was bruised but the bone was intact.

Steve caught the first flight to San Diego from Denver. The orthopedic surgeon told him they put a rod in Kerry's leg so the bone could heal properly. No novice, Steve looked at the X-rays after surgery. The rod looked too long and he said so. The surgeon insisted it would be fine. Steve backed off.

Kerry had already missed weeks by the time she returned to work in her last year of residency. Surgery was always the most competitive department for new docs, and it's hard to even land one of the coveted surgical resident positions. Kerry hobbled around and tried her best to catch up, but her leg wasn't healing. For months she dealt with debilitating pain, but never complained. She couldn't. Her boss, the macho residency director, didn't have much sympathy for her plight. Eventually, she had to have a second surgery (Steve had been right about the rod), and her boss didn't like that much either. With just weeks to go before her residency was over, he cut her from the program on a technicality. Steve wanted her to go over his head and fight for her job, but she didn't have the strength. She fell into a shallow depression and wallowed before starting over and landing in a family practice residency program. So close to being a surgeon, she'd have to begin again from year one.

That's where their problems began, although her new gig afforded her more free time—time enough to discover freediving. Steve had lost respect for her, and it showed. He became more controlling, and she responded by shutting down instead of fighting back. Though they trained and competed together, the tension built until it broke on the flight to Italy.

Kerry's old house felt dark and foreign when she got home. There wasn't much furniture, just a sofa, a coffee table, and a mattress on the bedroom floor. At first she was excited for the newness of single life 2.0, but as the hours passed, her perspective darkened, and everything about it felt empty. There was no Steve, no precocious thirteen-year-old novelist hiding in her room typing away on Wattpad, and Nutnut would not be coming over for dinner anytime soon. What did squirrels know about heartbreak, anyway?

For the past three months she'd taken time off and geared her entire life toward training in Kona and competing at the world championship, and now that was in the rearview too. Instead, she had the dog days of the longest residency on record at East Carolina University medical school to look forward to. She was a family practice doc on a convalescent rotation, with the odd nightshift in the ER. There were no exotic locations or urgent competitions on the horizon. Life couldn't get more ordinary. Forty was just around the corner. She lived in fucking Greenville, alone, with no eligible life partners within a hundred miles, and she'd probably have to drive farther until she found one who would tolerate her compulsion to don a mermaid fin and swim deep enough until her lungs were the size of Nutnut's acorns. In rural North Carolina, that's not really a thing.

As the self-pity swirled, her many gifts were cloaked as flaws. She couldn't remember feeling so alone, and there wasn't any wine or whiskey in the house to keep her company, so tears would have to do. They washed over her in waves, rattled her rib cage, and wrenched her gut as she doubled over and wept. Then, suddenly, her iPhone rang, and she was shocked back to reality. She wiped her eyes and looked at the screen. It was Dr. Gilliland, the forensic pathologist Kerry had recruited to help her make sense of what had happened to Nick. Kerry had been waiting a long time for this call. Maybe she finally had some news.

"Hi, Dr. Gilliland," she sniffled, "how are you?"

ON THE DAY Nick died, Kerry was at work in the hospital, sneaking away whenever she had a spare moment to check Facebook for updates on Vertical Blue. That's how it is for serious competitive freedivers. If there's a big comp, they keep tabs. If there's a record, they want to know about it. Kerry was especially keen to know if Nick bagged that Constant No Fins record. What she found instead was an official statement about his tragic death posted by the in-house media team.

"I didn't believe it at first. I just kept reading it over and over," she said. When it finally hit her that Nick was gone, she lost it. She began dry heaving and hyperventilating. Two doctors watched her break down but they let her be. Sobbing, she called Steve, who was working on the house. Pretty soon, he was crying too. "This doesn't make sense," she told him. She was having the most trouble correlating a depth of 72 meters to a mortality. Yes, it's certainly not an easy dive, especially without fins, but the world record was another 30 meters beyond it. She would have had an easier time believing an athlete had died pushing the edge of human limits, trying to set a new world record, but 72 meters? She'd been down that far.

"We had this construct in our head that you can't die in competition, that it was this safe endeavor because of the safety training we've had," said Steve.

Blacking out never scared Kerry and Steve because they understood the physiology and knew it was the brain's response to low oxygen levels. "That's why there are safety divers," Kerry said. "They protect your airway and get you to the surface and you should breathe. If your throat had closed to prevent you from drowning, then the safety divers should give you rescue breaths to break the laryngospasm (an involuntary closing off of the throat), and you should breathe."

"And if you don't, then we keep giving you air, and eventually you should breathe," added Steve. "We didn't have any reason to believe that you could damage your lungs so badly that you could hit the surface and not be taken care of."

After hanging up with Steve, Kerry called Ashley, who told her that Nick had a massive hemorrhage. "I'm thinking, fuck, did he tear something in his lungs from the pressure? A major blood vessel? If that was the case, there was nothing anybody could do to save him."

As word spread throughout the Water Tribe, Kerry's phone rang nonstop. Francesca from US Freediving called, as did Kirk Krack and John Shedd. AIDA was MIA, and they all agreed that there was no time to waste. Someone had to try and get the family to sign over Nick's organs for research. Francesca called Paul and Belinda. In the midst of grief and shock, they listened. So little was known about the effects of pressure on an athlete's organs, Francesca told them—perhaps Nick's death could advance knowledge and prevent a future tragedy. More accommodating than most, the family agreed, hoping to salvage meaning from loss.

Dr. Shedd was already in touch with Dr. Caryn Sands, the Nassau pathologist who received Nick's remains on Monday, November 18. Shedd also reached out to the head of hyperbaric medicine at the University of Miami, while Kerry called Dr. Richard Moon, the chief of hyperbaric medicine at Duke. Neither institution would agree to take the remains on such short notice, so Kerry called forensic pathology at ECU and talked to a tech. She told him that if ECU accepted custody, she would continue to work and find a more permanent home for the organs. With a residency to finish, Kerry had no intention of doing the research herself, but she also had no clue that with custody comes liability, and once ECU received Nick's remains, the university was legally obligated to research his case. In the mad, last-minute scramble, she'd accidentally suckered her own university into a commitment they had to see through.

Kerry and Steve were ordered to the morgue to discuss the case with the pathologist in charge. When they got there, they came face to face with Dr. Mary G. Gilliland. Not quite five feet tall, with bobbed gray hair and a strand of pearls draped over her blouse, along with a large gold cross, she sneered with suspicion. Kerry smiled back. They knew each other.

When Kerry was just an intern, she'd lost a patient in ICU, and thought she'd made a fatal error by inserting a chest tube in someone who'd bled out. Once a week new residents are forced to discuss lost cases in front of their peers and professors as part of a Morbidity and Mortality meeting. Kerry had been nervous heading into that meeting, but Dr. Gilliland turned up and told the room that Kerry hadn't done anything wrong. If she had done nothing, the patient would have died even sooner. It wasn't just what she said, but the way she said it that intrigued Kerry. Dr. Gilliland was tiny yet expressive, with wide eyes and an acrobatic brow—the kind that can communicate disbelief, suspicion, anger, and joy without a word.

In the halls of the morgue, Dr. Gilliland's face flashed with recognition, but she'd just had a new case dumped on top of a pile of old ones, and wasn't particularly amused. She marched Kerry and Steve to her office, sat them down, leaned against her desk, exhaled, and said, "Okay, so once there was a diver named Nick, and . . ."

They told her all they knew about the sport and Nick's case, although they were still fuzzy on details. They hadn't yet seen the video footage, but what they did know was enough to pique Gilliland's interest. Nick had been a healthy young man who was doing something he loved and was good at, and that was perceived as safe. He was doing it within the guidelines of the sport and still ended up dead. Gilliland longed to have her eye in a microscope and her brain on a puzzle. She found purpose and poetry in the dissection of medical records, witness testimony, police reports, and, of course, corpses. She was a natural-born sleuth, and it was her kind of case.

Med school in the 1960s was something like the tech industry now. There weren't many women. Gilliland was one of four in her class of eighty-eight. One was a nun. She'd dealt with her own hard knocks as a young female doctor and was naturally sympathetic to Kerry's story, which she'd heard through channels. Both whip smart, Kerry knew diving, Gilliland knew forensics, and the case intrigued them both. It was a natural pairing, and they decided to team up and investigate Nick's death together. Of course, the typical caseload for a forensic pathologist can feel like a blizzard that never ends. Files pile up, and some cases are more urgent than others, so it took awhile for Gilliland's techs to prepare slides of Nick's lung tissue.

In the meantime, Kerry retreated into the literature, trying to find out what the medical community already knew about how depth and pressure can impact an athlete's lungs. She ran searches on PubMed, an online medical research database, until her eyes hurt, and ended up with forty research papers printed out and piled on her kitchen table.

Most documented the mammalian dive reflex, blood shift, and

bradycardia within divers. One study suggested that perhaps it was the hyperinflated lungs and the squeezing effect of pressure on the chest that compresses the heart and causes it to beat so slowly, though that was just a hypothesis. A Swedish study from Erika Schagatay, a researcher held in high regard within AIDA circles, was the first to document spleen contractions. In terms of the health risk, there were a handful of papers to consider. One suggested that the packing of air could cause embolisms that could stop the heart or cause a stroke. A Canadian study by J. R. Fitz-Clarke at Dalhousie University documented a computer model that determined 235 meters to be the absolute limit for freedivers. After that, the report said, total lung collapse occurs "and the chest simply becomes an incomprehensible mass of solid tissue and blood."

But Kerry was more interested in pulmonary edema, for that was the cause of death given by Dr. Sands. One article she found, "Fear the Squeeze" by Peter Scott, included the following passage:

> *The greatest danger of severe lung squeeze is that it can cause secondary drowning. Meaning instead of drowning under water, you drown in your own blood, as your blood coated alveoli can no longer exchange carbon dioxide for oxygen. Not a nice way to go.*

Was that what happened to Nick? Kerry wasn't so sure. Besides, Scott's article was based on anecdotal knowledge of the sport. It wasn't a scientific investigation. Another study seemed to hold at least a clue. It was conducted in 2008 by Mats Liner and Johan Andersson, at Lund University in Switzerland. They were looking at the mammalian dive reflex and its possible negative impacts on athletes.

In freediving classes, the dive reflex is pushed as a purely positive physiological response to depth. As the lungs shrink due to pressure, the blood vessels in the extremities constrict, and blood floods the thorax. This also means that pressure in the lung's capillaries is ratcheted up, and because the blood gas barrier is so thin in the alveoli, edema is one likely outcome. A similar phenomenon can happen to mountain climbers. The Liner-Andersson study followed nineteen competitive freedivers through a competition to find out if any had edema after their dives. Six of them had fluid—blood and plasma—in their lungs hours after surfacing.

As for long-term effects, Kerry didn't find anything at all, but the final passage from a 2005 German study, "Physiological and Clinical Aspects of Apnea Diving," stuck with her.

> *Although the absolute limits of apnea diving are not yet known, it is increasingly clear that the quest by extreme apnea divers to find those limits could come at a potentially high physiologic and medical price if those limits are exceeded.*

While Gilliland's team worked on Nick's tissue and Kerry dug for gold on PubMed, a video of Nick's dive and the resuscitation attempt surfaced, and Kerry did not like what she saw. For weeks she'd assumed, based on what she'd heard from those at the scene, that Nick had a catastrophic lung injury, and that's why he wasn't resuscitated. The video that John Shedd sent her, taken with Daan Verhoeven's GoPro camera, told a much different story.

Kerry and Steve watched it together. They rewound it over and over, and paused it here and there to vent and take notes. They were appalled to see that the doctor at the scene, Barbara Jeschke, the same doctor who had cleared him to dive, didn't follow Advanced Cardiac Life Support procedures appropriately. The more times Kerry watched the event unfold, the more it became clear to her that Nick Mevoli should have lived.

That's not what the AIDA report said when it was released the following January. In it, Johan Dahlstrom, a Swedish physician and former competitive freediver who finished in the top ten at the world championship in Constant Weight in both 2005 and 2009, writes that "with the wisdom of hindsight, Nick should not have been allowed to dive," but Dahlstrom's report does not hold Jeschke responsible for clearing him. In fact, it specifically mentions that by rule, she did nothing wrong at all. As for dissecting the resuscitation attempt, Dahlstrom writes how calm and efficient the treatment was. He points out a few problems, but also asserts that should things have gone differently, there was only a very small chance that he would have survived. Dahlstrom goes on to place cause of death as pulmonary edema.

The report troubled Kerry to no end, and she didn't even know that Dahlstrom, AIDA's chief medical officer at the time, had not debriefed Dr. Jeschke over the phone or in person, or that the bulk of his report was based on emails and witness reports written by safety divers and Jeschke, among others. AIDA president Kimmo Lahtinen never spoke to Jeschke about Nick's death either. Erika Schagatay, the scientist who has published fifty papers on freediving physiology, wrote a supplemental report as well. In it, she claimed that she spoke to Jeschke, but when asked directly about their conversation, she retracted that and said she communicated with her by email. An athlete died for the first time in the history of AIDA, and nobody in a position of authority talked to the doctor.

Schagatay was less willing to concede that the cause of death was pulmonary edema until more research was complete, but both her report and Dahlstrom's made it clear that AIDA was more concerned about the culture of squeezes within the sport and the need to reverse it than they were about trying to figure out exactly what happened to Nick, and they went out of their way to avoid blaming Dr. Jeschke for her failures.

After reading the AIDA response, Kerry, Steve, and John Shedd filed a rebuttal. They singled out Jeschke for allowing Nick to dive.

Shedd had benched divers in the past, and they were unwilling to accept AIDA's premise that the absence of an explicit rule giving the doctor the right to suspend an athlete prevented Jeschke from doing the right thing. They also went into great detail about when and how Jeschke diverged from basic and advanced life support practices. (Dr. Jeschke declined several requests to be interviewed for this book.)

Kerry and the others were also troubled by the cause of death being listed as pulmonary edema so quickly. Nick had been given CPR for almost ninety minutes by the time his death was called. That alone can produce pulmonary edema. Kerry believed there must have been some underlying reason why he went into respiratory distress after getting to the surface under his own power and breathing on his own for nearly a minute. She met with Dr. Moon, at Duke, and showed him the video.

"This is not a hypoxic death," Moon said, "because he was communicative for what looks like about a minute after he surfaced, and you'd expect his oxygen levels to rise." Moon also doubted edema was the proper cause. "He wasn't spewing out blood, his lungs weren't full of blood, so what could it have been?" Moon believed it had to be an embolism—an air bubble that leaked from the lungs into the bloodstream and got lodged in his heart, causing arrhythmia and sending him into cardiac arrest. If that were true, he would have needed a defibrillator to shock his heart back into rhythm. Jeschke didn't have access to a defibrillator on the platform, so perhaps there was no saving him, after all?

Kerry was polite in the room, but doubted Moon's theory. Afterward, she stood on the roof of a parking structure, stared over Duke's modern and gleaming medical complex that put ECU's to shame, binged on gummy cola bottles, and chewed on the case. Dr. Sands had specifically tested the heart and brain for embolism—submerging them in a bucket of water to look for bubbles—and found none. She also reported no damage to the heart, which should have occurred had there been cardiac arrest. Moon was wrong, and Kerry was more convinced than ever that only Nick could help solve this medical mystery, but it wasn't until October 2014 that she saw slides of his lung tissue.

Then again, it was perfect timing. Dr. Gilliland's call helped her forget her troubles and reignited her passion to find the answers. The next morning she pulled herself together and drove her Toyota Tacoma past Greenville's historic brick facades and the towering southern live oaks that shade East Carolina University, and arrived at the hospital before her shift. Early enough to spend some quality time with her favorite forensic pathologist.

As Kerry put her eye to the microscope, Gilliland slid a thumbnail slice of lung tissue into the light and pointed out macrophages. Macrophages are cleanup cells. After an injury, they report for mop-up duty to digest red blood cells. That's how the human body heals. Each successive day, the macrophages eat more red cells, and as days pass, the macrophages digest and accumulate more iron. Gilliland had added dye to the slide in order to reveal the iron in a given piece of tissue. She was hoping to determine how fresh each injury was, and her dye stained those cleanup cells several shades of blue. The blood from his final dive was never mopped up, so the lightest blue macrophages were determined to be from the Friday dive, and yet there were additional macrophages dark enough to mean he'd had similar injuries several days before that. The cellular trail suggested that Nick had been squeezing and diving injured for weeks.

Gilliland kept pushing new slides under the microscope and she and Kerry kept taking turns looking for macrophages as well as interstitial fibrosis, or scar tissue. Scar tissue is denser, less permeable tissue created by repetitive injury, and if present in the alveoli (air sacs) can impede the exchange of carbon dioxide and oxygen. If Nick had that, it would mean his string of injuries dated back a lot farther than a few weeks, and it would also mean that freedivers who suffer repetitive injuries may be damaging themselves at a level they've never imagined, and could be putting their lives in jeopardy. It didn't take Gilliland long to find collapsed tissue, a telltale sign of fibrosis, but there also looked to be ample healthy lung tissue in his alveoli.

With each answer more questions bloomed. How much scar tissue did Nick have and where was it located? Could that be the reason he had trouble breathing after coming up for air? And was there so much damaged tissue that his resuscitation would have been impossible under any circumstances? Was Jeschke off the hook? It was too soon to tell. They would have to keep looking.

15

ONE-HUNDRED-METER MAN

Nick told himself it was just another dive, the natural next step, when he caught the boat from the white sand beach on West Bay to the competition zone a kilometer offshore. It was May 27, 2013, the fourth day of the inaugural Caribbean Cup, and the event had a world-class feel thanks to the presence of Will Trubridge, who had been a technical advisor, and the depth, which for the purposes of competitive freedivers, was limitless. There's a reason that self-trained explorer Karl Stanley settled and built a submarine on Roatan. Where else could he shove off from a pier and plummet two thousand feet below into the Cayman trench, taking willing tourists and scientists along for the ride?

Less than an hour later, Nick floated above that trench in warm crystal-clear blue water, wearing a two-piece wetsuit, his legs black, his hooded top silver. Friends floated all around him. Ren was there, and so was Ashley, who was six months pregnant with Ani. Ren had been spotting Nick while he trained for the past several weeks. He and the Chapmans met up in Long Island, Bahamas, and sailed for

Port Antonio, Jamaica, aboard *Nila Girl,* where Nick began building his depth, moving from 60 to 70 meters into the 80s and 90s. "It was a little bit cowboyish," Ren said, and after all the lessons the sea had already taught him, Ashley hated seeing him make those big leaps, but the Chapmans had learned to bite their tongues. Nick was going to do what he wanted and there was no team element involved, no pressing reason to rein him in. If he squeezed, they thought, he would only spoil his own competition, trash another opportunity to get better. All of his training dives were in Constant Weight, and Ren noticed his kicks were smoother, his technique cleaner. It was obvious he'd spent a lot of time in the pool.

It was a brand-new year. Nick had cut his hair short, and he'd let go of all the disappointment he felt toward the end of 2012. He'd even overcome a separated shoulder, which he'd injured snowboarding in January. He looked great, he felt great, he was on a mission, and he carried that energy into his early dives in Roatan.

He dove to a personal best 92 meters in Constant Weight on day one. After turning early on a Free Immersion attempt to 75 meters the following day, he decided to put all his focus back onto his monofin and broke Rob King's American record with a dive to 96 meters on May 25. The following day was an off day, and he spent it with Will, who was his roommate and coach at the competition. They discussed visualization and other preparatory techniques, blended smoothies, made curries and pasta dishes together, and became good friends. Although Nick had a wobble on the surface after his dive to 96 meters, he got the white card and thought it was the right time to attempt triple digits.

Will treaded water nearby as Nick breathed up. He noticed the strong current and checked the line, which fell at an angle thanks to the drift. Will figured it would take a 105-meter effort to get to 100 meters in those conditions, but if Nick made it, he would be the fastest man in AIDA history to triple digits and the first American to ever freedive to 100 meters. Nick's trajectory had the entire sport on notice. "It wasn't unreasonable to believe that within two to three years he could have been at the level of divers like myself and Alexey," Will said, "challenging world records."

Iru Balic was there too, flowers in her hair. Nick had gotten to the island early to train and in the days before the competition shared a casita with Iru in the Rasta hamlet of West End, a $1 water taxi ride away. She'd transited back into his orbit despite herself. Their relationship lines were still blurry, and he told her he couldn't have sex because it disrupted his chi. "Fine, keep all your chi," she snapped back. "I don't care. You can have it." She didn't realize how serious he was. He hadn't had sex in four years.

Regardless, their connection was sweet and meaningful enough to keep her interested. Although she hated his new haircut, she welcomed his fresh perspective. Nick wasn't brooding. He was diving with joy and skill. He was an elite athlete on the rise and she adored watching him. She was in a zone too, pushing her personal bests with a real chance to win gold. Until the competition began they shared a bed and he'd make her breakfast and bring her flowers to wear in her hair every day. "He told me I shined when he did those kinds of things," she said, "and he liked seeing me shine."

Nick had envisioned the dive several times, and as the count ticked down, he once again visualized an effortless duck dive, six strong, then six softer kicks, his arms straight as an arrow overhead. His alarm would chime at 20 meters, when it was time for his grouper call, which would bring air from his lungs into his mouth so he could equalize the rest of the way. He'd become streamlined, and with one last kick begin freefall. He would relax his gut and shoulders, tuck his chin one millimeter more, then sink soft and slow until his alarm chimed again and he was ready to kick back to life.

Nick was never so comfortable in the water as when he dove with fins, and his new monofin felt like an extension of himself. It was like having rocket boosters strapped to his ankles. With every smooth gyration of his hips, that fin cut through blue water and sent him thundering down. On the way up, his kicks felt supercharged and he knew he could make it back clean. He'd ditched the fluid goggles by then, leaving his eyes naked and burning in salt water, which he found liberating; one less item to deal with in the hypoxic fog after a deep dive. The more he visualized, the more certain he was that he would be America's first 100-meter man, and when the time came for peak inhalation he did not delay. He sipped and packed air to the zenith, flipped, folded, and began to swim.

Though he'd made peace with his disappointing 2012 season, he wasn't blind to the cause. He knew he had trouble controlling his urge for depth, his need to prove himself to himself, to fill a bottomless void. He also saw it as egotistical and vain, and during his long, boring Brooklyn rehab after his snowboard accident, he wondered if his injuries and setbacks weren't signs from God that his chosen sport was too dangerous, perhaps even too sinful, to pursue?

One Sunday after church he approached Father Wlodzimierz Laz as the congregation filtered out. "Father, do you know what freediving is?" Nick asked. Father Laz loved sports, and had been an athlete back in Poland, where he grew up. These days he's a paraglider, and in his downtime enjoys reading about extreme tales of risk and exploration. Nick had approached the right preacher man. Laz was a sympathetic ear. "I think I have a special gift from God. I can dive for over five minutes on one breath, but what I want to know is, is it a sin?"

"You want to know if your sport is a sin?" Father Laz asked.

"Yeah, because the bible says *thou shalt not kill,* and I'm wondering if maybe the risk is too great, and if I push too hard, if that isn't the same thing?" Father Laz considered the question. He had long admired Nick, the way he came to church every week, and prayed so intensely. He saw the kid as a throwback to more genuine times and wished there were dozens more like him.

"Well, it's true that when we put our lives on the edge we are only one step from killing ourselves," he said, "but it's also true that we can manage risk. If you train wisely, and perform within the rules . . . then, no, it's not a sin." He told Nick about his own paragliding fix, how alive he felt when leaping off a cliff face and soaring 1,000 feet over the sea, but how he always tried to temper his desire for adventure with pragmatism. "When I go to the mountain, if I don't like the wind or the cloud formations, I don't fly. It should be the same for you. Do you understand?" Nick nodded, pensive. There were questions he didn't ask. What if he couldn't stop himself? What if the drive to win and achieve was too much to control? Would that be a sin? For once, it was more comfortable to linger on the surface than dive too deep. "If God has given you a gift," the priest continued, "you should use it."

Nick went home and brainstormed his goals for the 2013 season. He would study to become a freediving instructor and lure students by breaking every American depth record in the AIDA books. Along the way, he'd become the first American to 100 meters, quit production, and leave New York behind. When he was finished, he read his list and tacked it to the fridge. He started a pot of espresso, walked to his window, and looked out over his neighborhood.

Williamsburg had become a brand-new place. Once it had attracted those in dire need of coke, willing to snort low-grade snow in vinyl booths shoulder to shoulder with crooked cops in the bar two floors down. Now it attracted those in dire need of an olive oil decanter. Nick laughed at his own resentment of the great yuppie invasion that hipsters like him helped launch. Sure, he avoided Bedford Avenue at all costs, but Williamsburg was still home, and there were still corners of authenticity, and nice Polish girls like Denny around. He watched her shuffle home from her Sunday morning swim. Her hair was wet, her swim bag slung over her shoulder, as she struggled to climb her front stoop.

The very next Sunday he was back at church, and this time he brought his swim stuff along. Denny noticed. When they ran into each other at the pool, she asked what he was doing there? "Just doing my Sunday morning swim," he said cheerfully.

"Oh, okay," she said. She didn't buy it. She always swam on Sunday mornings and he'd never been there once, but the next week he was back, and the week after. On the third Sunday, they walked home together and he made her promise to meet for coffee the next day. By the following afternoon she was hurting and in no mood, but as she approached his building, she saw him sitting on the front step and ducked behind a parked car, praying he hadn't caught a glimpse. Nick walked around the car with a smile on his face.

"Hi," he said.

"Hi," she said, sheepishly, still kneeling on the concrete. "How was your day?" She cringed and stood. Here they were. She had two choices. Cancel now, to his face, or have a cup of coffee with a cute boy.

She had tea. Nick sipped espresso, of course. They sat on a sofa in a neighborhood café and talked for three hours, about everything: his family, his work and his diving, her upbringing in Philly, her dashed photography dreams, and her new life as an acupuncture student. They talked about holistic healing and nutrition, something that had become important to him now that he was living the freediving lifestyle. They discussed everything, that is, except her suffering. By then it was obvious that he wouldn't bring it up and after the walk home, his suspicious Sunday swims, and a lovely afternoon of conversation, Denny felt he deserved to know, so she told him her whole story.

They became friends, sharing texts and swimming together regularly. When he caught a cold, she made him chicken soup, and when his bad shoulder acted up in the weeks leading up to his first big competition of the season, she gave him an acupuncture treatment.

He accepted her help and never bludgeoned her with pity. He was a link to life for her. Before he gently bulled his way into her world, she'd been in dangerous territory. Isolated, desperate, and miserable. She'd pushed everyone away so hard she'd forgotten what it was like to let someone in and enjoy a good friend.

"He made me feel like I was still alive. Which is really hard to do when you can't see, and you can't walk and you can't feel," she said. "Swimming brought me back, which is why it meant so much to me, but he brought me back too. Here was this person that didn't care about my disability, he just kept wanting to talk." He also needed her help. Days before he was about to leave for the Bahamas to meet Ren and Ashley, he asked if she would water his plants, collect his mail, deposit his checks, and look in on his place while he was away. That meant climbing three flights of stairs several times a week. It meant challenging herself and staying connected to the outside world. "It took me a really long time to understand just how much he understood," Denny said, looking back. She agreed.

As Nick fell toward the plate, 100 meters below, there was a palpable tension on the surface. Everyone leaned in, on edge, as the announcer followed Nick's movements on sonar. He touched down and there was a shout and a buzz from the crowd, though they knew the hard part had just begun. When he hit 60 meters, Ren, the first safety diver, dropped to meet him at 30. The final leg of the ascent would tell the tale.

On his 96-meter dive he'd had a bad samba on the surface, and it had looked like he might black out, but with Will preparing for his own dive, Carla Hanson had been coaching Nick that day, and her voice pierced his haze and led him through a clean protocol and to a national record. Carla wasn't coaching this time, and everyone wondered if he'd make it up safe and healthy.

The answer came when after a dive of 2:45, he rose to the surface in complete control and grabbed the line as Will yelled, "Hook! Hook!

Get that nose clip off!" Nick took his hook breaths, ditched the nose clip, and flashed the sign. "Say it!"

"I'm okay," he said, breathless.

"Keep hooking, keep breathing," another diver said.

"I'm not a hooker," Nick joked, as he continued to breathe, without any semblance of fog or discomfort. He got a big laugh, though Ashley rolled her eyes. She felt it was just another sign that he didn't have the proper respect for the depth or the sport. In her mind, he wasn't out of the woods. The white card hadn't been awarded yet, and he needed to be breathing, saturating his blood and brain with needed oxygen.

She needn't have worried. Nick was home free. He flashed his tag, and the crowd began to cheer a bit louder, though the judges still had to confer. He hung on the line in anticipation, and when the white card came he went berserk. He held the line with both hands and shook it back and forth letting out a primal scream, while spectators splashed the water around him into a white froth. The safety divers mobbed him as he leaned back and looked into the sky, staring past patches of cottony clouds and into the heavens. He wiped away his tears. He'd done it!

Rob King, the vice president of AIDA and the second-deepest American man of all time, called it "one of the two iconic dives in the history of American freediving."

Logan Mock-Bunting was taking pictures that day. "He had so much genuine emotion and happiness," Logan said, "he was glowing. There was some chest beating. He was very excited that he'd done it, but there was genuine humility too. That it wasn't just physical and emotional for him, but a spiritual experience. That he was not alone."

"God is great!" he shouted as he moved toward the platform, getting bear hugs from Will and Ren along the way. Will won the Caribbean Cup and Nick took bronze, behind Walid Boudhiaf but edging out Carlos Coste, with a final 81-meter dive in Free Immersion, just a few meters from a national record. His 56-meter dive in Constant No

Fins was another personal best. Nick had progressed across the board. His first competition of the season could not have gone better.

Iru won gold in the women's division, setting new Venezuelan records in both Free Immersion and Constant Weight. She was proud of Nick, who always led the cheering section when Iru was in the competition zone, but she wanted more from him. At the party the night after the competition she cornered him. "Dude, you are being the most perfect person ever, why don't you kiss me or something?" she asked. He shrugged. Something was stopping him short of romantic love. He enjoyed doting on her, he said, but what she heard was that he didn't love her. She banned him from giving her flowers for the rest of the trip, and left without saying goodbye.

Nick's next stop was Central Europe, where he competed in a small pool event in Brno, Czech Republic, before meeting up with Australian freediver Tanc Sade and renting an apartment in Belgrade, Serbia, for the AIDA Pool World Championship. In odd years, world championship events crown the best individuals in each discipline, and depth and pool competitions were held in separate venues. Nick met Tanc at the LA Apnea Challenge, a small pool comp held the previous April. Nick didn't fare well there, suffering two disqualifications and topping out in Dynamic at just 106 meters. But it wasn't a completely wasted week because he met two kindred spirits. Vanessa Weinberg, a beautiful blonde, blue-eyed yogi and actress, was a new freediver specializing in pool disciplines. She would post the second best Dynamic No Fins swim among all American women in 2013, and she and Nick would grow much closer as the year wore on.

Nick and Tanc, who had also burst onto the freediving scene out of nowhere, hit it off immediately. Tanc claimed two Australian records in the pool in his very first competition, with swims of 230 meters in Dynamic and 181 meters in Dynamic No Fins. He was a longtime spearfisherman and an actor, best known to American audiences for his role in the TV hit *Gilmore Girls*. Fit and handsome, with a mop of wavy brown hair and mischievous eyes, he'd been acting professionally his entire adult life, stitching together a living from disparate parts on American and Australian television. Nick and Tanc connected on all those levels, and they shared one more thing in common. They pushed themselves too hard, never satisfied with a depth or distance, obsessed with more. Always more.

"What I saw in Nick was something that was very similar in me," said Tanc. "There was a burning desire, a sense of emptiness, a sense of feeling less than, and that this obsession with getting some sort of validation, with getting some sense of self-worth is what drove him, which is a really unhealthy place to be. And I'm the same way. I hate losing more than I like winning, because winning is just sort of expected, and anything less than that is an absolute fucking nightmare. He would lose sleep, and if he didn't do well—what he defined as well—that was like, hell on earth."

It wasn't just their similarities that drew Tanc close to Nick. It was his generosity. On the first day they met, Tanc complimented Nick's retro Adidas jacket. He'd been looking for one just like it. Nick unzipped it and handed it over. "Take it," he said. "It's yours." Tanc refused. He'd been making small talk, and was overwhelmed by such a genuine gesture. "I'd give you the shirt off my back," Nick said.

But something much more significant would link them soon enough. On Tanc's last swim of the competition he tried for a new Australian record in Dynamic No Fins, and blacked out. The safety diver who had been following him on the surface had a delayed reaction, and when he realized something was wrong, had trouble bringing Tanc to the surface and laying him flat in an appropriate rescue position. Worse, Nick felt he wasn't reacting with enough volume or force to bring Tanc out of it. Tanc was stiff and his skin was gray, his eyes open and vacant, and saliva bubbled from his blue lips.

Nick ditched his jacket, dove into the pool, took Tanc from the safety diver and cradled him in his arms. "Breathe, Tanc. Breathe," he said. Instead of blowing gently as the safety diver had, he blew sharply across Tanc's eyes. When that didn't work he gave him a rescue breath. Tanc had been out for nearly a minute, and Nick brought him back. It felt to Tanc like Nick saved his life.

So it made sense that the two of them would room together in a Belgrade flat. When Tanc arrived, Nick vented about his previous week competing in Brno, when he failed to post even one clean dive. Only a few weeks removed from his triumph in Roatan, Nick was lost in the pool.

You wouldn't know it from his first attempt in Belgrade. On June 23, 2013, for his debut swim at the AIDA Pool World Championship, Nick just missed the American Dynamic No Fins record. He'd never hit 100 meters in that discipline, but when he got there this time, he felt good and kept on swimming, continuing more than two-thirds of the way to 150 meters, but by then he was too spent and hypoxic to put together a clean surface protocol and blacked out for a split second, enough for a red card. He'd hit 138 meters, one meter shy of an American record. That night, Nick was sleepless and despondent. The next day was the first round of the Dynamic competition, and breaking a national record seemed like a long shot considering what he'd posted lately. Tanc took him to the pool to get some work in.

"You have so much fucking talent," Tanc told him, as they dangled their legs in the water at Serbia's finest swim center, Sportski Centar 25 Maj. It looked like a resort compared to the public pools Nick was used to. He stared past the humming fluorescent lights, toward flags from more than thirty countries dangling from the rafters. "But your [pool] technique needs work." Tanc paced the gleaming tile deck and had him do laps. It was easy to see that Nick was kicking too hard, covering 50 meters in just five powerful flips of his monofin. "You're using too much force, mate. You'll be more oxygen efficient with nine or ten softer kicks." Tanc also got him to stop purging: a hyperventilation breathe up technique that lowers CO2 in the body and delays the urge to breathe. Some divers, including Will, feel that hyperventilation makes them less efficient in the water, if a bit more comfortable, and thus it's a net loss. They worked for hours and when they got home, Tanc gave Nick one more piece of advice. "If it hurts, keep swimming. As soon as you feel good again, come up."

"Why?" Nick asked.

"Because it's supposed to hurt, and if the pain stops it means you're about to black out." Buoyed by his training session with Tanc, Nick messaged Meir and Vanessa that he might push for the American record in Dynamic. When he arrived in Belgrade, Ted Harty still held that record at 170 meters, but Kyle Gion broke it on the eve of the World Championship during an independently organized record attempt in Honolulu that caught the American freedive community by surprise. Kyle had wanted to keep his attempt secret, in case it didn't go well. Now it was news. The new record was 184 meters.

Nick wasn't flustered. The next day as Vanessa and Meir kept tabs from their laptops, using the tactics Tanc shared, he hit his career best mark in the pool with a swim to 187 meters, over 30 meters farther than he'd ever gone before. When the white card flashed, he thought he'd nabbed the record. He didn't know that Kyle Gion had extended the American record a second time, to 200 meters, just before Nick pushed off.

He found out when he got out of the water, slumping onto a bench with a towel draped over his head. "I should have gone to the wall. I should have gone to the wall. I should have gone to the wall," he said as Tanc sat beside him. If he had, he would have made the final heat and had another crack at the record. "I don't know why I stopped. I felt so strong." Tanc draped his arm around Nick's shoulders and reminded him how far he'd come after just one night working on new mechanics.

"You cracked it, mate. You're gonna kick ass in the pool from now on." Tanc put up a good front but inside, he was furious with Kyle. He thought it was a chump move to extend a record during the week of the World Championship. Vanessa agreed, but Nick harbored no ill will. He sent Kyle a Facebook message as soon as he got back to the apartment.

> Congrats on your big swim, you are in the 200m club. Thank you for putting USA on the map, finally. Now at least we are not the laughing stock of the pool anymore. Are you thinking of coming to team worlds next year? You should. The pool is where we are going to win it.

When Kyle read it he felt relieved. He'd already taken some heat online, and at nineteen years old, he'd been following the advice of his coach and making the best decisions he could. He wasn't trying to hamstring anybody. Of all the congratulatory notes he'd received in the wake of his record, that's the one he valued most. He couldn't wait to compete alongside Nick in Sardinia in 2014.

Nick didn't have a hard time moving on from his latest competitive disappointment, thanks to Bojana Burnac, a Croatian filmmaker he met on the first day of the competition. She was in Belgrade shooting a documentary on her country's best freediver, Goran Colak, who dominated for the cameras, scoring gold medals in all three disciplines, and capturing a world record in Dynamic to boot.

On the day they met, Bojana was attempting to fix an underwater camera to the side of the pool. She needed to weigh it down, and someone grabbed one of Nick's neck weights at random and handed it to her. "Freedivers are very sensitive about their neck weights," she said. "Some believe it's bad luck for someone to touch your neck weight before a dive." When Nick realized it was missing, he asked for it back. She was apologetic, but he wasn't the superstitious kind. They stood apart on the tile deck and chatted about the film business. He liked her shaggy jet-black hair, her big eyes, and her worldly confidence. She wasn't classically beautiful, but he found her extremely sexy. She noticed him, too, and when he put on his neck weight and excused himself, she felt a sudden void she could not remember ever feeling before.

Five minutes later he was in the pool, doing his no fins dive. The timing of it all, his easy grace, valiant effort, and near miss, set her head swirling. Who was that guy? She wanted to know more about him. She needed to. One problem—she had a live-in boyfriend back in Zagreb she'd been with for years.

The next day, after his Dynamic swim, Nick sought her out and thus began a conversation that lasted three days. They went on long afternoon strolls with no destination in mind and dished about their families and their jobs. She was a freelance director of photography back home, and they exchanged tales from the trenches of production. They talked about his blackout, too. She was a decent freediver, and always enjoyed the theater of the blackout, and how different athletes responded in their own way. It told her something about them, she said, betrayed a personality quirk or even something a shade deeper. Some woke up sleepy. Others woke up startled. Nick always came to pissed off, and in Belgrade he threw another juicy tantrum. She happily filmed it and teased him a little. He liked her sass and took it well. He saw through her humor and felt her heart. He was falling in love, and she was too.

Belgrade wasn't a pretty town, but Nick dug it. The streets had energy, and the architecture was a byzantine swirl of Eastern bloc schlock, Ottoman relics, and art nouveau style. Plus, it was summertime and the weather was hot and sticky, Nick's preferred climate. They strolled the Knez Mihailova, a pedestrian promenade, to the old citadel, and found a smoky café in the Savamala quarter, which had sprouted from the ruins of Milosevic's awful war into Belgrade's creative bohemian nook. They rented bikes and rode along the Danube from the center of town into the outskirts, moving from an asphalt road onto a forest path until they were deep in the green. By the time they got back to town, they were famished, so they found a quiet place with candles and tablecloths and chose a back table where they kissed for the first time.

Bojana had been struggling with her feelings, because she wasn't just in a committed relationship, she'd been perfectly happy in that relationship. Then Nick showed up, and it was like a bomb exploded. She told him about her boyfriend, and he wrestled with the morality of that, but she wasn't married. After dinner they went back to her place and his self-imposed four-year drought came to an end.

NICK'S TRAVEL AND competition schedule had been so packed in the past two years that he hadn't kept up enough hours to stay in good standing with the union, and by the summer of 2013 his health coverage was about to lapse. To make up the time, he booked six weeks of work in New York, sandwiched between his pool competitions and the upcoming depth championship in Greece. But his flight home from Belgrade was delayed and by the time he'd landed at JFK, he was in danger of being late for his first day on the set of *Top Five,* a soon to be critically acclaimed feature written by and starring Chris Rock. Tardiness alone could cost him the gig, and his health coverage. It was early July and he needed four hundred hours before leaving town again in mid-August. He collected his bags, and sprinted toward the cabstand. It was overflowing. Then he saw a town car driver in a black suit holding a sign that read, "Hernandez." Nick thought about it twice, and decided Obama didn't need one more poor, uninsured bastard on his hands. "I'm Hernandez," he said.

"Very good, sir."

His six weeks in Brooklyn went by in a blur of sixteen-hour days and six-day workweeks. He fit in pool training whenever he could and on his one day off, he would catch a train to Jersey and do two days of yard work at his Grandma Josie's house in four hours. He had no downtime. No space to socialize, though his best Brooklyn buddies, Morgan and Yas, dropped by a few times. Both were in new relationships and happily inching toward domestic bliss. Despite his training, Nick allowed himself to smoke one more spliff with Yas. Stoned, they got busted sneaking fresh grilled bratwurst into a local movie theater, so they went down to East River Park and ate dinner on the riverside like old times.

Nick was happy, too. He had been in frequent contact with Bojana, texting and calling whenever he could. She hinted she would leave her boyfriend. He asked her to come live with him in Brooklyn or Florida, where he hoped to open his own freedive center once he got his instructor credential. She had no interest in the States, so he started mulling a move to Zagreb. She told him to give her time, and that somewhere, somehow, they would make it work. In the meantime, she said she would be on the Croatian coast filming Goran, while her boyfriend was working in the city. Nick decided to surprise her so they could be together and decode their future, and so he could get in some depth training before Greece.

By the time Meir dropped him off at JFK on August 13, his monofin bag on one shoulder and his backpack over the other, he'd logged his hours, made good with the union, and banked some cash. There was a woman by the beach he needed to see, and he was ready to do what he did best. Dive deep. He waved Meir off, feeling light and optimistic, as if everything up to then had been preparation, and the rest of his life was about to begin.

16

BLOODY WATER

It was breakfast time at the Elite Hotel, a modern three-star resort in Kalamata, Greece, and Nick couldn't bear the thought of leaving his room. He hadn't been sleeping, could barely eat, and it was far easier to hide than to venture out. There were too many friendly faces to dodge, and the last thing he needed was more vapid catch-up chat.

The Elite had been bought out by freedivers, with over two hundred athletes from thirty-six countries there to compete in the single largest freediving competition in AIDA's history, the 2013 Individual Depth World Championship. The opening ceremony had been the night before, and athletes grouped with their countrymen as usual. Draped in national colors and waving flag miniatures, they paraded along the wharf led by a local marching band. The discount Olympiad vibe was delightfully corny, and precisely the type of event Nick had been thrilled to be a part of in Nice the year before, but in September 2013 it was hard to fake a smile.

He was the only American at the competition. He'd had to pay out of pocket to come, and wasn't given so much as a T-shirt to wear at the opening ceremony or a flag to wave. All he had that was close to the correct stars and stripes color scheme was a striped blue-and-white sailor shirt. He took his ribbing well ("Look at the Frenchman!" "What's biting out there, captain?") but inside he was concerned. Was this the state of US freediving? Was his sport that insignificant back home? If he had to ask, he knew the answer, so he left the parade, strolled to the end of a pier, and watched the Greek fishing boats bob in the tide.

The next morning, instead of going to breakfast with the others, he fired up his camp stove and put on a bubbler of espresso. Coffee would help, he thought. Coffee always did, which is why he brought his own equipment. As he waited for the steam to rise on his makeshift kitchen counter (read: top of his hotel dresser), he surfed Facebook and saw that Iru was on the property. He hadn't noticed her in the parade and smiled at the thought of seeing her again. She was the one person who could save his soul.

Weary of the emotional roller coaster, Iru was hoping to avoid Nick altogether. He would never love her, she thought, so it was better to move along. Of course, she'd had a tough week. She'd blacked out underwater while training in Dahab, and had to be helped to the surface. As she came to she spewed blood and plasma. It was the worst lung squeeze of her life, and it threatened to keep her out of the world championship. Until his message blipped onto her phone, she'd been wondering why she'd even bothered to come to Kalamata. But Nick would understand why. He knew what she was feeling better than anyone—the burning desire to compete, the need to dive into the blue, and the lung issue that threatened to stop her. She invited him over for breakfast despite herself.

He knocked inside of two minutes. She answered, and without a word he pulled her close. They hugged in silence for fifteen minutes, and when she felt him melt into her, she knew something was bothering him, too. They drank coffee, ate fresh fruit, and planned an arepa party for later that evening. As usual she'd brought corn flour with her from Venezuela. Nick brought her to his room and showed off his DIY kitchenette. "It won't feel like a comp until we have arepas, Iru. You know that," he said. But they needed fixings to stuff the thick, Venezuelan-style tortillas. Nick had an idea.

"Where are we going?" Iru asked as he led them down the service stairwell.

"You'll see," he said, breezing past perplexed housekeepers and hotel staff, until they found the stainless steel double doors that led to the hotel kitchen. He pushed open one of them and peeked inside. Breakfast service had just ended, and lunch was still two hours off. The staff was away, smoking and napping in the sun. They'd arrived at slack tide, the perfect time for a dive.

Nick took Iru by the hand and led the way. They perused refrigerators and coolers, and explored the walk-in, where they found enough pulled pork and feta cheese for 10,000 arepas. Nick stuffed his pack with contraband and felt ten years younger, when food liberation was a matter of sustenance rather than convenience. Iru, nervous at first, couldn't stop laughing. She'd always lit up when she smiled, and it was no different under the fluorescent lighting of a Greek hotel kitchen.

They stashed their treasure in his room and walked to the supermarket for more supplies. This time, they'd pay cash. Along the way, Nick kept quiet. More quiet than usual, so she asked him what was wrong. He shrugged. "You are always in your head, you know," she said. "Too much." He knew damn well she was right.

Nick had landed in Croatia the month before, in love and convinced he'd found his perfect girl. One problem. He'd never told Bojana he was coming. The trick had worked before with Esther, the last filmmaker in his life. This time it backfired. Bojana was more shocked than excited. He tried to play it down and told her he'd come for training and to dive with Goran, whom he'd befriended in Belgrade, but she knew the truth. She didn't resent his coming. He was making a statement, and it touched her. Now it was up to her to decide what to do. She considered it in the downtime between her interviews with Goran, when they ate breakfast on the patio, and when they were in bed together and he was fast asleep.

She'd been perfectly happy at home with her man until Nick showed up. It was true that she felt more passion toward Nick than with her boyfriend, but part of her thought it was too much passion—that they would enjoy one another for a few months or years before burning out. And there were things about her boyfriend she couldn't lose: his intellect and understanding. He loved and respected her enough to empathize when she told him she'd met somebody and was confused. He didn't react out of jealousy. He gave her space to make her own choice. There aren't many guys like that, she thought.

For better or worse, Nick wasn't one of them. Sure, he'd led an alternative, bohemian life, but he was also old school. Of late, he'd been chatting with his sister, Jen, and his Uncle Paul about how much he craved the mainstream benchmarks of a successful life. Marriage, kids, and a promising career doing what he loved. He told Bojana he was ready for all of that and he wanted it to be with her.

The second time he proposed marriage they were naked in bed, just two days before he was leaving for Kalamata. "You should think more critically," she told him. That was her answer. He'd laid out his heart and she was glib. She'd made her decision. She wasn't detonating her life for Nick, and she didn't get his antiquated need for marriage. She didn't care if she ever got married, and couldn't comprehend his love of the church either. She thought the world would be better off without religion. Bojana was a modern, independent woman, and knew they were mismatched. "No matter how strong the feeling is between us, in life, you must be more critical, Nicholas. What we have is the beginning of something maybe, but . . . think about it, it can't work. We won't work." She was telling him it was over.

Her words sounded harsh in the afterglow, but she wasn't wrong. Truth is, neither of them had thought too critically. They'd responded to electricity in the moment and let it take them. Nick's best friends like to say that he was in love with being in love, and that impulse betrayed him in Croatia. He showed up on his magic carpet, unannounced, just as he had in Brooklyn after 9/11, and found that Bojana had been playing a part all along, teasing Nick by imagining possible futures over the phone because she craved distraction, and loved the attention, but she wasn't real. Nick had been surrounded by women his whole adult life who wanted nothing but to give themselves over to him, and the one he chose couldn't or wouldn't. His magic carpet crashed and burned.

He left Croatia in tears, and landed in Kalamata in time to compete in a smaller, warm-up competition, or mini-comp, before worlds alongside Mike, Alexey, and Natalia. He was in no condition to compete. He hadn't been eating or sleeping. Regardless, he donned his monofin, and tried to gut out a few training dives. On an attempt to 90 meters, he lost his mouthfill at 75 meters and couldn't equalize, so he came up. Aside from losing air, he felt clean, and breathed oxygen to make sure his lungs were clear. They weren't. Later that afternoon he developed a persistent cough, and with each hack he produced blood and phlegm. He thought about diving anyway, but with worlds days away, he did the pragmatic thing and withdrew. He did return to the competition zone the next day, however, this time as a spectator, to watch Alexey Molchanov attempt a world record and get the scare of his life.

The competition zone was in a deep blue bay, two miles and a mere ten-minute boat ride from the dock, which was across the street from the hotel. The weather was perfect, too perfect. Ideal conditions in Kalamata included a thermocline that bubbled up somewhere between 20 and 50 meters, depending on the day, and enough current to keep the platform moored at the proper angle, but on that day the Mediterranean was flat as a lake. Dublin-born safety diver Steve Keenan, thirty-six, noticed something was off while Alexey breathed up.

"The [platform's] mooring line wasn't stiff," he said, "and it was going down at a strange angle." In fact, it crossed the competition line, which could confuse any athlete, especially one who's narced from swimming to 128 meters and back. Steve alerted officials, and there was a ten-minute delay to get the line sorted out.

A marked characteristic of Russian divers is that they are seldom fazed by conditions or scheduling shifts, and the delay didn't disturb Alexey. Natalia, on the other hand, was rattled. She saw it as yet another bad omen and felt that Alexey should abort and wait until worlds to do the record attempt. He'd had a cold and was congested, she said, and proper preparation was key to the deep relaxation required to hit new depths safely. Alexey shook her off. For the past week he'd been hitting 126 meters—his world record at the time—without difficulty, and had been feeling good all season, aside from what he considered to be a mild sinus issue. He'd dealt with that before and it never interfered with business. He'd been feeling so strong, 128 meters didn't feel like a stretch for him. It felt like any other dive. It wasn't.

His descent was on time and went according to plan. He hit 128 meters at just over two minutes and when he touched down, most of those gathered around the competition zone cheered, but Natalia wouldn't celebrate until she saw him on the surface, alert and healthy. As he swam back toward the light, Steve prepared to meet him below. This wasn't his first time safety diving for Alexey. Steve was based in Dahab, where he was a full-time freedive instructor as well as a competitor, and had trained alongside the Russian for years.

"Alexey's not demanding with safeties," Steve said. "Normally you can belt it down to 15 to 20 meters and you'll see him belting up, and you'd have to start kicking hard to keep up with him." This was a world record attempt, however, so Steve left early, in time to meet Alexey at 30 meters. When he got there, Alexey was nowhere to be found.

"On the way up, I remember feeling dizzy. I had vertigo," Alexey said later. He had a reverse block—a condition that occurs when mucus in the sinus blocks the air used to equalize from escaping as the diver rises. There was pain and swelling in his inner ear, which threw off his internal compass. If the inner ear is off, one can be dizzy even on solid ground, let alone underwater. Alexey couldn't tell which way was up, and he began swimming at a 90-degree angle—horizontally into the endless blue, but that's why athletes are clipped to the line. His lanyard stopped him, and at that point, he realized that he needed to swim up, so he shifted direction. He was rising, but not in a straight line. He was swimming in circles, spiraling around the dive line. Instead of ascending at a pace of 1.2 meters per second, he had barely eclipsed .4 meters per second. It was a dangerously slow ascent, and nobody on the surface knew why.

Steve drifted down to 32 meters and hung there for forty seconds. His urge to breathe was building and he was getting worried. "I had that horrible situation that a safety always hates," he said. "You can't just stay there indefinitely, but you don't want to leave your man." Still, he hung on until he could see Alexey, hard as nails, fighting but struggling, and swimming around the line. Alarm bells sounded in Steve's brain and adrenaline kicked in. He finned down to 40 meters and grabbed Alexey.

Steve is a strong athlete. He has all the Irish depth records and one of the pool records, but he conceded thirty pounds and four inches to Alexey, who blacked out in his arms at 30 meters. Steve had already been down for two minutes by then, and now he was swimming for two. At 20 meters, a second safety, Andrea Zuccari, buzzed down on an underwater scooter and ferried Alexey to the surface. Steve was right behind.

Although he'd been underwater for over five minutes, Alexey was revived within fifteen to twenty seconds, but he was squeezed. "I had so much extra movement and tension at depth, I injured my lungs really bad. The worst I ever had," he said. Pink frothy spewdom came flowing out, and for the next five hours he was spitting bright red, oxygenated blood. Alexey couldn't breathe on his own for several minutes afterward; that was the worst part for him. "I was given oxygen and I was really weak. It was a scary feeling."

Steve was shaken as well, but he was even more alarmed when Alexey approached him later that night to thank him. "He came to me in total denial. He blocked it completely out. 'Oh, it was fine,' he said, 'just a small thing with the ear. Just a small squeeze.' Not that he almost fucking died," Steve said. "It just shows his resilience and determination and the psychology of the strongest freediver."

It also speaks to the freediving culture at the time. In September 2013, two months before Nick died, squeezes were considered more inconvenience than acute injury, and as far as competitions go, Kalamata was the worst example of a culture in denial. Throughout the mini-comp and the 2013 Individual Depth World Championship, athletes surfaced with lung injuries and dove again anyway. Nick was one of them. So was Alexey, who would attempt 128 meters again in just six days, with a world title on the line.

Nick and Iru did their shopping. They bought lentils and red wine, cold beer and avocados. On the way back he spat three times, each time spitting gobs of blood larger than a silver dollar. "Nick, that's not okay," Iru said. She knew he planned to compete the next day. It was the opening day of worlds, and the first discipline was Constant No Fins. Nick told her it was minor, and she let it go. But he'd soon write in a blog post that he'd been walking all over Kalamata spitting blood for the previous two days.

> I was donating blood to the sidewalk with each spit as I strolled aimlessly through town, wondering what the hell was wrong with me. . . . two days in the same pattern. Walking, thinking and spitting. . . . I have seen the inside of every grocery store

> and alleyway in Kalamata. I found where all the young people hang out and where the hardware stores are. I found many things except the answer . . .

But he already knew the answer. He couldn't stop pushing. He'd set his goals at the beginning of the year and he cared so much about achieving them that each dive became a referendum on his own value.

> . . . the need to achieve became an obsession. Obsessions can kill.

Perhaps those walks did him good, because finally, on the Kalamata streets, he realized how destructive that line of thinking was and that he had another choice:

> . . . to be kind to myself . . . to allow the performance to be an expression of my being and not define what my being is.

That evening he and Iru made batch after batch of arepas. She grilled and flipped them in a tiny pan on his butane burner. They left the door open, salsa blasting from the laptop speakers. Whoever passed by, hotel staff or athlete, would be called in to try an arepa stuffed with stolen and store-bought treats. He also made a pot of lentils, utilizing his trusty stash of spices he always smuggled into foreign lands, and they poured beer and wine. It wasn't the typical precomp meal, but it felt like good medicine. He'd already made his dive announcement for the following day. He would pull back a little rather than push his edge. Iru did the same. She would turn early, but Nick found his dive easy and it was the most successful he'd ever be on a world championship stage.

Some of that had to do with his late-night conversation with Grant Graves, one of the AIDA judges in Kalamata. Grant had become a consigliere for Nick over the past year. He'd dish out training tips and they'd discuss Nick's psychological blocks. Grant was one of the longest-tenured judges and coaches in the sport, and from his first dive in the Caymans the year before he had seen something special in Nick and, like Will, envisioned a day when he might challenge for world records. Before he went to sleep that night, Nick found Grant and told him about Bojana, and how much he'd been suffering. Grant listened and offered a nugget of wisdom that would help him in the water.

"The perfect dive isn't about how deep you go, and it's not about suppressing your pain," Grant said. "It's about finding those spaces between the thoughts, where you can live purely in the moment. That's easier underwater than on the surface, believe me. That's what I want you to work on tomorrow."

The Individual Depth World Championship surpassed Nice in scope. There were platforms for each of the three competition lines, a larger platform, which was the athletes' dry area, and three warm-up lines tethered to surface buoys. The event felt big, but Nick's announced dive of 65 meters was still shallow enough to make him feel anonymous. With no countrymen in the water, and no national record anticipation in the air, he could become the blank everyman. A happy ant, one of the many breathing up and dropping down, before the stars shined bright. He knew that six other athletes would dive deeper than he would, including Will Trubridge, and he wasn't even attempting a personal best. He had exceeded 65 meters in training. He was diving because that's what he loved to do. The dive itself would be his pause between thoughts, his respite of peace in the midst of pain.

His dive was as vanilla as he hoped. Unspectacular and uneventful, but the aftermath was not. After earning his white card, he caught the first zodiac back to the hotel and relaxed with coffee, chatting with Tanc over Facebook. Frenchman Thomas Bouchard was next on the line after Nick. He was headed to 68 meters, but turned at 64, so

Nick was officially still in first place by the time he got home. Next up were a Ukrainian and two Danes who planned to go to 71, 71, and 74 meters, respectively. But the Ukrainian turned at 41 meters, and the first Dane turned early as well.

"Dude, one more penalty and you're on the podium," Tanc wrote. Nick didn't believe him. When Stig Pryds, the second Dane, blacked out at the surface, Nick was guaranteed at least bronze. Tanc told him so. In fact, Nick was in contention for gold until Morgan Bourc'his, of France, took the no fins lead with a clean dive to 87 meters. Nick still wouldn't buy it.

William Trubridge was the last serious contender of the day. He'd announced 96 meters, when an announcement of 88 would have won gold. Nick understood why. It was the world championship and it didn't just matter *that* you won, it mattered *how* you won. When Will blacked out, too hypoxic to get through the surface protocol after making it to the plate and back, Nick couldn't celebrate, partly because Will was his friend, and also because in his mind, a 65-meter dive shouldn't have earned him a silver medal.

The Constant No Fins comp in Kalamata was rife with blackouts and red cards—there were ten on the men's side alone, but there were also quite a few squeezes among those who were awarded white cards. Jakob Galbavy of Austria, who came in fourth that day with a dive of 61 meters, remembers seeing a slick of blood on the surface while he was warming up, and the problem only got worse three days later during the Constant Weight competition when another diver described watching spoonfuls of blood dissipating in the current.

Steve Keenan remembers it well. He was a safety diver from the mini-comp through the six training days and on each of the three competition days, too. "There was quite a bit of squeezing there," he said, "and very little surveillance or screening. The athletes would come out on the boat, hit the lines, get back on the boat, and be back on the beach and gone. It was up to them really if they wanted to [get examined by a doctor].” He remembers one French diver who asked to be checked out and a member of the safety team accompanied him to the hospital, but if the divers kept it to themselves the organizers, judges, and competition doctor wouldn't pursue it.

In a competition with arguably the most significant squeeze problems in AIDA history, not one diver was disqualified from competition for medical reasons. Athletes were pushing themselves to the limit, injuring their lungs and coughing up blood, and nobody batted an eye. “I have to admit that at the time, I wasn't massively concerned,” Steve said. “I have to admit—myself, as I was training to go deeper, I had quite a few squeezes. Chasing numbers, basically.”

Nobody was chasing a bigger number in Kalamata than Alexey Molchanov. The day after his squeeze, he felt tension on each inhale. The deeper he breathed, the more he felt it, but there was no more blood. He'd told Goran Colak what had happened, and he suggested Alexey do four 15-minute sessions a day on oxygen to aid recovery. It worked. When he woke up the following morning the tension in his chest was gone; later that day, he was back in the water. There wasn't a medical protocol in place, so Alexey didn't need to seek clearance from a doctor, but his mother was beside herself with worry.

“I say to him, stop competition for you, and for me too. We go. Not important this competition,” Natalia said. Alexey wouldn't budge.

“If you don't want to dive, you can go,” he said, “but I want to compete.”

Alexey's first dive after the accident was just 45 meters. He wanted to make sure his lungs could withstand the pressure, and he came up clean. “I felt pain in the ligaments and muscles around the rib cage, but the lungs were fine,” he said. The next day he pushed to 75 meters, and felt normal. In his mind the only question left was how deep to push. Should he just try to win gold, or should he break the record and shock the world? On September 18, five days after his squeeze and the night before the Constant Weight competition, he announced 128 meters, sending ripples of shock and concern through the freediving community.

"Considering the depth and what was involved to do something like that [six] days later," Steve said, "none of us could believe he was doing it again."

Calm seas weren't a problem on September 19, 2013. The Mediterranean was choppy and the temperature had dropped 2°C/5°F. Half of the athletes would turn early that day, Nick included, but no matter how frustrated they may have been, they forgot themselves when Alexey was in the water. His dive was the talk of the tournament.

In his gold hooded suit, he breathed up on the line as the announcer ticked the minutes and seconds down to his top time. "I was a bit more nervous for sure," Alexey said. "I was worried about my ability to withstand hypoxia and I knew that my fitness level dropped because my body had exhausted resources for recovery instead of preserving them to compete, but I knew if I would focus on that, I'd lose." Instead, Alexey pretended that the bad dive never happened and tuned in to the weeks leading up to Kalamata, when he'd been making incredible progress, going deeper and getting stronger with each swim. "When you do repetitive deep dives in training, you get this level of confidence, and I was able to get it back during the dive."

His entry was crisp, his kicks elegant, smooth, and powerful, the Mediterranean a perfect blue. He was at the plate before two minutes had elapsed, grabbed the line with his left hand and the tag with his right and in two seconds was swimming back to the surface. That was the hard part, swimming against the pressure with nitrogen narcosis reverberating and twisting his brain. Diving deep, day after day, builds tolerance to narcosis, but he'd had several days off, and got a full dose. He willed himself to ignore the madness nipping at his synapses, and kept kicking.

As he approached the 10-meter mark, his form began to slip. His dolphin kick broke down, and instead of undulating his upper body and snapping his hips, he looked like a stunned rocking horse. His pace slowed to a crawl. Once again he started circling the line. Luckily he was positively buoyant, and the elements were pushing him to the surface despite himself. Steve was certain he would black out, and he might have if he hadn't accidentally bumped the line with his forehead.

"It kind of woke him up," Steve said. "He was far from clean, but he made it." At the surface he took his time, taking five hook breaths before removing his nose clip and running through that bumpy protocol, which nearly brought a protest from Will. White card. Alexey had come to Kalamata to win gold and break his record, and he'd done both, overcoming the worst injury of his career along the way.

The moral of the story for those in attendance, including Nick, was one of superior will, supreme athleticism, and natural talent, but there were implicit messages too. That diving on a squeeze can't kill you. That bloody lungs heal fast, and that if an athlete wants a record bad enough, has trained hard enough, and has some God-given talent, it's best to tune out the negative chatter, prove everyone wrong, and go get it.

Alexey and Will were the stars in Kalamata. Will took silver in Constant Weight and gold in Free Immersion with a dive to 115 meters. Alexey also won silver in Free Immersion, while Nick turned early yet again, but he'd already earned his bling. At the award ceremony America's only athlete stepped onto the podium, bowed his head, and accepted his medal, but it didn't make him happy. At the closing party, Nick found Grant at the bar and slipped silver into his pocket. "You deserve this more than I do," he said, before drifting into the shadows.

Iru and Nick collided later that night, as well, and it wasn't pretty. He kept circling while she danced with Johnny Sunnex. He wanted to cut in, but she was weary of his antics. She didn't like that he seemed ungrateful for his medal or that he was continually leading her on, and most of all she was pissed off about Bojana. Someone else finally told her why he'd been so sad. She didn't have all the details, but she'd heard enough. In her mind, if he didn't want to be her lover, he should have at least been a friend and told her everything. She demanded he keep his distance. She was through being his consolation prize.

She tried to leave Kalamata without saying goodbye, but he showed up at her door the next morning with an armful of gifts, set them down, and gave her another bear hug. Nick was dramatic, hilarious, stubborn, troubled, and passionate. Just like her. They didn't have the love affair she'd hoped for, but they loved each other all the same. She stood there, limp, arms at her side, while he held her. Until she gave in and hugged him back tight enough to feel better.

"I'm glad I did," she said, "because that's the last time we saw each other."

17

NICK'S LAST DAYS

Nick was back in Brooklyn for less than twenty-four hours before he had to leave again. Barely enough time to do laundry and pack for the tropics. He was on his way to Curacao for Deja Blue 2013, then Long Island, where he and Johnny Sunnex would assist Will Trubridge's upcoming freediving class and enjoy weeks of training in Dean's Blue Hole. There wasn't time to see friends, so he didn't tell anybody he was stopping through, besides Denny. She'd become his de facto assistant, cold calling public pools across the country, trying to find places that would allow Nick and Goran to teach freediving classes on their upcoming cross-country road trip. Goran was flying out in January, and their trip promised to satisfy both halves of Nick: the bohemian rambler and the serious athlete. It would also be the first step into his new career as an instructor.

When Denny showed up, he gave her a bottle of Greek olive oil as a thank-you gift, and they hung out on his rooftop. It was nighttime, a crescent moon hung low in the sky, and a light breeze kicked up from the East River. Nick was backlit by streetlights as he sat on the ledge facing Denny, who stood, leaning only slightly on her cane.

One of Nick's favorite things about Denny was the way she could chew a fanciful, philosophical straw to the nub. Once she talked about how much more fun it would be if she could tell time with bouquets of flowers. "Think about it," she'd told him. "Instead of saying I'm twenty-one years old, I could say I'm 1,372 bouquets old."

This time she had a more serious topic on her mind. She'd begun taking a cutting edge MS drug, Tysabri, over the summer. It was her first time taking medication, and it was working. Her vision had drastically improved, her pain had subsided, and she could move better than she had in years. Slowly, she was becoming herself again. One problem: Tysabri made her susceptible to a rare, deadly, and incurable brain infection known as the PML virus. Within the first year there would be a 1 in 1,000 chance that she'd get PML, which was essentially a death sentence. After two years, there would be a 1 in 333 chance, and after four years on the medication, it could be as high as 1 in 76. If she were to quit the medication, however, her symptoms would most likely return. Hell, they might come back anyway. MS is vicious like that.

Denny, feeling her mortality, explained the risks and rewards, her improvement, and her fear; then they sat in silence while her mind conjured the image of a bonfire at summer camp when she was a teenager. She remembered an old tree stump reduced to glowing embers, transitioning from yellow to orange to red with hints of blue, purple, and white in between. Dead wood was the canvas for the entire spectrum as it was consumed by its own beautiful destruction. She painted the picture for him. He nodded and smiled.

"Wouldn't it be great to be consumed by a passion?" she asked. "To be short lived, but to have given it your all?" She was thinking about her own choice. Whether to endure blows from a fucked-up disease or to go out standing, with balled fists and full faculties. "Do you think it would be worth it?" He stared at her, as he flashed to his own quest for records still unbroken, for the life he longed to live, perhaps forgetting that he was already on the path. His penetrating eyes made her momentarily shy. "Don't listen to me," she said. "I'm just being silly and stupid."

"It's not silly," he said. "It's not stupid. It's profound, and you know it."

HE WAS A latecomer to Deja Blue, forgoing the two weeks of training before the event and landing just in time to compete. His connecting flight had been delayed, so he drank beers and watched baseball in an airport lounge and didn't land in Curacao until 11 p.m. He'd already messaged in his dive announcement, and when he woke up that morning he learned he'd be the deepest diver of the day, and the first man in the water. This time he hadn't had the time to bond with the other athletes, and few of his friends were there. He wasn't part of the tribe, but an outlier, the rock star silver medalist and American record holder. The natural. His 90-meter dive was clean and easy. He blew everyone away.

Two days later he hit 68 meters in Constant No Fins. Again he was clean, and he felt so good that he high-fived Kirk Krack after completing the protocol. That was a violation. Divers aren't supposed to touch anybody within that thirty-second window after surfacing. When the red card came, he flipped out. He punched the water and screamed. He climbed onto the dry boat and started kicking things. Someone tried to console him. "Don't talk to me!" he shouted. For an hour he pouted and steamed, and then he was calm again. He felt terrible and made his round of apologies. Kirk included, but the damage was done.

Nick dominated the rest of the competition. He did another 65-meter Constant No Fins dive, and got to 75 meters in Free Immersion.

His pool numbers were solid and he won gold. With over a month to train on Long Island before Vertical Blue, he was in perfect position to close the season on a high note.

Before he left Curacao, however, he had to sit down with Kirk. He'd been in the midst of the PFI teacher training course and was hoping to complete it and get certified before he left the island. Kirk had him run through a lecture, which could have been tighter, but it was his antics in the water that gave Kirk pause.

He didn't certify Nick. In their final meeting Kirk encouraged Nick to reconnect with his love for freediving. "If you find that enjoyment again then when you hit the numbers, that will just be the cherry on top." Nick nodded and listened. He knew Kirk was right, and Kirk had left the door open for him to refine his teaching skills and eventually get certified, but he would have to shift his relationship to the sport. "I don't care how good you are," Kirk told him, "you need to walk the walk."

Nick arrived in Long Island for the last time on October 13, moving into a split-level house on a hill with Johnny Sunnex. The digs were small but stunning, with wood floors, an open floor plan, and two bedrooms, one upstairs and one down. Not to mention a wide terrace with spectacular, 180-degree views of a turquoise lagoon sheltered by barrier islands and the deep blue Atlantic Ocean beyond. The pair cooked, trained, and worked together, and the more time they spent, the more common ground they found.

Both were products of tough childhoods. Johnny, trim and chiseled at five feet ten with wavy, shoulder-length hair, was from a poor town in rural New Zealand, thirty minutes from the coast. "Most people aspire to work in the frozen food factory," he said. "If you get a good trade behind you, like an electrician, you're doing pretty well." That's what Johnny did and it was his ticket out. He ended up working in Australian mines and, like Nick, making great money for a young kid with no college degree, but it wasn't fulfilling. Between mining gigs, he'd travel and ended up a dive master at a scuba shop on the Great Barrier Reef, practicing freediving in his spare time. Eventually he'd travel to Ko Tao for a class from Christina Saenz de Santamaria, the 2014 Caribbean Cup champion, and her husband Eusebio.

There were other similarities too. Neither diver was afraid of taking big jumps during training—an oft-criticized tactic—and both were squeezed in Kalamata at the Individual Depth World Championship where Johnny became close to his countryman, Will Trubridge. Johnny won bronze in Free Immersion, with an impressive dive to 95 meters, but upon surfacing coughed up bright red oxygenated blood. As October days passed, however, neither appeared to be injured. Training with each other along with Will almost daily, both Johnny and Nick had the same goal for the competition: an overall bronze medal.

"From the first time I saw his name, when he'd hit 91 meters, I knew we were on a collision course," Johnny said. Nick felt the same way, and they even joked about it as they trained together. Nick knew something else, too; if he managed to win bronze, the depths required would mean he'd have bagged those two American records he wanted so badly.

Secretly, though, Nick was exhausted. Even minor physical effort left him gassed. On dives, he'd have an urge to breathe at 20 meters, which was not like him. It was as if his superpower had betrayed him. Nick was supposed to be the guy who could tolerate pain and discomfort better than anyone, and now his body was rejecting the very thing that made him special. These were telltale signs of an overtrained athlete. Overtraining leads to performance black holes and the only way to get back on track is to rest, which allows the muscles to rehydrate and repair. What he needed was a break.

His days would brighten during the last week of October when Johnny and Nick embraced Movember tradition, growing delightfully revolting mustaches to raise awareness for prostate cancer, and when Vanessa Weinberg flew into Deadman's Cay. Nick and Vanessa had been messaging, Skyping, and talking over the phone since they'd met in Los Angeles the previous April. They talked about training and yoga, philosophy and family. He gave her tips on how to find a monofin. She gave him pranayama exercises to help him relax. They shared snapshots from her road trips and his travels. They flirted. They analyzed their dreams. When she snagged a small role on a network comedy, he cheered her on. When he was at a competition, she helped settle him down beforehand and checked in afterward to see how it went.

There was a one-month period when Nick wasn't in contact. It coincided with his trip to Croatia. He resurfaced while still in a funk over losing Bojana. "I'm a bit of a mess," he wrote. "Didn't get what I wanted in Croatia." As the weeks wore on and the pain began to recede, Vanessa was eager to hear from him, and extended only positive vibes. Bojana hit with the force of a hurricane; Vanessa delivered sunshine. Part of him wondered about her since the spring, but she lived three thousand miles away from a home he rarely lived in. Suffering from a broken heart, he also wondered if she wasn't just another sweet illusion.

Vanessa grew up in Los Angeles. She was a California girl who moved back east for school and was into yoga and theater. Tall and athletic, she had long blonde hair, blue eyes, and Eastern European roots, and she was poetry in the pool. But she'd been unlucky in love. Forty and unmarried, she wondered if she'd ever find her soul mate. Nick ticked a lot of boxes for her. He was handsome and strong, kind-hearted, fun, and adventurous, and on the day they met, she had an intuition that he would become an important part of her life. For months she went about her chores, teaching yoga and auditioning for bit parts on big-time TV shows, or for major roles in small films, and messaged him only because she wanted to. Because it felt good to connect with a good man. She was optimistic yet realistic.

Days after winning his silver medal, while still in Kalamata, he invited her to join him for Vertical Blue. Instead, she arrived a bit earlier, which was perfect. Most of the athletes wouldn't show until the day she left on November 5. She and Nick would have nine days with minimal distraction, enough time to figure out what they were.

After a day of training, and on Vanessa's first evening on Long Island, he took her to the St. Peter and St. Paul Catholic Church. Long Island has dark nights, and the starry sky was patched with clouds, which were being chased by wind from one horizon to the other. He led her into the sanctuary and up one of the twin bell towers. The ladders were rickety, the passage cramped enough that they had to tuck their shoulders to squeak through. She was timid. He helped her feel safe, and they emerged onto a thin wraparound lookout platform with the best views on the island. It was misty, and they huddled close. When she arrived the night before, they'd slept in separate beds. That night, in the wee hours, she climbed in bed beside him.

They didn't kiss until a few days later when Will and his wife, Brittany, threw a Halloween party for the athletes and safety divers who had already arrived. He and Vanessa danced throughout the night When they got home he kissed her for the first time. They climbed into bed, kissing and touching, until she stopped him. She was falling for him, and she needed to know that they had a chance, and weren't just a fling.

"What are you looking for in a partner?" she asked.

"Well," he said, rolling onto his back. She laid her head in the crook of his arm. "I really want to date somebody that lives close enough I can make them chicken soup when they're sick."

"I want you to make me chicken soup when I'm sick," she laughed as he ran his fingers through her hair. She understood his point. They were long distance. The odds were not in their favor. "God! I have such bad luck in love!" she shouted. He leaned on his elbow and looked into her eyes.

"If that's true, then so do I," he said, and kissed her again. This time she didn't stop him. Soon they were naked and he took his time as he explored every inch of her. He was having so much fun he started squirming.

"You're like a dolphin doing a happy dance," she said, laughing. He nodded. "I'm being intimate with a dolphin." They didn't have sex. She made him wait for that, but they went everywhere else.

On November 4, the day before Vanessa left the island, Nick hit 70 meters in Constant No Fins, a new personal best, and it was super clean. For weeks, Will had been diving alongside Johnny and Nick to watch their form and coach them up, and he knew that Nick had been moored on a plateau. This was a major breakthrough. Vanessa had been off to the side watching. He swam over to her.

"Are my lips blue?" he asked. "Do I look okay?"

"You're fine. Your lips aren't blue at all," she said, giddy. Vanessa had come to Long Island, brightened Nick's world, and it was starting to show where it counted most. Underwater.

Athletes, photographers, and safety divers arrived every day in the lead-up to Vertical Blue. Among them was Dr. Barbara Jeschke. Will had met Jeschke, also a competitive freediver, during Team Worlds in 2012, where she was the lead physician. The event website that year included a profile of Jeschke, and on that page was her personal statement about her qualifications and her role in that competition:

> I know about emergency medicine, and, being an athlete myself, I know about the risks freediving can bring. So, in case of need, I will give my very best to help! But deep in my heart I hope that nobody will really need me during this World Championship ;-)

Forget for a second that an emoticon in a doctor's bio is never a good sign, and that statement is still troubling. It reads lighthearted and far too casual given her role in a sport where athletes push the very limits of their physiology.

Before Nick died, there was a feeling among athletes that doctors who knew the sport well or, better yet, were freedivers themselves were ideal candidates to work competitions because they knew the health risks best. There are good examples of freediver docs. John Shedd, a freediver and an ER doc for twenty-five years, is the long-tenured event physician for Deja Blue and runs arguably the most thorough safety program in the sport. Each year he brings a full emergency kit with him when he arrives on location.

Jeschke, on the other hand, arrived on Long Island empty handed. She'd expected Will to have the necessary gear waiting for her. The ER docs and emergency professionals interviewed for this book found that expectation mind-boggling. Doctors headed to a remote island prepared to lead an emergency response team, they reasoned, should always bring their own medical kit and be prepared for the worst-case scenario at all times. Jeschke's preparation level hinted that she wasn't sufficiently on guard and perhaps, as a freediver herself, was so familiar with the perceived risks inherent in the sport that she'd gotten comfortable. In other words, just like the athletes, she assumed competitive freediving was perfectly safe.

When Dr. Jeschke arrived to find Will's medical gear incomplete, she swung into action. She recruited Joe Knight, one of Ren's safeties and a former paramedic from Byron Bay, Australia, to help her scavenge medical supplies. "Barbara and I ran around the whole island trying to find gear. It was cannibalized from so many different areas," Joe said. "If the doctor had come in [with her own kit] and said, this is my kit and I'm super happy with it and nobody fucks with it, I think that would have been better."

Vanessa left the island on November 5. That morning, Nick rose early, made her breakfast and cracked two fresh coconuts. He drove her to Deadman's Cay airport where they found a bench and some shade, held hands and waited for her plane to arrive from Nassau. They made plans to meet up in New York, and again during his and Goran's upcoming cross-country freediving tour.

When her plane finally landed, Vanessa felt a twinge in her heart. A handful of freedivers—new arrivals, including photographer Daan Verhoeven, disembarked and gathered around the alfresco baggage claim area. They waved and smiled at Nick as he and Vanessa began walking toward the prop plane idling on the runway. On the tarmac he pulled her close, and kissed her deeply. And again. His heart seemed to be healing along with his body. With the competition five days away, he simply had to repeat the dives he had done in training and the records were his for the taking. He would open with a dive to 72 meters without fins.

He failed on his first attempt, losing his mouthfill and turning early at 60 meters, so he made the same announcement the following day. When he failed again, he was furious. This time he had technical problems. The strap for his lamp, which divers wear around their forehead so they can see at depth, broke and he lost his light. His computer malfunctioned as well, so his alarms never sounded. He had to guess when to call up his mouthfill from his lungs and had no idea how far he was from the plate. When he got to 69 meters he couldn't equalize any further so he swam back to the surface. Instead of running through the surface protocol to earn a yellow card this time, he threw a tantrum and stormed off. Johnny didn't go to the hole that morning. It was an off day for him, so when Nick came back he asked him how it went. Nick grabbed the balcony railing, shook it, and screamed, "Seventy-two fucking meters!"

"He really shook the fuck out of it," Johnny said. "He almost ripped it off." That night he messaged Vanessa on Facebook, and told her he'd been feeling pressure in his lungs beyond 15 meters. That's the kind of thing beginning freedivers experience, not competitors at the top of their game.

> **Nick:** I don't want to compete any more this season. It all feels so awful that I can't relax. I want to do well and I think that is where the pressure is coming from.
> **Vanessa:** I certainly understand the wanting to do well part . . . I think we all know that you will get it soon. . . . Try to take the pressure off yourself and re-find the joy in diving.
> **Nick:** Tomorrow I am going to train early in the morning maybe do a CWT dive and then go spear fishing.

NICK HAD TWO off days in a row to rest and Vanessa tried to convince him to actually rest. Johnny did too. "For me he was in a state of overtraining," said Johnny. "A rest day is a proper rest." Nick wasn't hearing it. The next afternoon, after training in the blue hole, he grabbed a kayak and paddled out to the barrier islands from the beach below his house looking for lobster. A specific, monster-sized lobster he'd seen out there twice before, but had always eluded him. This time he didn't give up. He chased it into a crack and spent nearly half an hour waiting for a clean shot, finally spearing it with his Hawaiian sling. He'd never seen a lobster that big, and couldn't wait to tell his Uncle Paul and the Bonzo boys all about it. He thought about what he'd say on the long paddle back to the beach where he rejoiced and posed for pictures with his eight-pound prize on the sand. It would be his final victory.

Nick was back on the line two days later, going for a national record in Free Immersion with a dive of 95 meters. An 88-meter dive would have been enough to earn the record, and after coming up short twice in Constant No Fins, exhausted and joyless, he was going 7 meters beyond what was necessary to achieve one of his main goals. Instead of reading the signs and pulling back, satisfied merely to score or perhaps grab one American record, he refused to concede in his pursuit of bronze. He still wanted it all.

If he had announced 88 meters, he might have earned a white card. Instead, he hit the high 80s, couldn't equalize any further, and went for it anyway. That's when he thought his eardrum burst and surfaced with blood dripping from his mouth.

As the event wrapped for the day, Ren Chapman led the safety divers through an emergency evacuation drill. They practiced bringing a diver up from depth, placing him on the platform, sliding him onto a backboard, and loading him into their de facto ambulance. Along the way, Dr. Jeschke practiced using her unfamiliar kit. They did the same drill every day twice, just in case.

Meanwhile, Johnny and Nick walked to the car, and Johnny saw Nick spit blood. It wasn't a lot, but it was enough to concern him considering he'd been out of the water for nearly an hour. When they got home, Nick stomped off to the beach to do a series of dry breath holds known as static tables.

"Dude, you shouldn't be doing that," Johnny said, "that's not good." But Nick wasn't listening to Johnny, who was feeling strong and had kissed 105 meters in Constant Weight on opening day. As far as Nick was concerned, Johnny was a competitor, just like Ted Harty, and he wouldn't take advice from a rival in the middle of a competition. He was once again locked into that self-destructive loop he'd escaped in Kalamata when he blogged about roaming the streets, "donating blood to the sidewalk." In that same blog he wrote:

> Any one who knows me at all knows that I don't quit. I don't let anything stop me from diving. Not squeezes or anything else.

As he loped toward the sand, it dawned on Johnny that once Jeschke determined Nick's ear to be sound he would dive again, and soon. She'd already checked him on the beach before they'd left Dean's Blue Hole. In her accident report following his death, she wrote:

> *As far as I know Nick Mevoli was a healthy young man and a world class freediver. On November 15 he had done a 95m FIM dive, where the safety divers had to assist him to come up. He thought that he had broken his eardrum. There was some blood coming out of his nose, as we often see it after a dive with equalisation problems. After the competition I examined his ear, the ear drum looked o.k., and he did neither cough nor complain about anything else.*

Numerous eyewitnesses reported seeing blood coming from Nick's mouth, not his nose, and a photograph taken that day by Daan Verhoeven confirms it. Jeschke missed it. A sinus squeeze isn't nearly as dangerous as a lung squeeze, but in the presence of blood, most doctors wouldn't wait for an athlete to complain of symptoms, they'd take a proactive approach. Dr. Jeschke explicitly mentioned checking Nick's ear in her report, so it stands to reason that if she had put her stethoscope to his back and listened, she would have documented it. Based on her report, one can only assume that she never checked his lungs, yet still cleared him to compete.

Ashraf Elsayegh, the clinical chief of Pulmonary and Critical Care at Cedars Sinai Medical Center in Los Angeles, says it can take one to four weeks for the alveoli to heal after pulmonary hemorrhage. Former world record holder Bob Croft said that back in the pioneering days of freediving if a diver came up with blood coming from the mouth, he'd be out of the water for a month. "Diving again too soon after pulmonary hemorrhage," said Elsayegh, "can make further hemorrhage easier to occur." Injured divers, he said, also have less lung reserve, which means the volume of air and amount of oxygen they can bring with them on a dive is limited, and equalizing at depth becomes an even bigger challenge.

After attending a potluck hosted by the safety divers at Greenwich Lodge, drinking a Kalik, popping into the kitchen to help prepare dinner, and having some laughs, Nick drove home and stewed. His public appearance made it seem that he was happy and well, but when he got home he messaged Tanc complaining of pain and exhaustion. "My ears hurt, my lungs hurt, my body hurts," he wrote.

Tanc suggested he pull back and drop all expectations or better yet, not dive at all, rather than go for another record. "I told him really firmly, you're tired. You've had a long season. You're mentally fatigued, you're physically fatigued, you haven't had a break, and you're not in peak fitness." Nick wouldn't give in. If he wasn't going to go big, there was no point in diving at all. Meir received similar messages from Nick, and what he wrote back that night still haunts him:

Tommorow's your day. I can feel it.

On November 15, Jen was in Orlando at Disney World with her two daughters, in line for "It's a Small World," when word came in from one of Nick's friends that he'd suffered an injury. In that moment, she was struck by a dark premonition that knocked the wind out of her and sent her to one knee. For the past two years Nick had maintained his policy of keeping his family in the dark during competitions. He'd call to check in, so they knew where he was, but he didn't want them stressed out, waiting for results. Often he wouldn't tell them how he did, even and especially when he won a medal or broke a record. They'd have to search it out for themselves on Facebook. Jen didn't even know he was diving that day, so the news came out of nowhere. She collected herself and messaged Nick directly to ask what happened and make sure he was okay. That night she would hear back:

> I am F'ed in the head is what happened. I am not relaxing on the way down. I am not performing to the best of my abilities . . . because I am so burnt out and ready to go home. I need to let it all go and give up . . . not having fun.

Jen knew Nick needed a pep talk, or perhaps permission to quit, but when his message came in she was putting her two kids to bed. It was Elizabeth's birthday weekend. Her eldest had just turned five, and Jen had a house full of family and friends. There wasn't time to sit down and compose a proper response. She planned to do it on Sunday evening, when she had time to think. By then it was too late.

The last person Nick wrote on the night of November 16 was Vanessa:

> **Vanessa:** Hope your ears are okay . . .
> **Nick:** Doc says that there is no hole.
> **Vanessa:** nice and you?
> **Nick:** I feel like offing myself. Frustration is oozing from my pores.

Vanessa suggested he go outside and yell into the wind to get it out; she offered a series of yoga postures and mudras that yogis use to release frustration and help reset the nervous system.

> **Nick:** I am not sure if it will help reset 31 years of anger . . .

In retrospect, his comment about "offing" himself seems much more an angst-ridden, off-the-cuff reaction than a serious threat, but considering what he would say to his friend, Junko, on the beach just before his dive, ("I hope I see you again") it's obvious that he wasn't thinking straight and that he was in dire need of intervention. His friends tried to talk sense to him from afar. Johnny urged him to pull back, but nobody on Long Island threw themselves in the path of a train barreling toward disaster, because nobody in the freediving community could ever have imagined what would happen next. If anybody should have seen the signs, it should have been Dr. Jeschke, but her exam was less than thorough.

Nick knew he wasn't right, yet he still floated to the line willing to risk it all to grab his elusive second American record. In that infamous Kalamata blog, he wrote, "Numbers infected my head like a virus." Well, the virus was back, and one number loomed larger than all the rest.

Seventy-two meters.

18

NICK MEVOLI'S LAST DIVE

After a week of mostly rough weather, it was a beautiful day at Dean's Blue Hole the day Nick died. As he breathed up on the surface, some divers wondered why he would choose to dive 72 meters a third time. Athletes often get superstitious with numbers that don't pan out. Instead of 72, they might have chosen 73, just to shift the energy. Nick wasn't superstitious.

He looked relaxed as he lay on his back, eyes closed, and to those treading water around him, it felt like just another dive. Judges and fans chatted off to the side as Sam Trubridge ticked down the time. Daan Verhoeven had the most reliable video footage of the entire episode. With about twenty-five seconds to go, he kicked to 15 meters and waited for Nick, whose descent was smooth. It took just four strokes to get to 10 meters and he looked comfortable as he drifted past the sandfalls.

Sam and Dr. Jeschke leaned over the sonar monitor together and Sam announced his progress. Seconds after passing 60 meters, Sam noticed that Nick had halted his descent, and hung there, trying to equalize. At that depth his lungs would have been compressed to what's known as residual volume.

After a typical inhale and a full exhale, there will still be a thimble of air left in the lungs. That's residual volume, and underwater, when a diver's lungs are compressed to that point, it's dangerous to attempt to access more air to equalize because it requires too much effort from the diaphragm, and when under pressure any unnecessary tension or movement in the core can cause injury. "He told me that he'd used his diaphragm to force air into his lungs in that depth range before," said Johnny. That was his first thought when Nick started to recommence his descent, and if Johnny was right, it may have caused Nick's lung injury. Bottom line, if Nick lost his mouthfill, as many suspect, he should have surfaced.

Instead he fell toward the plate head up. He had less control, and had to scull with his hands to maneuver. At depth, any pronounced or awkward motion in the upper body can also tear tissue. Though it's impossible to know if that was a contributing factor to his squeeze that day, some, including Grant Graves, believe it may have played a part.

"Be ready for this one," Sam warned the safety team as he began to ascend. Nick's dive time was a concern. He'd burned nearly thirty seconds trying to equalize at 68 meters, and hypoxia and underwater blackout were likely. But he didn't black out. He swam his ass off. Joe Knight duck dove and kicked down to meet Nick at 30 meters. Ten seconds later, Ren Chapman sliced the surface and met them at 20 meters. Daan followed Ren and waited at 15 meters. By then Nick was gassed. On Daan's footage Nick is seen fighting to get to the surface, Joe and Ren facing him at an angle.

"I remember looking at his face and thinking it didn't look right," said Joe. At 10 meters he thought Nick was blacking out and went to grab him. "He was just working too hard. He wasn't streamlined. He looked like a level 1 freediving student coming up from 20 meters."

Ren shook Joe off. He wanted to give his friend every opportunity to get his record.

Nick's final 10 meters were slow. He exhaled and a storm of bubbles rippled toward the surface. Again Joe went to grab him, thinking he was losing motor control. This time Nick shook him off, and Joe backed away once more. Nick surfaced a few feet from the line, and offered the okay sign, saying the words before removing his nose clip. That's an improper protocol, but it didn't matter yet, because the sequencing only begins once the diver clears his face of any equipment. Nick still had time to book a white card. He lunged and grabbed the line, while shouts of "nose clip!" went up from the athletes and spectators, everyone pulling for him. But he was hypoxic and teetered backward. Ren was there and held him upright with a gentle hand. He removed his friend's nose clip as Nick gripped the line, unable to speak. "You were almost there, buddy," Ren said.

Nick looked to be breathing on his own, but instead of recovering, his color got worse. He'd been at the surface for over thirty seconds, yet hadn't had a nourishing breath of air in almost five minutes, and he wore a thousand-mile stare, a telltale sign of distress.

"Sorry Nick," said Carla Hanson as she removed the competition's official dive computer from his wrist. For about ten seconds he seemed to improve and relax, but then he took another dip, hyperventilating, struggling for air. Still nobody came to his aid. After twenty more seconds he could no longer hold himself upright on the line and he fell backward into the arms of the safety team. One minute after surfacing, he was still conscious. Ren and his crew moved him toward the platform, while Nick groaned, his condition deteriorating. He was pulled onto the platform 1:20 after surfacing and within seconds he was out.

"I'd never seen a competition blackout like that," said Ren. "Usually you'll black out within the first fifteen seconds, within the first three breaths. Something definitely was not quite right."

"I feel something in his lung," said Marco Consentino, who

attended to Nick along with Joe Knight, while Dr. Jeschke moved in with a bag valve mask, an ideal piece of equipment if used properly.

"Bag valve masks require two people," said Kerry Hollowell, who has shown the video to dozens of colleagues and watched and analyzed it over a hundred times. "One person with two hands on the mask to create a seal and the other to squeeze the bag." Jeschke attempted to use it alone, and it was not hooked up to oxygen. "If it was hooked up, it could have given him 80 percent [oxygen]. Instead she was pumping air, which has 21 percent oxygen."

Jeschke had already been late on the jump and now she was misusing her equipment. The mask and bag attachment came apart after two pumps. She reattached it and started again, still without a proper seal and without hooking it up to her oxygen tank. She was not off to a good start.

"He can't breathe because he's full of blood," said Marco. "His lungs are full of blood."

Nearly three minutes after surfacing Joe and Jeschke moved him into the rescue position, on his side, in anticipation that blood might come pouring out. Jeschke continued to pump away with a poor seal and the mask continued to fall apart. The third time it happened she had to fish the mask out of the sea, while Nick's head lolled and bloody saliva seeped from his mouth.

Jeschke reattached the mask to the bag and placed it back over his mouth, but by then Nick was almost on his belly, his neck kinked. There was no way to monitor chest rise, and nobody was checking a pulse.

"At that point he should have been on his back," said Kerry. "One person should have created a seal with the mask and another person bagging it. [Jeschke] should have stepped back and made sure everything was running smoothly. Is the bag valve mask attached to oxygen? No it isn't, let me do it. Does he have a pulse? Cut his wetsuit off, get that wetsuit off! And she should have been asking, Do we have chest rise? Do we have a good seal? Is there blood in his mouth? With Nick on his side his left lung was compressed, it couldn't expand normally. She was behind the eight ball already."

He'd been out of the water for 3:30 and hadn't had a nourishing breath in seven minutes. His time was short. The resuscitation did not improve and neither did Nick's condition. The bag valve mask kept falling apart, and wasn't hooked up to oxygen until seven long minutes had passed, though several people attempted to point that out to Jeschke, including Daan, the videographer. If Nick still had a pulse at that time, it's difficult to tell because according to the video, Nick's pulse was not monitored consistently.

Joe and Jeschke as well as two nearby volunteers attempted to get a peripheral pulse—a pulse at the wrist—from time to time. But ER doctors argue that it is difficult and often impossible to monitor a peripheral pulse during such an emergency because the pulse is almost always too weak to register at the wrist. Joe did check the carotid artery in Nick's neck a handful of times, often with gaps of twenty seconds in between.

Through it all, Nick remained unresponsive. At the 9:00 mark they finally cut off Nick's wetsuit, though he remained on his side. At the 11:30 mark Jeschke checked his pulse herself, again opting for a peripheral read on his wrist. She seemed to feel something, and went back to pumping the bag, which continued to fall apart. This all happened in front of a rapt, concerned group of freedivers in disbelief. Johnny was appalled at the resuscitation effort. "It was like watching a bad movie unfold," he said.

"I can't see his chest move or his stomach move," said Daan, hoping to trigger a response from Jeschke. It wasn't until Nick had been out of the water for thirteen minutes that he was placed on his back, the preferred position to access his airway. By then he had no pulse, and nobody involved in the rescue effort could pinpoint when his heart had stopped.

"Barbara was out of her comfort zone," said Joe. "She told me that." Dr. Jeschke is an anesthesiologist, which means she's an expert in airway management. If anybody should have been able to get chest rise in a patient like Nick, who was in the midst of respiratory arrest, she should have been able to do it. "She had the right medical background," Joe added. "She was just a little bit uncomfortable we weren't in a hospital, her normal place of work."

She also didn't bring the advanced airway equipment she was comfortable using in a crisis with her to Vertical Blue from Germany. Nick was never intubated at the scene—a process that allows a doctor to funnel air through the trachea directly into a patient's lungs. Jeschke, an anesthesiologist, should have been proficient in intubation, but because her kit was cobbled, she likely did not have the proper equipment with her on the platform. She did have an oropharyngeal airway, which elevates the tongue and makes it easier to ventilate a patient, but she didn't use it until it was too late.

Joe doesn't believe any of that impacted the rescue effort. "The protocol went perfectly," Joe said. "Clinically, it was perfect as far as how I've been trained. Yeah the mask fell off and bits and pieces went wrong because the kit was shit, but overall it went exactly how we trained it. It felt good because it showed that our training worked."

Joe Knight runs popular waterman courses—a blend of water safety and freediving—in his native Australia and internationally. He hasn't been a paramedic in the field since 2010, but he was hands on, and is convinced he felt a pulse and saw chest rise throughout the first thirteen minutes. He also contends that he and Jeschke established an airway. Unfortunately, the video tells another story.

"The rescue was completely botched on so many levels," said Kerry. "It's painful to watch."

"This physician did not do a very good job of maintaining his airway," said John Shedd. "She was having problems with the bag valve mask, she was confused, there were times when oxygen was not connected. You can't get adequate vital signs with his wetsuit on. It was one fuck-up after another."

Unlike Kerry and John Shedd, Larry Stock, fifty-two, is not a freediver, but he has been an emergency room physician for twenty-five years. He's on the board of the American College of Emergency Physicians and teaches emergency medicine at UCLA medical school. He has also delivered emergency care in remote locations, ranging from the war zones and displaced people camps in Eastern Myanmar to the aftermath of earthquakes in mountainous Pakistan to the Ebola wards of Liberia. He watched the video twice, and though he qualified his opinion through the lens of hindsight bias—a measurable factor which implies that knowing the outcome can color a doctor's opinion of how a medical mortality was handled—he felt that from the moment Nick was on the surface, precious little went right.

"Immediately after surfacing, any experienced emergency physician should see that this guy's in serious life-threatening trouble, and that he is going to stop breathing and go into full cardiopulmonary arrest very soon. He's awake but he's not alert," said Stock, who like Kerry and Shedd, said he would have shown up with his own medical kit. "The best time to resuscitate someone is before they arrest, because once they arrest, their body starts shutting down and goes into something called metabolic acidosis. Acid starts building up in their blood, and the heart gets irritable, and it's a downward spiral. It gets harder and harder the longer they're in arrest to resuscitate them."

Stock believed Jeschke should have read the signs and stripped Nick's wetsuit right away. He also agreed with Kerry and Shedd that Jeschke never established an airway or got an adequate seal with the mask, that Nick should have been placed on his back, and that neither Joe nor Jeschke checked the pulse correctly or frequently enough. "I didn't see a lot of pulse checks going on. To me it looked as though he could have lost his pulse long before they began CPR; it's possible at least."

Joe Knight and Grant Graves, the lead judge that day, have been supportive of Dr. Jeschke's efforts, as have officials within AIDA. When confronted with criticism, they've responded that most of it was coming from Monday morning quarterbacks who weren't at the scene.

Most, but not all. Marco Consentino couldn't sleep for four nights after Nick died. "If proper emergency management had been given to him, Nick would still be alive," he said. "I will always think his life could have been saved. [Jeschke] was completely in panic. She was unprepared for this kind of emergency."

Ren has since learned proper advanced cardiac life support protocols and is also upset at how Nick's case was handled. "[Jeschke] was an anesthesiologist, which is what you want," Ren said. "They are trained in airways, the first thing in the ABCs. Airway, breathing, circulation. You establish an airway, then you establish breathing, then you establish circulation. She didn't do that."

Fifteen minutes and thirty seconds after Nick surfaced in distress, Jeschke finally got her team organized. She and Joe operated the bag valve mask, and Ren began chest compressions. As Will swam toward the platform to help, Jeschke prepared and administered three shots of epinephrine, or adrenaline, which might have jump-started his heart if given immediately after it stopped. They had no effect, which suggests that his heart had stopped beating minutes earlier.

When Ren, Jeschke, and Joe finally moved Nick from the platform to the beach, over twenty minutes after he'd surfaced, there was a pause in CPR. Not long, but enough to snuff out any hope he had left. Ren and the others kept up with chest compressions anyway. They refused to give up as Will drove over sixty miles an hour along Long Island's ribbon road toward Vid Simms Memorial Health Clinic. According to Dr. Yvette Carter, the attending physician, once Nick arrived at the clinic, Jeschke intubated and ventilated him and there was chest rise without any need to drain his lungs. By then, of course, it was much too late.

"When he came in there was no pulse. We worked on him a long time," Carter said. "Nobody wanted to give up. People were sobbing, people were praying."

There is no doubt that mistakes were made during resuscitation, but in the aftermath of the event, AIDA's position was that no matter Jeschke's faults, there was no saving Nick. His lungs, they said, were beyond repair. Kerry was never comfortable with that theory, and she didn't believe pulmonary edema told the whole story.

If his lungs were so filled with fluid, why was Jeschke able to get chest rise once he was at the clinic? If pulmonary edema killed him, why wasn't there more blood in the water? Nick hadn't regurgitated that much blood. There had to be a better answer. She and Dr. Gilliland found it as they continued to examine Nick's heart and lungs.

They followed the trail of blood and macrophages, or repair cells, and found extensive damage from multiple episodes of pulmonary hemorrhage, which they were able to correlate to lung squeezes he was known to have had. They marked off the squeeze from Sunday and the previous Friday, and continued to follow the trail as it extended weeks and perhaps months back.

Pulmonary hemorrhage is not a burst blood vessel but rather an overengorgement of alveolar capillaries—blood vessels in the air sacs of the lung. Those vessels have permeable walls to allow for oxygen and carbon dioxide exchange and when they become engorged due to extreme pressure, the walls can be too permeable. Think of pantyhose stretched to maximum. Those tiny holes get bigger and bigger until they rip. Too often on Nick's dives, his capillaries stretched and the walls weakened, and red blood cells showered Nick's alveoli, which were riddled with microtears. Those tears required repair, and like any wound if they're reinjured multiple times, the result is scar tissue or fibrosis.

"Think if you wound your knee—like when you are learning to ride a bicycle. The tendency is to take care of it and not fall on that knee again until it is all healed up," said Gilliland. "If you have an operation you don't want to play with that scar and pull the stitches out or you'll have a broad scar, and if you tear it again you could have a broader scar."

In Nick, the resulting fibrosis was found in his peripheral lung, where most gas exchange occurs, which may explain why he had such a difficult time recovering from his dive, though he was still conscious for over sixty seconds. "It takes a lot of pressure to get the lungs open after a dive when the air sacs can be stuck together," Kerry said, "but like a balloon the more air that flows in the easier it becomes to blow up. A damaged lung is like a stiff balloon. In Nick's case because he'd done so much damage to the lungs—chronic and recent—and then did a longer, more stressful dive than he'd planned, he didn't have the capability to recover from that dive on his own."

Translation: the chronically damaged area limited Nick's capacity to reoxygenate. But that alone should not have killed him. "There was enough healthy tissue to resuscitate him," said Gilliland. If Jeschke had managed to recognize Nick's condition immediately and access his airway properly, there were enough intact alveoli, or air sacs, for Nick to begin to exchange carbon dioxide for oxygen and come around.

What Nick's case reveals about long-term risk to freedivers is up for debate. "There are two types of alveolar damage," said Elsayegh, the Los Angeles pulmonologist. "There's an acute damage such as pneumonia, and pulmonary hemorrhage, which will clear up and the lung will heal, but chronic damage to the alveoli will not heal. Whatever tissue is scarred is damaged for life."

Still, neither Dr. Elsayegh nor Dr. Gilliland believes Nick's lungs were yet damaged to the point where it would have impacted him on a day-to-day level. "It was only a problem because he was at the absolute extreme of hypoxia," Gilliland said.

Yet Kerry and Gilliland also found systemic changes in Nick's heart. His right ventricle was enlarged and the walls thickened, as were several pulmonary arteries, a condition known as right ventricular hypertrophy and a sign of either right heart strain and/or pulmonary hypertension, symptoms common among patients who suffer from congestive heart failure or valve disease. Nick didn't have those problems, and given that his left ventricle was normal, it was likely not a function of his advanced fitness level either (athletes with left ventricular hypertrophy are often diagnosed with athletic heart syndrome). Gilliland and Kerry believe it's related to the fibrosis. Their theory is that because his lungs were damaged in the periphery, it took more effort to exchange gases. As a result his heart and arteries were forced to pump harder, which caused them to grow thicker.

The good news for freedivers, Kerry said, is that while the severity of a lung squeeze is difficult to reliably diagnose in a living patient [though Elsayegh suggests they undergo annual pulmonary function tests to be safe], hypertrophy is diagnosable through an echocardiogram, a noninvasive ultrasound of the heart. "It's a tool already used in the clinic to define pressure in the pulmonary artery and determine the size of the heart muscle wall. If an athlete is determined to have pulmonary hypertension," she said, "based on Nick's autopsy, we can hypothesize that they have interstitial fibrosis in their lungs." Elsayegh adds that if that happens, the athlete should stop diving until the hypertension is under control. Competitive freedivers are frequently involved in medical studies and have been since the dawn of the sport. Based on her investigation into Nick's death, Kerry sounded poised to launch a study of her own using cardiac ultrasound. "Coming to a freediving competition near you," she said.

Given the volume of evidence, it's clear that Nick may have been saved with better emergency care, though that isn't a sure thing, and it's important to remember that his poor resuscitation was merely the last domino to fall. If any of eight things had gone differently, Nick would have survived. If he hadn't recommenced his descent, and made unorthodox movements at extreme pressure, perhaps his squeeze would not have been so severe. If he'd been examined more thoroughly and held out of competition, he would have lived to dive another day.

Squeezes had been a problem in freediving for years, but judges, event doctors, and athletes everywhere had been ignoring the signs and pushing for records and personal bests while injured. That's the culture Nick came up in, it's what he witnessed, and if there had been better awareness among his peers and leaders within competitive freediving, perhaps he might have recognized the risks in time or wouldn't have been taught the skills to go so deep before his body had adapted to pressure.

Most important, if he had listened to his own body, and opted out on Sunday, November 17, he would have lived. When he died, a handful of athletes and writers, as well as AIDA officials, were quick to pile on Nick Mevoli. They called him reckless and egotistical, thoughtlessly diving for numbers. His uncle, Paul Mevoli, has other ideas.

"Rarely did he talk about his success unless I pried it out of him," Paul said. "He never even told me about the silver medal at the World Championship. He was the second best in the whole frickin' world and was like, ah, no big deal. That's just the way he was. He wasn't egotistical. He was humble." Paul, a competitive racecar driver, knows what it's like to want something so bad that you come to believe you need it—when your mind flips, and the passion that has fueled and challenged you to pursue a dream and achieve, turns against you. That's what he thinks happened to Nick.

"He wasn't reckless, he was fixated. Mentally fixated. I saw that many times chasing fish out at Seven Mile Bridge. He won't quit. Believe me, my nephew had just as much fault as anybody. He was the one that dove, he knew how he felt, and he kept going down when he had already turned around, but they need to make some changes. To give the next kid who shows up like Nick a fighting chance even if he makes a mistake. Because as it is, if you make a mistake, it can be lethal."

19

VERTICAL BLUE 2014
LONG ISLAND, BAHAMAS

At 11:06 a.m. on December 2, 2014, Will Trubridge floated into the competition zone in Dean's Blue Hole. It was day five of Vertical Blue 2014, with thirty-five athletes from eighteen countries on the island looking to break records and push personal limits. Will among them. If successful on his 102-meter Constant No Fins dive he would break his own world record.

That was no sure thing. For weeks Will's training had been hit and miss. He'd take a step forward on a Monday only to stumble on Wednesday. On his final training dive, however, he'd hit 100 meters and come up squeaky clean. That day 102 meters seemed not only possible, but a likely next step. Then on his first competition dive he blacked out after what was supposed to be a warm-up jaunt to 93 meters. That did not bode well.

The very next day he got a white card after a dive to 94 meters, reestablishing positive momentum, but 8 meters was a huge leap, and Will knew that better than anyone. To make matters worse, after a dominant year, Alexey Molchanov had put himself in position to win Will's home tournament, with white cards after a 123-meter dive in Constant Weight on day three, and a 114-meter dive in Free Immersion only thirty minutes before Will got in the water. True, Alexey had blacked out on both of his attempts to hit 97 meters in Constant No Fins, but he was still in command, and after Will's record attempt there were only two days left in the competition. Will would have just one dive each to score in the two remaining disciplines. If he failed to get his record, he might as well kiss competition gold goodbye as well.

Alexey wasn't the only external stressor in Will's head. His record attempt was big news back home in New Zealand, thanks to Will's sponsor, Steinlager, who along with NZ TV One was broadcasting his 102-meter dive live on national television. After the National Geographic record attempt fell apart, New Zealand's national beer brand stepped in and became Will's main sponsor, paying him $150,000 to train hard, shoot a riveting commercial, and deliver a new record to his homeland, if only the weather gods would cooperate.

Those ideal conditions Dean's Blue Hole was known for had not been so perfect over the past week. The night before, big waves thrashed the limestone bluffs, sending a halo of whitewater fifty feet high. The morning of the record attempt, winds were upwards of thirty miles per hour, bringing cool wind and rain, which had competitors shivering before their dives. This was a major problem, because shivering muscles burn much more oxygen than when they're warm and loose, and several athletes struggled with conditions.

Then something magical happened. Swatches of blue sky opened above the hole as a bright shining sun tried to burn its way through to clarity. Behind Will, a minimalist Steinlager banner hung from the bluffs. Its message was simple: 102M. Across New Zealand, viewers were glued to their televisions, and about seventy athletes and fans were crowded around the competition zone, treading water and aiming their GoPros above the deep blue. All of them hoping for history.

Will's dive time had been the most reliable indicator of success or failure over the past weeks. If his sink phase was too slow or his ascent lagging, the dive would stretch beyond 4:10, which would leave him too hypoxic to maintain consciousness at the surface. Whenever he managed to get closer to four minutes, however, his dives had been clean. On December 2, Will's dive was supposed to take 4:04. Like a great stage actor, all he had to do was hit his marks and perform what he'd rehearsed countless times. He was the best no fins man in history, and it was time to prove it to New Zealand, to his rival, and to himself, once more.

For nearly six minutes Trubridge lay on his back, faceup with a foam float beneath the crook of his neck and another beneath his knees. His breathing was slow and steady, and as the anticipation grew, he looked like he was sleeping. With forty seconds to go, he arched backward, dipping his face in the sea, filling his goggles with water, stimulating the nerve endings around his eyes. With twenty seconds to go he built toward peak inhalation, beginning with his belly, moving up into his chest and into the subclavian air pockets beneath his shoulder blades. Forty sips and packs later, he flipped onto his stomach and duck dove, his long, elegant strokes propelling him toward his goal.

Within three strokes he passed the sandfalls, and after three more he'd reached negative buoyancy in the midnight blue. His arms at his side, his chin tucked, he became streamlined. He closed his eyes and let gravity do the rest. "Shut down, shut down, shut down," he told himself, hoping to keep his mind blank. Thoughts take energy. Thoughts consume oxygen.

Steve Keenan, the safety diver from Kalamata, had flown in to manage the platform and announce the dives. He squinted into the sonar monitor and announced Will's progress. "Okay, I've got him. Dive time thirty seconds, diver's at 30 meters." Will was past 50 meters when the clock struck one minute. Thirty seconds later he'd reached

81 meters, and before two minutes had elapsed, he'd touched down, grabbed the tag, and started swimming back. His timing had been perfect. Optimism bloomed at the surface of Dean's Blue Hole.

Among those monitoring Will's progress more seriously was Johnny Sunnex. Just like the year before, Johnny was Will's right hand in the weeks leading up to Vertical Blue. Whenever Will was training, Johnny was there, spotting him, lending an ear, and helping Will analyze and troubleshoot. But Johnny wasn't a competitor in 2014. He was head safety and would be the first man down. He'd greet Will at 40 meters and escort him all the way home. He checked his dive computer, marking time, and as soon as Will had passed the 80-meter mark, he duck dove to meet him. His nickname, "Johnny Deep," was visible on the blades of his bi-fins as they sliced the surface and disappeared.

Johnny hadn't been looking forward to coming back to Long Island. The memories were too fresh, too dark. After Nick died, Johnny packed all his gear for the family, and found Nick's passport to help get him back home. The following January, he was spearfishing in Dubai with a group of buddies. One got separated. He wasn't found until the next day, when his body washed up on shore. Johnny harbored a lot of guilt for losing contact with his friend, and was overcome with grief.

"I lost my passion for freediving for a while," he said, though it was hard to tell from the outside. He still taught freediving courses and lived the carefree life of a handsome, thirty-year-old breath-hold gypsy—traveling to Turkey, Egypt, Greece, Croatia, and more. Yet part of him was missing. He stopped training. He lost the fire to push his limits. What did it matter if he could swim like a superhero, when his fellow divers kept dropping dead? When he arrived at Dean's Blue Hole, he knew it was time to dive for himself again, and what better way to restart than to spot his friend, mentor, and countryman—the best freediver in the world.

Johnny started with shallow dives, for him anyway. He tapped 50 meters, then 55. Soon he'd progressed to 70 meters. New freedivers enjoy the feeling of their first freefall from 20 to 30 meters, but it still feels like effort. As the slow, steady sink phase gets extended, however, the easier it is to feel the sea squeeze and time expand. Experienced divers say the real fun begins below 50 meters, when freefall becomes even dreamier, and if an athlete can relax deeply and there's no pressure to achieve or win, the mind opens as the heart rate drops and they feel blank, pure, completely at one with the water and within themselves.

As it had for Nick, freediving had become too much about competition for Johnny, and these deep, agenda-free dives were infusing him with that inner peace he'd lost. Deep water was his ally again. At least until the day he dove to 80 meters, and came up coughing. He climbed onto the platform and spit into his palm: blood.

ALEXEY AND NATALIA chose to build their sport, diver by diver. Will Trubridge builds the sport with a broad media reach. Will's deal with Steinlager, a major beer brand, was freediving's first six-figure sponsorship. He's had a documentary made about him and been featured on *60 Minutes,* when Scott Simon visited Dean's Blue Hole, and he uses his celebrity in New Zealand to promote ocean conservation projects.

He also does the dirty work to make sure Vertical Blue happens, whether that's recruiting other athletes; seeking corporate partners, like the dive computer manufacturer Suunto, to stuff the champion's purse; or taking apart and towing the dive platform in and out of Dean's in his blue pickup, his Vertical Blue logo on the driver's side door. Each day, piece by piece, he personally cleans out the plastic that drifts into the blue hole and collects on the beach from the open water, and he's also part of the registration team when the divers arrive. Such is life even at the top of the freediving world, a diverse community that is strongest when everybody plays a role. "Compared to other sports, there have been so few competitors and almost zero financial backing, so that's the way it is," he said.

Imagine the best marathoners or triathletes on earth organizing their own races, and even helping block off the streets ahead of time. That's what Will does. In competitive freediving, elite athletes are also the brick and mortar when duty calls. But Will's most important contribution to competitive freediving is putting Dean's Blue Hole on the map to begin with. It began with a rumor, which led him to inquire about it on the popular freediving forum, Deeper Blue. Nobody seemed to know anything concrete, so he decided to see for himself.

"The first time I rocked up to the blue hole, I could tell straight away it was gonna be as good as I'd hoped," he said. A few of the locals he'd met had warned him of dangerous whirlpool currents and resident bull and tiger sharks. They told him to stay away. He didn't. "The first few dives were a little creepy, a little ominous, because it gets quite dark," he said. "If you go deep enough it gets black, but the freefall is better here because there's no current."

Will's initial trip to the hole was in 2005, and for the first few years he would come for four to six months at a stretch, spending the rest of the year competing or teaching in Italy. He befriended a local waterman and Hawaii transplant named Charlie Beede, who spotted him whenever Will needed it. Charlie had a granddaughter from Daytona Beach who was a student at Florida State. When he introduced her to Will in 2008, their worlds merged. They were inseparable for three days, exploring beaches and bays together, talking for hours, falling in love. But she had another year at school and Will had to go back to Sicily. They kept in touch and Will went to Tallahassee to visit. In 2009, they bridged the distance and married on Long Island.

Will is very much an island man. He and Brittany built a modest but charming house on a patch of land, ten-minutes drive from the hole. He rarely wears shoes, spearfishes fresh catch for dinner, and cracks his own coconuts; Brittany ferments their own kombucha tea. When an island festival is on, they attend, eating barbecued pigeon—shot or caught on the island—if it's on the menu. In fact, the only time he eats meat is when it's locally sourced, which means beef is out of the question. Once in a long while he may eat goat, if he's invited to a friend's ranch for Sunday lunch. But flavor is secondary to Will.

Food is fuel. This is partly due to an early career sinus injury that damaged his sense of taste, but mostly because Will is a world-class athlete pushing his body to do things nobody has ever accomplished. His mostly vegetarian diet, complemented by whatever he can forage, as well as regular green protein shakes and home-baked power bars, keeps him thin. But he's not scrawny. Will is all muscle, with six-pack abs, broad shoulders, and a slender waist.

"Life is quiet," Brittany said. "It's an everyday routine in preparation for his dives. It's all about his training."

Will trains eleven months a year. Each morning begins with yoga, including a series of apnea stretches to loosen the intercostal muscles and increase rib cage flexibility. He'll stand on his head, do arm balances and down dog, then ripple and contract, relax and contort his diaphragm, stuffing it beneath his rib cage. That kind of thoracic flexibility allows a diver like Will to pack over 20 percent more air for Static breath holds or Dynamic swims, which he does in his own 25-meter lap pool to build lactic acid and CO2 tolerance. The thoracic stretches also help his lungs withstand atmospheric pressure at depth. Because his core is so flexible, he can remain loose and relaxed on a dive, which means his lung tissue doesn't get bruised or battered. Will has had his share of blackouts, but he claims to have never been squeezed.

Of course, adaptation to pressure comes naturally when living down the road from the best freediving terrain in the world. Nothing prepares one's physiology for depth and pressure like reps, and Will dives deep four days a week, year round. He spends the island's quiet nights analyzing his dive profiles on his computer. If his sink phase is a few seconds slow, as it was in the lead-up to Vertical Blue, he'll add weight. In this case he had a 400-gram tungsten rod shipped just in time. If his ascent is too quick it usually means his oxygen efficiency will be off. Sometimes he consults freediving innovators like Eric Fattah for advice, and he's always analyzing and contemplating, looking for an edge. But he works in enough sunset strolls, virgin beach patrols, and starry-night stare-downs to keep him calm and peaceful. He does live in paradise, after all, and each morning as he rolls over the rutted dirt track that leads to his favorite place on earth, he feels blessed.

Dean's Blue Hole is a mecca for a reason, and whenever Vertical Blue draws near, travel plans, car shares, and roommate arrangements ripple through Facebook. Spouses win permission for an extended trip away. Businesses shutter for a sabbatical; apartments and homes are house sat and sublet from Santiago to Warsaw, from Tokyo to Tel Aviv. Will is not the only diver who longs for the hole, after all, but he is the only man on earth who works there full time.

In November 2014, athletes began to trickle into Long Island three weeks before the competition began. Among them were Mike Board; Carlos Coste; Iru Balic; Marianna Krupnitskaya; the ladies of Team Japan: Tomoka Fukuda, Hanako Hirose, and the Japanese national record holder Misuzu Okamoto; rising Slovenian star Samo Jeranko; and Alexey Molchanov.

Alexey's confidence was at an all-time high. His training in Croatia prior to arrival in the Bahamas had been spectacular, and he hoped to build on his dominant year by adding enough depth in Constant No Fins to make a run at Will's world record. And if that didn't work out, save his last dive for a potential Constant Weight record attempt at 130 meters. When asked if he would focus more on records or try to win, he said, "I won't try to win. I *will* win."

The athletes came along with the usual entourage of judges, media, and safety divers. Carla Hanson was a judge again. Daan and Logan would be in the water with camera gear, and Marco Consentino was back as a safety. Johnny's squeeze turned out to be minor and his lungs had cleared by morning. From then on his dives were shallow and his focus was on making Vertical Blue the safest it had ever been.

Event medic Tom Ardavany, sixty-three, an ER and flight nurse who specialized in remote-area care and airlift rescue, made sure of that. Tom brought a robust medical kit with him, and it included a defibrillator. Thirteen years in medical air transport and nine years in a trauma center taught him one thing above all: "Play with your own toys," he said. Kerry sent him the drills she and Ren ran in Roatan, and Johnny and his team ran through them several times a day, while Tom augmented them and led additional rescue seminars at Greenwich Lodge each night. Before the competition had begun, it was clear that Tom and Johnny helped Vertical Blue take a major leap forward in terms of health and safety.

Although the official response from AIDA in the aftermath of Nick's death was lacking, the General Assembly did vote through three rule changes in the hopes that nothing similar would ever happen again. The first one limited announcements to 3 meters beyond that diver's personal best. That rule alone would have prevented Nick from attempting his 95-meter Free Immersion dive the Friday before he died, because his deepest successful Free Immersion dive on record was 81 meters. The second rule banned recommencing descent, and the third and final rule authorized event doctors, medics, or judges to suspend divers who've been squeezed. Although Deja Blue had given its event doctors that jurisdiction for years, AIDA had not. That's why Walid was so upset to be suspended from the Caribbean Cup in Roatan. Doctors had never had that kind of power before, but Nick's death was seen as a tipping point. AIDA had to change.

Although the rules passed in a summer landslide, they wouldn't take effect until January 2015. Will saw no reason to wait and implemented them at his event anyway. He also added an oxygen saturation test designed to detect lung squeezes. Oxygen saturation is the percentage of oxygen carried by red blood cells in the bloodstream. A level of 95 to 100 is normal for adults, and if an athlete scores below 95 when taking the test on the beach within thirty minutes after surfacing, it could indicate a lung squeeze. In that case they would be examined by Tom and given another saturation test that same evening. If the symptom or the reading persisted, the athlete would be suspended for a period of time. It was a well-intentioned plan that proved controversial, as more than one athlete scored above 95, then spit blood all afternoon. Because they'd passed, and kept their injuries to themselves, however, they were free to dive the very next day.

Mike Board touched off the controversy when he suffered a blackout on the second day of competition. He had been going for a personal best and a new UK national record of 103 meters, but it was a stormy morning. The wind was blowing and the water was a touch colder than normal. With no sun, Mike warmed up in the water by hanging onto a line at 20 meters, then waited on the chilly platform for his turn in the competition zone. Shivering and depleted, he still went for it. The dive never felt right and when he met the safety divers at 30 meters, he asked for help. As they swam him to the surface he blacked out in about 5 meters of water.

As he breached the surface, saliva bubbled from his lips as his girlfriend, New Zealand record holder and internationally known yoga instructor Kate Middleton (no, not that one), watched in horror. Mike came around quickly and breathed oxygen as Tom checked him out. He would go on to take the oxygen saturation test and pass, but he knew he was squeezed. He felt moisture in his chest and spit some blood. It was mild, but it was there, and given what he'd witnessed the year before, he felt it appropriate to tell Tom and get checked out again that evening.

Tom wouldn't discuss Mike's case, but by then, Mike said he was fine and that Tom told him he was symptom free. Still, the judges banned Mike for three days, which they claim was on Tom's recommendation. Mike appealed. "Why did you give me three days instead of two, five, or ten?" he asked. The judges had no answer, but held firm. Mike was right that the ruling was arbitrary. There was no way to know how mild or severe the damage was to his alveoli. Dr. Elsayegh said it can take one to four weeks for most similar injuries to heal, so what good would three days do? Freediving was still in the wilderness, and there was no road map.

Meanwhile, Mike's housemate, Yaron Hoory, the Israeli national record holder, blacked out on day one going for a 66-meter Constant No Fins dive. He failed the oxygen saturation test on the beach, but passed that night when Tom examined him, and was cleared to dive. Like Mike, he'd spit blood, but never confessed. He took a day off to rest, but could have been in the water on day two if he'd wanted. "I am mature enough to decide for myself when I can or can't dive," he said. "If I think being honest is gonna get me banned for the rest of the competition, I'm gonna swallow my blood."

It got weirder later in the competition when UK freedive blogger and physician Chris Cranshaw, who trained with Mike in Indonesia before Vertical Blue, came up after a no fins dive to 68 meters and earned a white card. While waiting for his turn to breathe oxygen on the beach, he offered a foghorn cough and spit blood. He kept coughing and spitting, sometimes specks, and sometimes teaspoons. He passed the oxygen saturation test on the first try.

"It's obvious, we need a better way to diagnose a squeeze," Mike said.

"Let's not kid ourselves," Chris added. "There is no objective measure. I've just passed the objective measure." He felt terrible for Mike when he was suspended without adequate explanation, and believed decisions like that might encourage other divers to hide their squeezes. "What you want to do is to encourage openness with athletes, so they are honest with the doctor or medic and honest with themselves. The best way to keep athletes safe is to encourage them to keep themselves safe."

At Vertical Blue 2013, before Nick died, the chatter was about how the general public, and more specifically the media, didn't understand how safe the sport really was. Nosebleeds and blackouts scared exactly no one, and few were fazed by lung squeezes. If questioned, athletes would deny the sport's inherent risk. Now Chris hoped those same athletes would hold themselves back, but would they?

In the face of change, athletes had begun to admit that risk is part of the draw. A large part, the same as with high-altitude mountain climbing, big-wave surfing, or base jumping. It's the exploration of dangerous terrain and the pursuit of an experience few will ever know—that Zen hit during freefall, which is the physiological equivalent of deep meditation—combined with an uncertain outcome that heightens the rush. These men and women live to dive deep.

"You could tell me every 100-meter dive damages your lungs, and that's not gonna stop me from doing it," said Mike, who would nail his 103-meter dive on his second attempt. "You can't legislate risk out of the sport."

Samo Jeranko put it plainly after hammering an elegant dive to 107 meters with his monofin. "At the surface you have to accept that you might die," he said. "You must have no fear."

His words were a harbinger of a coming tragedy that would shock freedivers everywhere and make international news. On August 2, 2015, Natalia Molchanova would disappear while freediving off the coast of Formentera, an island in Spain. She'd been teaching a small group of students, who also happened to be friends. They were beginners, and she trailed them on instructional dives to 5, 10, and 15 meters. Between those dives she demonstrated proper technique off the line, and dived to about 15 meters each time, while her friends watched. After about an hour she plunged off the line again, without fins, this time for pleasure, on a dive thought to be between 35 and

65 meters. Untethered, she was swept away in one of the fierce underwater currents the area is known for, and surfaced 60 meters away. Her friends saw her briefly, hopped in their boat, and motored toward her, but she slipped below before they could reach her. She most likely suffered a surface blackout, and disappeared forever. Search efforts lasted nearly a week but were fruitless. "It seems she'll stay in the sea," Alexey said, heartbroken, three days after her disappearance. "I think she would like that."

There is no doubt that Natalia went out doing what she loved most, and from a wide angle, her story—the one about a forty-year-old divorced, single mother, who took up a new sport and practiced it passionately and brilliantly—is inspirational. Over the course of her career she accumulated forty-one world records, twenty-three world titles and became the most decorated athlete in the sport's history by far. But her death also revealed, yet again, just how thin the margin for error is in freediving, even for the very best.

On December 2, Will ascended deliberately, working his perfect breaststroke, and met Johnny at 35 meters. "He looked strong," said Johnny. "He looked determined." But at the 10-meter mark he peeked toward the surface, and that's when Johnny knew he was in trouble. Though his dive time was on the money—the dive would take only 3:58—Will had reached his physiological limit too soon that day, and began pulling the line. Johnny grabbed him and hustled him to the surface. His lips were as blue as the water, and he quickly lost motor control and blacked out.

Brittany was his coach, but when Will surfaced in Johnny's arms there was nothing for her to do but watch and hope. "When he has a blackout, I feel it," she said, "I get emotionally exhausted." This time he was gone for only a few seconds, and when he came to, she could relax as he received a warm round of applause.

Will gracefully met his obligations. He did his interviews with New Zealand television, and Steinlager supported him all the way, unveiling a new tag line on Twitter: *When you push boundaries, success isn't guaranteed, but our support is.* That message was echoed by the Kiwi public, who before and after the event flooded the Steinlager website with encouraging messages. Nervous the night before, Will read several, which made his failure even more poignant.

He left the beach despondent. When asked about his next move, he said, "Well, I have two more dives left. I guess I'll try to get on the podium." To do that he'd have to nail dives in Constant Weight and Free Immersion, disciplines he hadn't been working on much in the lead-up to Vertical Blue. Most expected him to post a modest announcement, all but concede the comp to Alexey, and try to edge Samo for silver. Instead, Will announced a 120-meter dive in Free Immersion, just one meter off his world record.

All over the world, freedivers chimed in on Will's announcement. Many called it irresponsible, considering he'd had two blackouts in his first three attempts. Some called for rules to prevent an athlete from diving the day after a blackout. Of course, that one had been proposed along with the new rules passed earlier that summer, and it was voted down. Alexey defended Will's choice. "He isn't squeezed, and his announcement is within the rules," he said. "It's a sport, and in our sport we push limits." Alexey was right. Will's announcement was legal. It was also ballsy. If he missed, he'd be out of the medal hunt in his own playground.

Judging by the online commentary, Will's decision was also a little dangerous. Embedded in the posts and tweets flying around the freediving social media sphere was underlying concern that tragedy might strike again at Dean's Blue Hole. Brittany has lived with that worry for years.

"There's times when nobody is on the island and it's just me holding the line and those thoughts cross your mind," she said. "What if he doesn't come up? What am I going to do? It's a deep, low-grade anxiety that I live with, and I don't think about it because it's not healthy and it's not good for him. Every once in a while I feel sorry for myself. But you have one life and you have to realize your potential in whatever field you choose, and this is what he loves to do." (She and Will would separate within a year.)

The wind had died down and the sun was shining when Will drove up to the beach, over an hour before his Free Immersion dive. He looked relaxed and fresh. He waved to a neighbor who had come out to watch, took photos with athletes, and watched a kiteboarder carve the bay beyond the hole, then sat beside Alexey in the shade. With the hoopla of the record attempt behind him, he looked more relieved than anxious. He had nothing to lose.

All athletes work hard to build and repeat their habits, and Will's breathe up didn't change. Free Immersion is the slowest discipline, so his descent of .9 meters per second wasn't alarming on its own, but with two recent blackouts there was no telling if he had the reserves to withstand another long dive. He touched down in 2:16 and knew he needed to pick up the pace. He did just that, pulling and gliding, pulling and gliding, first the right hand, then the left. His pace was steady but the contractions began punching him in the gut when he hit 60 meters. He'd been in the water for 3:20, and was moving at 1 meter per second. Then, as if an internal alarm sounded, he began pulling and gliding faster and faster. He covered the next 30 meters in twenty seconds, and was back on pace, gliding the last 10 meters toward the surface. When he was 3 meters away he nodded to himself, the way he did when he knew he had it, though he wobbled at the surface. Luckily, Brittany was there to lead him home.

"Goggles, William!" she belted. He inched them onto his brow, flinching slightly. "Nose clip! Make the sign! Do it! Now breathe!" Will did as his wife demanded, his surface protocol was clean, and when the white card came, he was back in the game.

After clean dives by Mike and Samo, Alexey would have his say. He'd announced 95 meters in Constant No Fins. He'd been so close in his last attempt to 97 meters, he figured taking a small step back would give him the space he needed to make the dive. If he made it, the gold medal was his for sure, as he'd have won two of the three disciplines outright, including Will's best. Nevertheless, it was a puzzling choice. He didn't need to win the no fins battle. He could have announced 92 meters or 93 and made up what he'd lose in points by pushing out his Constant Weight depth on his final dive. Instead of trying to win the competition with his best weapon, he'd made an all-or-nothing choice on no fins. Then again, he'd focused on Constant No Fins all year long, and had the best year so far of any diver in the water. Elite athletes trust their preparation, so that's what Alexey did.

"I expected him to make it," said Will, who was in the water to watch.

Alexey also analyzes the forensics of every failure, and knew he needed to be fifteen seconds faster than he had been on the last dive. He was, but the dive was miserable. He felt discomfort almost the entire way, yet he fought through it to stay on pace. As he approached the surface, however, something was off. He'd abandoned the breaststroke and started to dolphin kick. Without fins that doesn't help much, and it looked and felt like a desperate choice from an athlete on the verge. He managed to reach the surface and grabbed the rope high but his grip slipped, and he flopped backward, shaking. He'd lost motor control but he'd managed to keep his airway above the water, and the safety divers hadn't touched him yet. He still had a chance as long as his airway didn't slip below the surface.

"Nose clip," his coach screamed. "Nose clip!" His words cut through the fog, Alexey popped vertical and grabbed the rope again. He ditched his clip and flashed the okay sign, saying the words. The judges watched it all intently, and checked their stopwatches. His protocol was shaky, but clean enough. Only it took seventeen seconds, two seconds too late. Red card. Alexey had left the door open. Gold was there for the taking, and it was up to Will to grab it. If he could hit his 117-meter dive in Constant Weight the next day, it was his.

On the last day of Vertical Blue 2014, with eighty spectators watching, Will floated into place with six minutes to go. When the time came, he disappeared into the dark in just three swipes of his monofin. Streamlined, he felt good all the way down, averaging 1.1 meters per second. On the way up he was even faster. He whipped his legs with power and grace, channeling all his desire and passion, disappointment and love into his final competitive dive of the year.

Before he hit the 2:30 mark he'd already passed the safety at 30 meters and knew he had it in the bag, but he kept pumping, flying by the next safety diver at 20 meters, enjoying that blue hole dawn when the halo of turquoise light above bleeds into the darkness, and when the elegant sandfalls drift into his peripheral vision. It was like seeing a gorgeous yet familiar view, a friendly reminder that he was almost home. The last 10 meters were a joy. He floated up and rocked the protocol. Will had saved his cleanest performance for last. He flashed the tag to extended applause, shoved it in his mouth and chewed, enjoying the breakfast of a champion. Then he kissed his beautiful wife for good measure.

When the day was done and the final diver had surfaced after a humble 33-meter Free Immersion dive—proof that freediving is a sport with all levels of competitors—the athletes, judges, photographers, and safety divers relaxed on the beach as Will brought out two tubs of icy Steinlager. Johnny was first man to the cooler, and Will wasn't far behind. They'd been hustling and training hard, and now it was time to play.

Even in defeat, Alexey had a blast. All competition long he'd been leading group swims, spending hours in the sun, enjoying homemade gourmet seafood dinners with the Eastern bloc—divers from Croatia, Russia, and Serbia—almost every night, chasing a former Latin American beauty queen around the island, and spending long nights with her under the stars. Perhaps that's why his game was slightly off. But if so, he'd take living over a gold medal this time around. After all, there was always 2015, and he still hadn't turned twenty-eight years old. His athletic prime had only just begun.

When his mother died eight months later, his belief in living for each day was only reinforced. He'd prove it less than two weeks after her disappearance when he celebrated her life by diving the arch in Dahab's blue hole: her favorite underwater terrain in the world.

Will smiled as he watched Alexey laugh and swim with his friends, while he sipped his second cold one on the white sand. Three days earlier his hopes had been thrashed against the bluffs. Even the podium seemed ambitious. Two money dives later, everything had changed. Will's was a comeback for the storybooks.

"It was a little topsy-turvy," he said, staring over the blue hole, "but it does feel really good to have finished this way."

On top, he meant.

Still the best freediver on planet Earth.

EPILOGUE

"We lost Nick," Ren choked through tears. "I'm sorry," he kept saying, "I'm so sorry."

Belinda hung up and staggered out of the stall. It was a busy Sunday afternoon in IKEA and the bathroom was wall to wall. Her face was contorted with shock and pain, and all eyes were upon her. She pushed through the door onto the showroom floor and stood there, sobbing. Alone. Most gave her wide berth, but one stranger came over, held her, and prayed for her, until she found the strength to walk into the pale Orlando sunlight and drive to her daughter's house to break the news.

When she heard, Jen went into type A crisis control, calling funeral homes and a friend who was a US attorney in Miami, trying to get her brother back home, but soon collapsed in tears on her living room carpet.

Ren showed up the following night in St. Petersburg. Paul had him flown in on a friend's private plane with Nick's things. The family gathered to meet him and he attempted to answer all their questions, though was often at a loss.

Will Trubridge and Vanessa Weinberg were among those who attended Nick's funeral, held in St. Petersburg on Thanksgiving Eve. They mourned with Nick's family and with members of his many tribes. Aaron, Justin, Clayton, and Sol from the Tally vegan crew were there. Akia and his theater friends showed up, and Morgan did too. A similar phenomenon occurred on an even larger scale at the Brooklyn memorial held a week later at Esther Bell's thriving café in Williamsburg, where the full cast of characters from every period of Nick's rich life came together to grieve and rejoice in his memory.

In *Exist,* while standing on the rooftop at 3rd and Berry, Nick's character said, "I have faith in the fact that we never really die . . . that we perpetuate ourselves by the pieces we give others."

Denny's cane snapped the day after Nick died. When she heard the news, she was consumed by a crushing guilt, as if their last conversation contributed to his terrible mistake, but when her cane broke she felt Nick behind it, nudging her toward a better life.

On the verge of graduation with a masters in acupuncture, nearly a year after Nick's death, Denny's days had become active and full. She was a sales rep for a Chinese herb and holistic medicine distributor, had trips to Japan and the Yucatan on the horizon, and spent her free time with a community of new friends. Together they paddled the Delaware River, ate out at funky ethnic joints in Brooklyn, the Bronx, and Queens, and on her birthday they went skydiving.

With a handsome Aussie instructor strapped to her back, she leapt into the blue sky over a leafy western Pennsylvania countryside banded with autumn colors. She extended her arms, the wind rippling her cheeks, and experienced her first freefall. When Nick met her, she was a shut-in. Now she was new.

For those who don't just love, but need the ocean, each surf, swim, paddle, or dive can be a baptism. It can wash away the dread and pain, loss and confusion of the day and deliver pure elemental connection, reminding them that no matter what else is happening in their world, the ocean exists—in all its beauty, mystery, and fury.

Each time Nick suited up and floated into the blue, with each reef dive and lobster hunt, whether he was in the Gulf, a blue hole, or the open sea, it was an opportunity for renewal and connection. A simple YouTube search will turn up freedivers riding the dorsal fin of great white sharks or surrounded by a pod of dolphins, 150 strong. They are dressed in monofins swimming with mantas and sperm whales, or they're freefalling barefoot into Dean's Blue Hole. Nick Mevoli's 100-meter dive is there, and no matter the clip, each diver shares a common motivation. They do it because it is in the ocean where their soul feels free.

What was most important to Nick was to live, not merely exist. He reached beyond the norm, rebelled, chased dreams, worked hard, reused what others threw away, listened more than he spoke, and gave all he could whenever he could. Sometimes lost, most of the time right where he belonged, Nick was bruised and battered, but he had a soul full of goodness, a heart full of love, and he glowed, until he was gone.

The memory of Nicholas Mevoli was everywhere at Vertical Blue 2014, especially during the Apnea Games, held in his honor on an off-day during the competition. Athletes gathered on the beach and shared Nick stories, then competed in cliff jumping, tandem no fins diving, bubble ring blowing, and underwater somersaults. The cove was filled with their laughter all afternoon. It was just the sort of event Nick would have adored.

But Will and Brittany made sure there were opportunities to remember him every day. The 2013 medals—awarded for the top three in each discipline and for the top three overall men and women—were never handed out when the competition was canceled after he died. In 2014, they were left at the check-in table for folks to grab as keepsakes or, better yet, as an offering.

Some let them slip through their fingers and watched them disappear into the darkness. Their blue hole, their wishing well. Others placed them on a stone that Paul Mevoli had engraved in Nick's memory. It read: *Dive into Your Dreams with Passion*.

Two weeks prior to Vertical Blue, Paul piloted his prop plane into Long Island with Nick's father, Larry, and Scotty, Paul's *Bonzo* buddy, to deliver the stone. After his son died, Larry suffered heart problems, and had a pacemaker installed. His second marriage had ended years before when his business tanked. So did a subsequent relationship with a woman who finally figured out he was broke. He would be homeless, living in Jen's guestroom, if it weren't for Nick's life insurance policy. When he bought it all those years ago, he'd declared himself the beneficiary.

It paid $100,000 tax free, enough for a mobile home in Orlando and a brand-new black Mustang convertible. A hustler to the end, losing his son changed him. He'd become one of Jen's most reliable caregivers for her two girls, who can frequently be seen in his backseat on the way home from preschool and first grade, top down, their hair tangled and wild, their smiles ear to ear. Their mother can only shake her head and roll her eyes when Larry roars into her driveway, and whenever a rainbow rises she points to the sky and says, "Look, girls. Uncle Nick says hi."

Weighted down by the stone, Will walked it across the sandy bottom, underwater, as the three men swam on the surface. Together they placed it beneath a small overhang in the bluffs near Dean's Blue Hole. They shared a round of thoughts and a moment of silence before Scotty said a final prayer.

"I gotta let him go now," Paul said, fighting tears. "I gotta let him go."

ACKNOWLEDGMENTS

While on what I thought would be a routine assignment to Long Island, Bahamas, covering a top competition in a niche adventure sport for the *New York Times,* fate turned when Nick Mevoli died, and the scope of both that assignment and my interest in the athletes and the art of competitive freediving changed forever. This book is the result, and it would have never happened without the inspiration and collaboration of photographer Lia Barrett, or the interest, faith, and responsiveness of Jason Stallman, Tom Connelly, Sam Dolnick, Becky Lebowitz, and Jim Luttrell at the *New York Times* sports desk, as well as fellow reporters John Branch, Mary Pilon, and William Broad.

I would also like to thank my friend and agent Byrd Leavell and the wonderful Julianna Wojcik at Waxman Leavell as well as Nathan Roberson, my editor at Crown, who believed in this book from the beginning and saw what it could become before I did.

Of course, there would be no book at all without the patient collaboration of so many generous people. For over a year, they shared memories—painful, beautiful, and hilarious—and pushed me to do my best work. If you've read the book, you already know who they are and I won't list them all here, but I would like to especially thank Nick's family. They were partners in this book from the beginning and for that I am forever grateful. So thank you, Jen, Joe, Elizabeth and Alexandra, Belinda, Fred, Kristine and Katie, Larry, and Terri, Ashley, David, and Paul. I'd also like to thank Nancy and the late Josie Owsianik, Nick's grandmother, who passed away just fourteen months after Nick. It was a joy to meet you and watch your last dance.

Nick's nonfreediving friends were just as generous. Thanks especially to Justin Pogge, Aaron and Katie Suko, Soliman Lawrence, and Clayton Rychlik from the Tally Vegan crew; Esther Bell, Morgan Sabia, Yasunari Rowan, Denny Kowska, and Akia Squitieri in New York City; Jessica Mammerella and Jennifer Kates in Philly, and Jana Turcinkova and Roman Susil in Czech Republic.

I'm also grateful to the many dozens of competitive freedivers, judges, safety divers, pioneers, innovators, and AIDA board members who shared their stories and opinions with me, but special thanks goes out to my most staunch allies from the freediving realm: Meir Taub, Ashley and Ren Chapman, Kerry Hollowell and Steve Benson, Mike Board and Kate Middleton, Yaron Hoory, Bobby Kim, Marco Consentino, Goran Colak, Alexey Molchanov, the late Natalia Molchanova, Carlos Coste and Gaby Contreras, Lena Jovanovic, Marina Kazankova, Mandy Sumner, Kyle Gion, Carla Hanson, Grant Graves, Beatrix and Ricardo Paris, Tomoka Fukuda, Hanako Hirose, Misuzu Okamoto, Tetsuo Hara, Sofia Gómez Uribe, Iru Balic, Kirk Krack and Mandy Cruickshank, Francesca Koh Owings, and William Trubridge. Big respect also to Daan Verhoeven who was shooting both stills and video the day Nick passed. With a tragedy unfolding, Daan let his camera roll and thanks to him there is a video record of everything that happened. I relied on it heavily throughout my research and showed it to dozens of doctors—including the generous and thoughtful Larry

Stock and Ashraf Elsayegh. Without it, Nick's cause of death may have remained a mystery, and a family left wanting for closure.

I also have my own friends and family to thank. First I should thank my mother and father, Trude and Richard Skolnick for raising and believing in me and for offering their lovely home in La Quinta as a valuable retreat as deadline day loomed. Thanks to Heather Barbod for making time for me whenever I came through the city and for sending me on the road with a sweet, shining totem in my pocket. Massive thanks to Paul Feinstein. Trapped beneath a bloated, unwieldy first draft, with a week to go before d-day, Paul parachuted in and together we found, shaped, and polished what I hope is a beautiful book. He helped shape several drafts after that one too. In addition to his editorial wizardry, he was a confidant and counselor from the beginning of this project to the end. I could not hope to have a better friend. Speaking of amazing friends, thank you Liz Gilbert and Kelton Reid. Liz has been a mentor to me since we met all those years ago and Kelton has been a partner and brother in our quest to make a living as writers from day one. Both read early drafts of the book and their guidance and support has been legendary.

Then there's John Moore, my defacto patron, ace deuce rival, and enabler of my drifter tendencies. Ever since the week after Nick passed away, I have been a nomad, roaming the globe in search of freedivers and those with insights into his past. Often I'd come through Los Angeles and John's door and his guestroom were always open and available to me. I wrote a book proposal and most of this book in his beautiful home. But even before that, John gave me the greatest gift of all. He encouraged me to take up open-water swimming, which he's been doing religiously with our friend Jacklynn Evans for more than a decade. Swimming in the deep blue Pacific with John and Jack, I have encountered and enjoyed swarms of sea lions and pods of dolphins, many whales and seals and thousands of fish. There is nothing I love to do more, and it's because I need it and have become so passionate about it that I understand better than most why freedivers must do what they do. I doubt I can ever repay him. Thank you doesn't begin to cover it.

Finally, I'd like to thank Nicholas Mevoli. I knew him for less than a week of his life, but that was enough to get that he was one special dude. I just didn't understand how special until I got to know him through those he left behind and through his own words. He wasn't perfect, but he possessed an uncommon generosity of spirit and time. His heart was big, his soul was real, and his actions backed it all up. I wish he could have found more peace on this sweet earth, but I know he found more than his share of joy, love, and adventure, and moments of solace and serenity too. Nick Mevoli lived! For others and himself. His is an example I intend to follow. I hope others will too.

INDEX

Note: The initials "NM" in index entries stand for Nick Mevoli.

INDEX

L

M

N

O

P